Early
American
Crafts

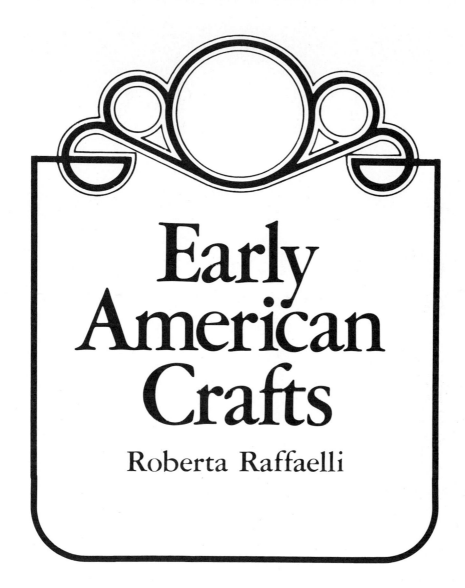

Early American Crafts

Roberta Raffaelli

CHL CREATIVE HOME LIBRARY®
In Association with Better Homes and Gardens®
Meredith Corporation

designed by Allan Mogel
photography by Ike Uyeda, Los Angeles, except for page 227, by John Garretti,
New York City

⌂ CREATIVE HOME LIBRARY®

© 1974 by Meredith Corporation, Des Moines, Iowa
All rights reserved
Printed in the United States of America
First Edition. Third Printing, 1976

Library of Congress Cataloging in Publication Data

Raffaelli, Roberta.
    Early American crafts.

    1. Handcraft—United States. I. Title.
TT23.R33   745.5′0973   74-13359
ISBN 0-696-19990-4

Contents

About the Author

Roberta Raffaelli has been actively involved as an artist, author, and teacher of crafts for twenty-five years. Many of her craft creations have been published in national magazines. Although interested in all crafts, Roberta's first love is eighteenth-century decoupage. She is a nationally renowned decoupage teacher, holding such positions as a lead teacher at Connoisseur Studio's national seminar held in Louisville, Kentucky; she is also one of the founders of the National Guild of Decoupeurs. Roberta has a private studio in Granada Hills, California, where she researches, develops new craft methods, and teaches crafts.

Preface

Throughout the many years that I have been involved in craft work, I have worked toward two goals—perfection and authenticity. Within these two goals, I have always tried to experiment, updating yesterday's techniques with today's methods and equipment, and to share my newfound knowledge with others. Sharing knowledge is what this book is all about.

My experience in teaching crafts has proved conclusively to me that the best method of teaching is the project method. In other words, the best way to learn how to perform a skill is actually to do it. It is with this knowledge that I have written *Early American Crafts*.

The instructions for each craft presented were written with the assumption that the reader has no knowledge of the particular craft. The fundamental techniques for each craft are, consequently, discussed in depth. Projects vary in regard to degree of difficulty, enabling the reader to learn while creating. A complete list of materials and tools accompanies each project. The projects are presented in a step-by-step format with explanatory photographs and diagrams to guide the reader. Every effort has been made to enable *anyone* to complete easily each and every project in the book.

It is important to remember that in order to do a craft well, it is first necessary to master the techniques. I encourage you to make this your primary objective. Try to do each project as well as you possibly can. You will find it a great morale booster to see your efforts rewarded with a design piece that is truly beautiful. At the same time, you will have increased your skill and gained enough confidence to branch out and design your own projects.

The ultimate goal of this book is to acquaint the reader with enough information to do each craft well and to inspire her to create her own projects.

1

Quilling

The art of quilling, sometimes called quillwork or paper filigree, is a technique of creating designs with narrow strips of paper that have been rolled, shaped, arranged, and glued on a background. At one time, featherless quills of birds were used as the rolling tools; thus, the terms *quilling* and *quillwork.* The other term, *paper filigree,* sprang from the fact that quillwork was often done with gilt paper and very much resembled ornamental gold filigree work.

Quilling seems to have had its origins in fifteenth-century Italy. Italian and French nuns used the technique to embellish religious plaques and relics. Sometimes entire walls surrounding statue niches were decorated with the lacelike paper filigree. Over the next two centuries, quilling spread throughout Europe and the American colonies. In America, the craft was used to decorate various household items, such as candle sconces, furniture, shadow boxes, mirrors, and screens.

Interest in quilling has recently been revived in the United States, and the craft has become very popular. It is now being taught in many hobby and craft shops across the country—where, incidentally, precut paper strips in every color of the rainbow and other needed materials are readily available. Modern-day quilling is used to embellish all kinds of household and personal objects, such as jewelry, shadow box purses, flower plaques, and small tree and flower arrangements.

The designs in this chapter are all originals. Most of them combine standard quilling forms with new rolling techniques and arrangements. Although quilling looks like a complicated and difficult craft, once a few basic principles are mastered, it is really quite easy to do. These basic principles will be explained in the following sections. Be sure to read them before starting your projects.

Quilling Materials and Tools

Basically, there are five essential items needed for quilling. These are quilling strips, rolling tools, a quilling board, glue, and a pair of scissors. First and foremost are the quilling strips. One of the major updates in this craft is the availability of standard, precut quilling strips. These measure ⅛ inch in width and usually 25 inches in length. They come in many colors and can be bought inexpensively at craft stores. Although it is possible to cut your own strips using Strathmore or other smooth-finish, high-rag-content papers, it is difficult to maintain a constant width. Even with a paper cutter, it is a time-consuming chore and more expensive in the long run because of the waste involved. In any case, you will need a pair of scissors to cut your strips to their required lengths. Any pair of scissors will do, as long as they are sharp and clean.

There are several tools that can be used to roll the strips. For most quilling shapes, you will need a tool with a small diameter—less than $1/16$ inch—such as a hatpin or corsage pin. (See Photograph 1-1.) For those who prefer working

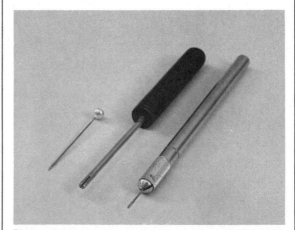

Photograph 1-1

with a handle, you can easily make a handled quilling needle. Use an X-acto knife for the handle and a needle for the curling section. (An X-acto knife is a metal handle fit with a scalpel-like blade, which is used by artists for cutting paper. It is available at stationery stores, hardware, and art supply stores. See tool on the right in Photograph 1-1.) Use a needle with an eye that is large enough to accept the ⅛-inch-wide strips. (A #7 embroidery needle is perfect for this.) Cut the needle in half with a wire cutter and insert the cut end into the X-acto knife slit. Adjust the slit so that the needle will not fall out. Then insert the end of the quilling strip into the eye of the needle. (See Photograph 1-2A.) You will then proceed to roll the handle, guiding the strip with your fingers as you roll. (See Photograph 1-2B.) You can either leave the eye as it is or file off the end with a metal file to form an open eye. There are advantages to each. While the closed-eye needle is strong and rolls the quilling strips with ease, it doesn't release the strips very easily. To free the strip from the needle, you will have to twist the needle in the opposite direction while holding the roll firmly in place. On the other hand, the open-eye needle offers easy removal of strips but is not as strong as the closed-eye needle and doesn't roll them as well. To find the type that suits you best, make one of each and practice with both.

For quilling shapes with larger diameters, you will need a tin can curling tool. (See center tool in Photograph 1-1.) Available in craft stores, these come in four sizes according to diameter—#00, #01, #02, and #03; or $3/32$ inch, ⅛ inch, $3/16$ inch, and ¼ inch, respectively. Actually, you probably have cylindrical items of these same diameters around the house. Knitting needles of various sizes, for example, will do nicely. Check and see what you can find before you buy.

In the projects that follow, you will be instructed to use either a quilling needle or a tin can curling tool. *Quilling needle* will refer to any of the smaller-diameter tools and *tin can curling tool* will refer to the larger-diameter tools.

Once you have rolled your shapes, it is time to arrange them. For this, you will need a quilling board. (See Photograph 1-3.) A quilling board, quite simply, is a flat work surface with see-through paper taped over it. The drawn or traced pattern is placed on the surface and held on with masking tape. A thin sheet of acetate or waxed

Photograph 1-2A

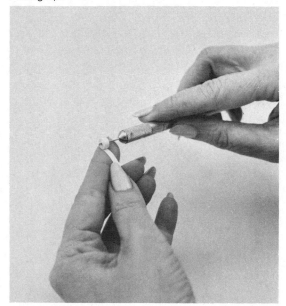

Photograph 1-2B

13

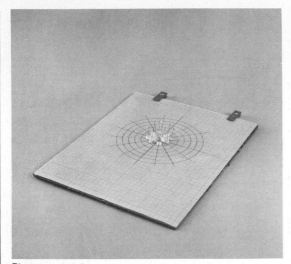

Photograph 1-3

paper is then wrapped around it and taped in place. The quills are placed over the transparent paper and arranged, following the pattern underneath.

The board can be made of corrugated cardboard, Styrofoam, or cork. Graph paper glued to the top of the board is helpful but not essential. Acetate sheets (.007 to .010 inch thick) are more transparent than waxed paper sheets and are therefore more suitable for this work.

Once the shapes have been assembled, they must be glued together. For most gluing, use a fast-drying white glue. White glue should also be used in certain shapes for adhering the end of a strip to the body of the roll. In some of the following projects, you will be elevating areas of the designs. For this you should use a silicone adhesive, such as General Electric Silicone Seal, Dow Corning Rubber Silicone Sealer, or Dow Corning Silicone Adhesive. Project instructions will specify when to use silicone adhesive.

Some of the other tools you will be needing are straight pins or corsage pins and bead wire. Pins are used for holding quilled pieces in place on the quilling board. Bead wire (24 gauge) is used for hanging purposes and for applying thin lines of glue. You will also need a pair of wire cutters to cut lengths of the wire.

Since quilling shapes are usually very small, they are often difficult to handle. A pair of tweezers is helpful for picking up pieces. The serrated type is best. To lift pieces that are stuck to the transparent cover of the quilling board, use a palette knife. Used by painters to mix oils, a palette knife has a thin, flexible blade and no cutting edge. Slip the blade under the piece and gently lift up.

Have a ruler on hand to measure quilling-strip lengths. You will also need 8½- by 11-inch paper sheets and tracing paper for drawing and tracing the design patterns. Keep some sharp pencils nearby too.

Since many of your quilling designs will be done on wood, there are certain materials you will need to treat the wood. For sanding wood objects and smoothing paint between coats, use #350 garnet paper or #400 sandpaper. Chemically treated cloths, called tack rags, are used for picking up dust and sanding residue. To seal wood or paper, purchase Treasure Sealer. It comes in spray cans or regular containers. You will also want some vinyl varnish to add a shine to the wood. Use separate brushes for sealing and varnishing. These should be pure bristle brushes, ½ inch wide.

Some of the projects in this chapter call for

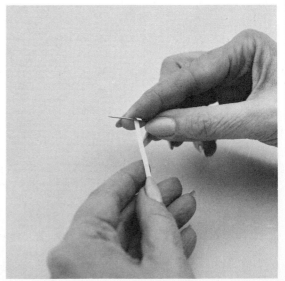

Photograph 1-4

Photograph 1-5

steaming paper into shape. For this you can use an ordinary kitchen strainer. Drop the paper shape into the strainer, and place the strainer over, not in, a pot of boiling water. After the piece has been steamed, shaped, and allowed to dry, apply acrylic spray. This protects the piece against moisture and helps it to maintain its shape.

In some of your quilling work, you may want to gild the paper strips. Gold metallic paint, called Liquid Leaf, can be used for this purpose. For painting quills, use two-ounce jars of water-base acrylic paint.

At the end of the book, you will find a list of these quilling materials and tools and where to find them.

Quilling Hints and Techniques

Following is a list of hints and techniques that will help you in your quillwork.

■ Always remember to keep your hands clean. The hours of time and energy spent in creating a design can be lost to a completed project that has been soiled by dirty hands.

■ If you are using a hatpin, corsage pin, or knitting needle to roll the strips, moisten the end of the strip slightly. Place it against the rolling tool and roll, while guiding with your fingers.

(See Photograph 1-4.) Starting the roll is much easier this way, since moistening the end of the strip makes it cling to the rolling tool.

■ When gluing, always remember to use glue sparingly. A little goes a long way.

■ To gild or paint just the edges of strips, place a few drops of the desired color in the center of a piece of polyurethane sponge. Hold the strip perpendicular to the sponge and draw the edge of the strip across the colored spot, as shown in Photograph 1-5.

■ Never assemble a design directly on the quilling board without using the acetate sheet. If you do, the white glue will stick to the board and you will have a mess on your hands.

■ At times, a design will stick slightly to the transparent cover of the quilling board. If this happens, you can easily lift it off with your palette knife or a kitchen spatula.

■ When rolling a large number of assorted quilling shapes, separate them into categories according to color, size, and shape. This cuts down on confusion and helps ensure accuracy when arranging the design.

■ When marking and measuring quilling strips, measure accurately and make pencil marks that are faint so that pencil lines don't appear all over the completed design.

Basic Quilling Shapes

The quilling shapes to be made in the projects of this chapter are explained in the following instructions, diagrams, and photographs. We will begin with the simplest shapes and progress to the more complex. For the time being, learn and practice each quilling shape with the rolling tool and quilling-strip length you find easiest to work with. Most quilling shapes do have small diameters, however, so that you will be using the quilling needle more often then the tin can curling tool once you have started on the projects.

For many shapes, you will be told to mark off a specific measurement or measurements on the

15

quilling strip. These marks designate points at which to fold or glue the strip. Be sure to mark off these measurements accurately. Careful marking helps ensure that your quills will be identical in size and shape.

When you are working on your own designs, the instructions for the basic shapes should still be followed. Choosing strip lengths and rolling tools is where your individual creativity enters in. Work with shape types and sizes that suit your artistic taste.

Since most quilling shapes use the rolling technique, it is important that you understand and master it thoroughly. Quilling shapes can either be tightly rolled or loosely rolled, depending upon the desired effect. Before advancing to more complicated shapes, you must learn how to make both tight rolls and loose rolls.

1. **Tight roll:** With a high degree of tension, wind the strip tightly around the tool, guiding the strip with your fingers. When completely wound, slide the rolling tool out of the center of the roll, gently holding the roll together with

Diagram 1-1

Photograph 1-6

your fingers. Put a small amount of white glue under the end of the strip, and adhere it to the body of the roll.

Tight rolls and loose rolls may have either open or tightly closed holes in their centers. This will depend on the diameter of the rolling instrument you have used. If you wish to make a tight roll with a tightly closed center, use the X-acto knife-needle tool. Make a tight roll, and glue its end to the body of the roll.

2. **Loose roll:** With a lesser amount of tension, wind the strip around the rolling tool, guiding the strip with your fingers. Slide the rolling tool out of the center of the roll. Allow the roll to uncoil a bit so there will be space between each

adjacent turn. Unwind the roll with your fingers until the desired diameter is reached. Put a small amount of white glue under the end of the strip, and adhere it to the body of the roll.

The amount that the roll unwinds—its spring-back—is a direct result of the amount of tension that was used to roll the strip. If a high level of tension was applied, the roll will not

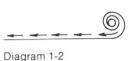

Diagram 1-2

Photograph 1-7

unwind as far as it would have had a low level of tension been applied. Learn to control the tension level by experimenting with different levels and observing the results.

If the quilling strip has been marked, line up the loose end of the quilling strip with this mark. Put a small amount of white glue under the end of the strip, and adhere it to the body of the roll.

Once you have mastered the tight roll and the loose roll, you are ready to progress to more complicated shapes.

3. **Tear drop:** Make a loose roll. Tightly pinch the spot at which the end of the strip has been glued to the body of the roll, allowing the opposite end to form an elliptic shape.

Diagram 1-3

Photograph 1-8

4. **Eye:** Make a loose roll. With one hand, gently pinch the spot where the end of the strip has been glued to the body of the roll; with the other hand, gently pinch the opposite end of the

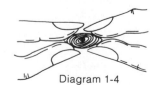

Diagram 1-4

Photograph 1-9

roll. The result should be an eye-shaped quill with a roll in the center.

5. Double circle: Lightly mark a quilling strip according to project directions. Turn strip over. Make a tight roll and remove the tool. Unroll the

Diagram 1-5A

End — Mark

Diagram 1-5B Glue end to mark

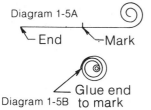

Photograph 1-10

outer end of the strip until the mark appears at the bottom of the roll. Allow the loosened strip end to spring back, forming a loose circle around the tighter portion of the roll. Glue the end of the strip to the body of the roll at the mark with a small amount of white glue.

6. Open tear drop: Make a double circle. Tightly pinch the spot where the end of the strip

Diagram 1-6

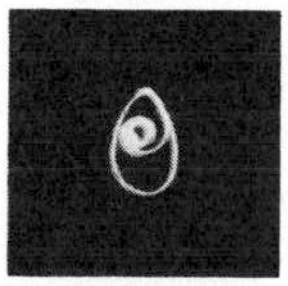

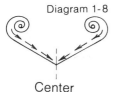

Photograph 1-11

has been glued to the body of the roll, allowing the opposite end to form an elliptic shape.

7. Scroll: Lightly mark the center of a strip. Make a loose roll from each end of the strip,

Diagram 1-7

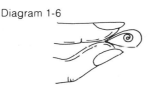

Center

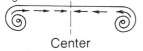

Photograph 1-12

rolling outward to the center. Allow the strip to uncoil. Do not glue.

8. Heart: Fold a strip in half, end to end. Make a tight or loose roll from each end of the strip, rolling inward to the center. Uncoil the ends and

Diagram 1-8

Center

Photograph 1-13

shape to form a heart. Glue the two rolls together at the point of contact to form a closed heart.

9. Petal: Fold a strip in half, end to end. Make a tight or loose roll from one end of the strip, rolling inward to the center, and another tight or loose roll from the other end, rolling inward but not quite up to the center. Uncoil the ends so that the rolls will fit "one on top of the other." Glue the rolls together at the points of contact.

Diagram 1-9

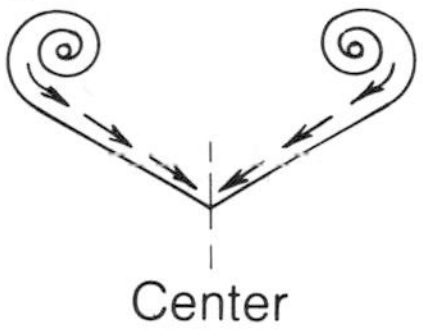

Center

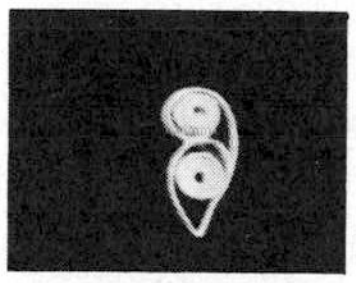

Photograph 1-14

10. V scroll: Fold a strip in half, end to end. Make a tight or loose roll from each end of the strip, rolling outward to the center. Uncoil and shape to form a V.

Diagram 1-10

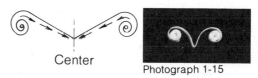

Center

Photograph 1-15

11. Reverse open scroll: Fold a strip in half, end to end. Make a tight roll from one end, rolling inward to the center. Make another tight roll from the other end, rolling outward to the center. Uncoil the rolls about one-half to one full turn. Shape as shown in photograph.

Diagram 1-11

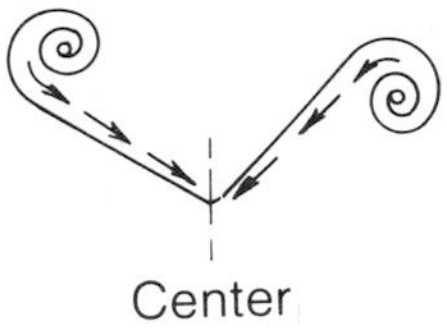

Center

Photograph 1-16

12. S shape: Lightly mark the center of a strip. Make a loose roll from one end, rolling inward to the center. Allow the strip to uncoil. Make another loose roll from the other end, rolling outward to the center, and allow the strip to uncoil. Shape to form an S. Do not glue.

Diagram 1-12

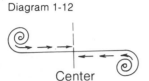

Center

Photograph 1-17

13. ? scroll: Lightly mark the center of a strip. Make a loose roll from one end, rolling inward to the center. Allow the strip to uncoil. Make a tight roll from the other end, rolling outward and not quite up to the center. Shape to form a question mark. Glue the tight roll to the body of the roll to close it up.

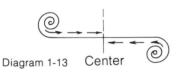

Diagram 1-13   Center

Photograph 1-18

14. Basic fan: Mark off 2 inches from each end of a 9-inch quilling strip. Divide and mark the center portion into five 1-inch segments, as shown in Diagram 1-14A. Make inward folds at each of the six marks. Gather the six folds together to form five loops. (See Diagram 1-14B.)

|← 2" →|←1"→|←1"→|←1"→|←1"→|←1"→|← 2" →|

Diagram 1-14A   Quilling strip

Diagram 1-14B   Crease strip at each mark

Glue together on each creased line

Diagram 1-14C

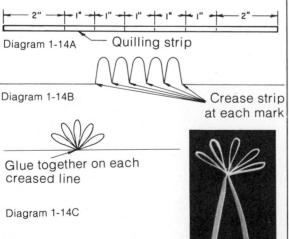

Photograph 1-19

Adhere them together at the bottom with a small amount of white glue, as shown in Diagram 1-14C, and hold the fan in place until the glue sets.

Fans can be made with any number of loops. To make a four-loop fan, for example, simply mark the center portion of an 8-inch quilling strip into four 1-inch segments.

15. Fan variations A, B, and C: Make 3 basic fans. Make a tight roll from each end of the 3 fans, rolling outward to the center. (See Diagram 1-15.) Uncoil and shape, as shown in Photo-

Diagram 1-15

Center

Photograph 1-20A

Photograph 1-20C

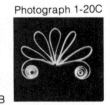

Photograph 1-20B

graphs 1-20A, 1-20B, and 1-20C. Glue the coils in variations A and B together at the points of contact.

16. Fan variations D, E, F, and G: Make 4 basic fans. Make a tight roll from each end of the 4 fans, rolling inward to the center. (See Diagram 1-16.) Uncoil and shape, as shown in Photographs 1-21D, 1-21E, 1-21F, and 1-21G. Glue the coils in variations D, F, and G at the points of contact.

Photograph 1-21D

Photograph 1-21F

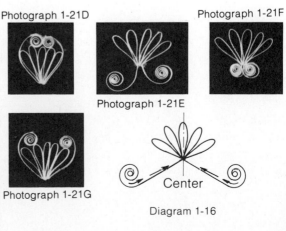

Photograph 1-21E

Photograph 1-21G

Center

Diagram 1-16

17. Basic comma scroll: Mark off ¾ inch from one end of a 1¾-inch quilling strip. Make a tight, inward fold at this mark. Using a #00 tin can curling tool, make a loose roll, rolling from the fold to the end of the strip. Slide out the tool and line up the two ends of the strip. Adhere

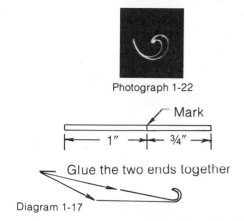

Photograph 1-22

Diagram 1-17

them with a small amount of white glue. Uncoil and shape to form a comma.

18. Double scroll: Mark off the center and ¾ inch from each end of a 3½-inch quilling strip. Make tight, inward folds at these marks. Using a #00 tin can curling tool, make a loose roll from each of the folded ends, rolling inward to the center. Slide out the tool and line up each strip

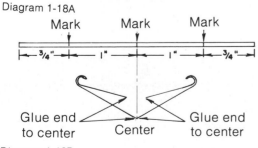

Photograph 1-23

Diagram 1-18A

Diagram 1-18B

end to the center. Adhere them with a small amount of white glue. Uncoil, shape, and tightly fold on the center mark to match the photograph.

19. Double scroll variations A and B: Make 2 double scrolls. Uncoil, shape, and tightly fold on center marks to match the photographs.

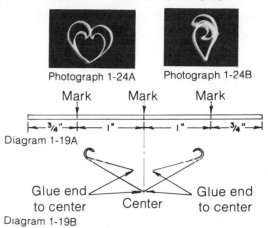

Photograph 1-24A   Photograph 1-24B

Diagram 1-19A

Diagram 1-19B

20. Double scroll variations C and D: Mark off the center and ¾ inch from each end of two 3½-inch quilling strips. Make a tight, inward fold at one of the ¾-inch marks on each strip. Make a tight, outward fold at the other ¾-inch mark on each. Using a quilling needle, make a loose roll from one of the folded ends, rolling inward to the center. Slide out the tool. Make a loose roll from the other end, rolling outward to the center. Adhere each end to the center with a small amount of white glue. Uncoil and shape to match photographs.

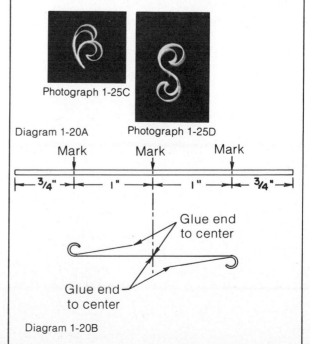

Photograph 1-25C

Diagram 1-20A   Photograph 1-25D

Diagram 1-20B

19

21. Running vine: Find the midpoint of a 20-inch quilling strip. Mark off ⅝ inch from either side of the midpoint. You now have a 1¼-inch segment. Mark off other dimensions of the five-loop fan section in Diagram 1-21A. Leaving ¾ inch on the right side and 1½ inches on the left side, mark two more fan sections. Make inward folds at each mark. Beginning with the centermost 1¼-inch segment, form an elongated loop by bringing the folded ends together. Place a small amount of white glue at the ends, match, and adhere them together. Do this for each adjacent section—the 1-inch and the ¾-inch segment on either side—thus forming a fan with five loops. (See Diagram 1-21B.) Measure ¾ inch from the right side of the fan section, and repeat this procedure; then measure 1½ inches from the left side of the fan section and do

Photograph 1-26

Diagram 1-21A

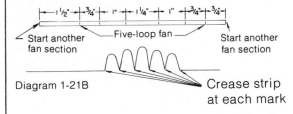

Diagram 1-21B

the same. Adhere the remaining strip lengths together, as shown in Diagram 1-21C. Shape the vine to match photograph.

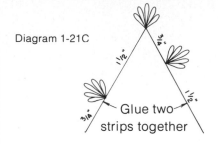

Diagram 1-21C

Glue two strips together

22. Continuous scroll: Make the number of loose rolls required in the project, leaving the ends unglued. Unroll the outer leg of each loose roll. Position it so that the leg will gently sweep from the top of the roll to the bottom of the adjacent roll. Use a small amount of white glue to adhere the end of the strip to the bottom of the adjacent roll. (See Diagram 1-22). Continue in

Photograph 1-27

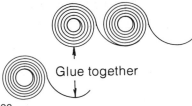

Glue together

Diagram 1-22

this way until the scroll is complete. The scroll can be made on a work surface or directly on the design. The same scroll can be made rolling two strips of different colors simultaneously.

23. Triple loop: Mark a strip according to project instructions. There will be a short, a medium, and a long section. Make an inward fold at the short section mark, and make an outward fold at the long section mark. (See Diagram 1-23A.) Make an elongated loop from the short

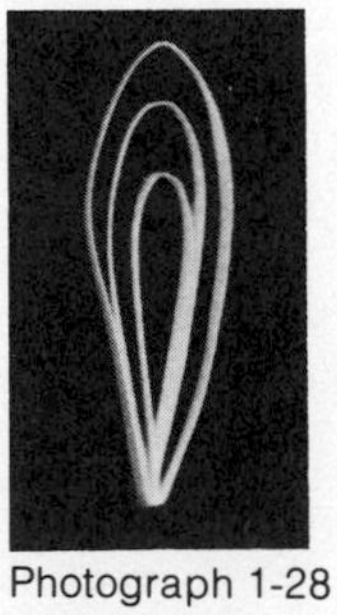

Photograph 1-28

Short

Medium

Long

Diagram 1-23A

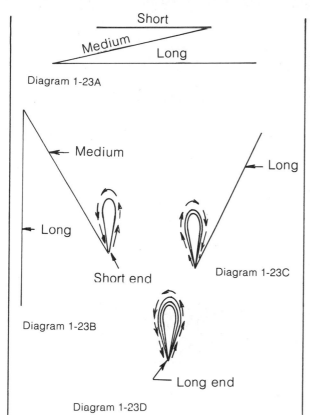

Medium

Long

Long

Short end

Diagram 1-23C

Diagram 1-23B

Long end

Diagram 1-23D

Photograph 1-29A

Mark — Curling tool

Glued area

Glue

Long end

Diagram 1-24B

Diagram 1-24A

Diagram 1-24C

Glue

Diagram 1-24D

Photograph 1-29B

Diagram 1-24E

section by bringing its end to the fold, as shown in Diagram 1-23B. Adhere at the bottom with a small amount of white glue. Bring the center segment back over the small segment, and adhere at the bottom with white glue. (See Diagram 1-23C.) Finally, bring the longest section back over the two loops and glue at the bottom, as shown in Diagram 1-23D.

24. Single spray: Mark a strip according to project instructions. Place the rolling tool (the tool used here was a #01 tin can curling tool) on the mark, and wrap the strip snugly around it. Apply a small amount of white glue to the two sides of the strip, directly below the loop. The glued spot should cover an area equal to the diameter of the rolling tool. In other words, if the rolling tool is ⅛ inch in diameter, the glued area directly below the loop should be ⅛ inch long. Remove the tool. Hold the strip firmly together until the glue sets. At the point where the glued

area stops, fold the longer side of the strip up. Apply a small amount of white glue below the fold, covering an area equal to the diameter of the rolling tool. Place the rolling tool on the fold, and wrap the strip snugly around it. Align the two legs of the strip, below the loop, and hold them together until the glue sets. Continue in this manner until you have made the number of loops specified in the project instructions.

25. Double spray: Make a single spray with the number of loops specified in the project instructions. Make another single spray with one loop less than the first one. Glue the two single sprays together, positioning the extra loop at the top.

Diagram 1-25

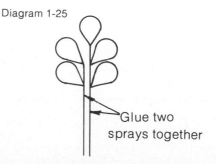

Glue two sprays together

21

Sailboat Shadow Box

This sailboat, with its red and white sail billowing in the breeze, makes an attractive piece for a game room or den. Alter the colors used for the sail, the boat, the frame, and the frame trim to fit the color scheme of the room you wish to use it in.

Materials

shadow box frame, 9 by 12 inches
1 piece posterboard, 9 by 12 inches, in white
quilling strips in light blue, dark blue, white, and red
quilling board
rolling tools
scissors
pencil
tracing paper
white glue
straight pins or corsage pins
1 Styrofoam egg, 6 inches in diameter
1 sheet aluminum foil, large enough to encircle egg
kitchen strainer and pot
1 can acrylic spray, clear
1 sheet Strathmore paper, 2-ply; or construction paper, in white
3 jars acrylic paint, 2-ounce size, in white, red, and light blue
1 paintbrush
7 inches floral wire, 18 gauge
1 felt-tipped pen, fine-pointed, in red
3 inches white thread

Instructions

1. See shape numbers on the following Quilling Instructions table. Refer to corresponding shape numbers in preceding Basic Quilling Shapes section and follow directions. Follow table for amount of each shape to make, lengths of quilling strips, colors, use, and tools needed.

2. Trace the heavy outline of the sail pattern onto tracing paper. Place tracing paper beneath transparent work surface of quilling board.

3. Place the S shapes between the traced lines, as shown—one forward, the next reversed. The red S shapes should be placed in the shaded areas and the white S shapes in the unshaded areas. Adjust the S shapes to fit within the outline. Apply a

Quilling Instructions

Shape and Shape Number	Amount	Strip Length (in inches)	Color	Use	Tool
S shapes (12)	75	2	red	shaded sail area	quilling needle
S shapes (12)	64	2	white	unshaded sail area	quilling needle
Open tear drops (6)	73	2, marked at ¾ inch	dark blue	waves	quilling needle
Open tear drops (6)	52	2, marked at ¾ inch	light blue	waves	quilling needle

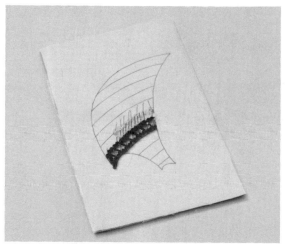

Photograph 1-30

Photograph 1-31

small amount of white glue to the S shapes, at the points of contact. Pin in place on the pattern, as shown in Photograph 1-30.

4. Wrap the Styrofoam egg with aluminum foil. Rub the surface of the foil with your hands to make it as smooth as possible.

5. After the glue on the sail has thoroughly dried (about 8 hours), place sail in a large strainer. Place strainer over an open pot of boiling water for 3 to 5 minutes. This steaming process will make the sail flexible. Remove the sail from the strainer, and immediately pin it on the Styrofoam egg. (See Photograph 1-31.) After the sail has been left on the egg for at least 1 hour,

spray it with clear acrylic. Once the acrylic has dried (about 15 minutes), remove the sail from the egg.

6. On tracing paper, trace the boat from the design pattern. Transfer the traced pattern to a piece of Strathmore paper. The easiest way to do this is to place tracing paper over Strathmore paper, with carbon paper in between, and draw over lines. Cut out pattern. Crease and glue together with white glue, as shown on the pattern. Paint white stripe with white acrylic paint and rest of boat with red acrylic paint.

7. Paint floral wire with red acrylic paint, and allow it to dry.

23

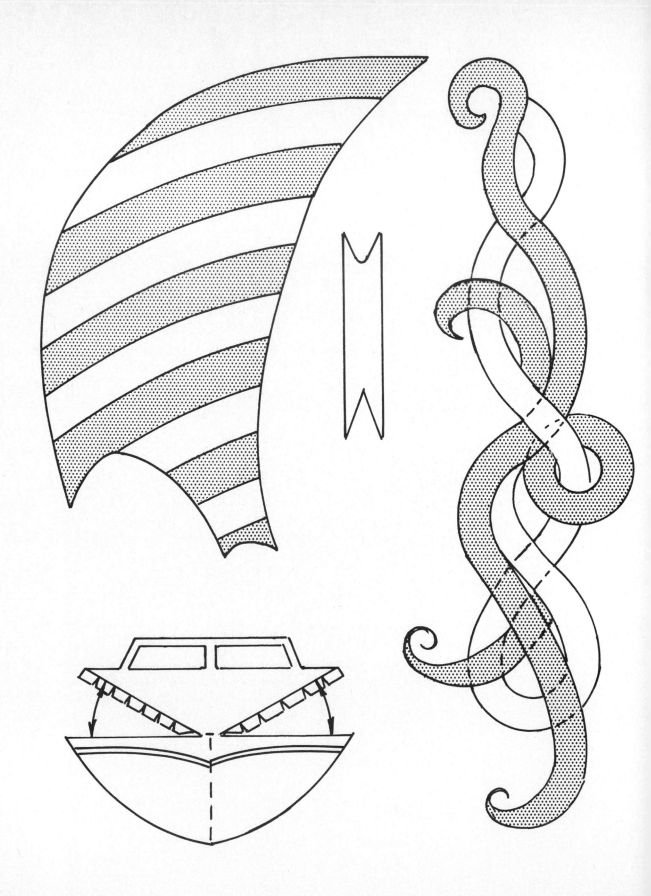

8. Trace the banner from the pattern onto a piece of tracing paper and transfer it to a piece of Strathmore paper. With the felt-tipped pen, make five horizontal red lines across the banner, as shown on the pattern. Cut the banner out, shape it, and glue it to the top of the wire. Glue the wire behind the centerpost of the windshield, allowing 6 inches to extend above it. (See Photograph 1-32.)

Photograph 1-33

Photograph 1-32

9. Trace the pattern for the waves onto tracing paper. Place tracing paper beneath transparent surface of quilling board.

10. Mark an 11½-inch light blue quilling strip into forty-six ¼-inch segments. Stand the strip up on its edge. Adhere the point of a light blue open tear drop to each mark on the strip. Place this strip over the unshaded portion of the wave pattern. Shape it and pin it in place. (See Photograph 1-33.) Note that at the left side of the

pattern, the loop forms a figure 8 and comes back across to the right. Where necessary, fill in curves with additional open tear drops. Shape and glue another 11½-inch strip of light blue quilling paper to the opposite edge of the wave, as shown in Photograph 1-34. Make the dark blue wave in the same manner, using two 13-inch dark blue quilling strips and the dark blue open tear drops. Shape the ends of the wave strip to form two wave tips.

11. After the glue has thoroughly dried (about 8 hours), place both waves in a strainer, and steam them over a pot of boiling water for 3 to 5 minutes. Intertwine the dark and light blue strips, as shown in Photograph 1-35. Position the two waves over the pattern on the quilling board. Glue the waves to one another, at the points of contact, and pin them in place on the quilling board. Allow the glue to dry for about 30 minutes. Unpin and remove waves from quilling board.

Photograph 1-34

Photograph 1-35

12. Place pins at $^1/_{16}$-inch intervals around the inner circle wave on pattern. Wrap a 1¾-inch dark blue quilling strip around the pins, overlapping it slightly at the ends. Adhere the ends with white glue. Glue 14 open tear drops to the strip, with the pointed ends in. Glue a 4¾-inch dark blue quilling strip around the circumference of the open tear drops. After the glue has dried (about 30 minutes), make a cut in the circle, as shown in Photograph 1-36. This allows the circle to be slipped around the light blue wave. Position the circle around the light blue wave so that the opening will be behind the wave. Glue the circle to the wave with white glue.

Photograph 1-36

13. To make the two center wave tips, mark a 2¾-inch dark blue quilling strip into eight ¼-inch segments. Place the strip on its edge, and adhere the point of an open tear drop at each mark. Place this strip over one of the wave tips on the pattern, position it, and pin it in place. (See Photograph 1-37.) Glue another 2¾-inch dark blue quilling strip to the opposite edge of the wave tip. Make another wave tip in the same

26

Photograph 1-37

manner. Adhere both wave tips to the wave at appropriate positions.

14. Paint the posterboard with light blue acrylic paint. Allow to dry. Use silicone adhesive to glue the boat to the posterboard in appropriate spot. The boat should be set at a slight angle. Center and position the wave 1½ inches from the bottom. Adhere to posterboard with silicone adhesive. (See Photograph 1-38.) Use silicone adhe-

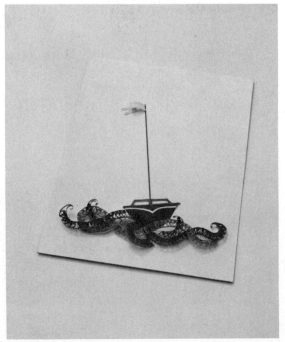

Photograph 1-38

Sailboat Shadow Box

Photograph 1-39

sive to adhere the sail in place, as shown in Photograph 1-39. Glue at the top and at the left bottom corner of the sail. To make a boom line, glue a piece of white thread from the right bottom corner of the sail to the boat.

15. Make the three gulls from white quilling strips. Make one from a 2-inch strip, one from a 1½-inch strip, and one from a 1-inch strip. Fold each strip in half widthwise. Use a quilling needle to make a two-turn tight roll at the fold of the longest strip. Remove the tool and glue the·tight roll to wing section. Make a one-turn tight roll in the 1½-inch strip and a one-half-turn roll in the 1-inch strip; glue in the same manner. With

Photograph 1-40

scissors, taper each end of the gull to a point, and shape. With white glue, adhere gulls to the sky area of the posterboard, as shown in Photograph 1-40.

16. Assemble the picture into the shadow box frame, following instructions given in the Helpful Hints chapter.

28

Butterfly Mobile

Any area of your home that receives a gentle flow of air will make an ideal spot for this mobile. I have mine hanging from the ceiling in my studio, positioned so that the current from the heating and cooling system will keep the butterflies in constant motion. Make five or seven butterflies for the mobile.

Materials

quilling strips in assorted colors
quilling board
rolling tools
scissors
21 sheets notebook paper, in white
ruler
pencil
X-acto knife
long $1/16$-inch-diameter rolling tool
8 seed beads per butterfly, #11/0
15 inches bead wire per butterfly, 26 gauge
wire cutters
white glue
tracing paper
straight pins or corsage pins
1 large hatpin
jars of acrylic paint, 2-ounce size, in assorted colors
1 paintbrush

Instructions

1. There are three types of butterflies in this mobile—large, medium-sized, and small. Each butterfly has a head, a body, and a tail. All three parts are made in the same way. Refer to Butterfly Parts table (following) for the dimensions to follow for each butterfly and body part.

2. For the head of the large butterfly, fold a sheet of notebook paper in half lengthwise. Measure across from the top folded corner of the paper to the width designated in the table—$1/8$ inch. Mark off this spot and label it "W." On the fold, measure down from the top corner to the length designated in the table—11 inches. Mark off this spot, and label it "L." Using an X-acto knife and a ruler as a guide, cut from point "W" to point "L." Make sure that the paper is held firmly in place while cutting. (See Diagram 1-26A.) Unfold the triangle, as shown in Diagram 1-26B. Moisten the wide end of the triangle strip. Place a long $1/16$-inch-diameter rolling tool against it and roll from the bottom to the point, as shown in Photograph 1-41. Make sure that you are

Butterfly Parts

Large Butterfly

Part	Width of paper	Length of paper
Head	$1/8$ inch	11 inches
Body	$1/4$ inch	11 inches
Tail	$5/8$ inch	11 inches

Medium-sized Butterfly

Part	Width of paper	Length of paper
Head	$1/8$ inch	10 inches
Body	$3/16$ inch	10 inches
Tail	$1/2$ inch	10 inches

Small Butterfly

Part	Width of paper	Length of paper
Head	$1/8$ inch	10 inches
Body	$1/8$ inch	10 inches
Tail	$3/8$ inch	10 inches

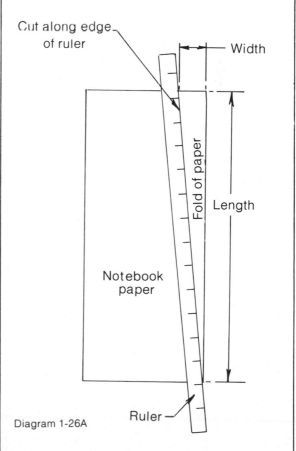

Diagram 1-26A

Fold

Diagram 1-26B

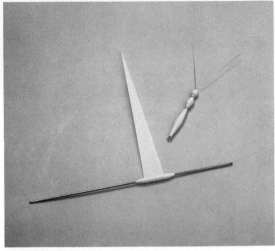

Photograph 1-41

rolling straight. The point of the triangle should be right in the center when you are done. Place a small amount of white glue under the point and adhere it firmly in place. Allow the glue to dry for 2 or 3 minutes. Slide the rolling tool out.

Repeat this same procedure for the head, body, and tail parts of each size butterfly, following table specifications for widths and lengths.

3. For each butterfly, thread two seed beads onto a 9-inch piece of bead wire. Fold bead wire in half so that the beads are in the center. Pass the ends of the wire up through the tail section, and position the tail section snugly against the beads. Pass the ends up through the body section in the same way. Put a small amount of white glue between the body and tail sections. Put the head section on the wire, in the same manner, and apply white glue between head and body. Spread the wire apart to form a slightly open V. This will hold the parts firmly together and form the butterfly's antennae at the top. (See Diagram 1-27.)

4. Trace the outline of each butterfly pattern on tracing paper. Place tracing paper pattern beneath the transparent surface of your quilling board. Pin butterfly body in place over the pat-

tern body. Place one pin through the wire loop at the tail and one at each side of the neck. Do not stick pins through the body. (See Photograph 1-42.)

5. See shape numbers on the following Quilling Instructions table. Refer to corresponding shape numbers in preceding Basic Quilling Shapes section and follow directions. Follow table for amount of each shape to make, lengths of quilling strips, colors, use, and tools needed.

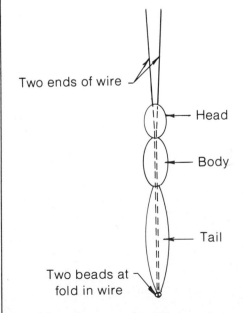

Two ends of wire

Head

Body

Tail

Two beads at fold in wire

Diagram 1-27

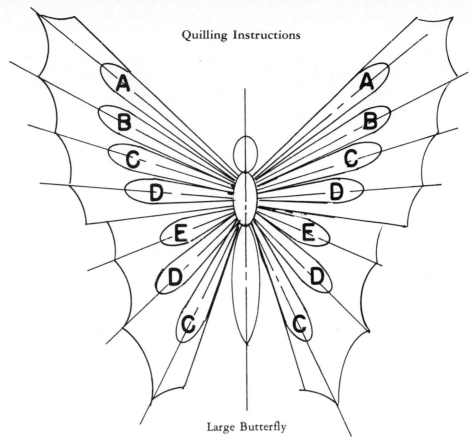

Large Butterfly

Shape and Shape Number	Amount	Strip Length (in inches)	Color	Use	Tool
Triple loops (23)	2	9¾; marked at 3¾ inches, 3¼ inches, and 2¾ inches	optional	Section A	none
Triple loops (23)	2	8¼; marked at 3¼ inches, 2¾ inches, and 2¼ inches	optional	Section B	none
Triple loops (23)	4	6¾; marked at 2¾ inches, 2¼ inches, and 1¾ inches	optional	Section C	none
Triple loops (23)	4	5¼; marked at 2¼ inches, 1¾ inches, and 1¼ inches	optional	Section D	none
Triple loops (23)	2	3¾; marked at 1¾ inches, 1¼ inches, and ¾ inch	optional	Section E	none
S Shapes (12)	60	2	optional	around wings	quilling needle
Scrolls (7)	2	2	optional	on top of wing	quilling needle
Open tear drops (6)	46	1¾; marked at ¾ inch	optional	around wings	quilling needle

31

Medium-sized Butterfly

Shape and Shape Number	Amount	Strip Length (in inches)	Color	Use	Tool
Triple loops (23)	2	8¼; marked at 3¼ inches, 2¾ inches, and 2¼ inches	optional	Section B	none
Triple loops (23)	2	6¾; marked at 2¾ inches, 2¼ inches, and 1¾ inches	optional	Section C	none
Triple loops (23)	4	5¼; marked at 2¼ inches, 1¾ inches, and 1¼ inches	optional	Section D	none
Triple loops (23)	2	3¾; marked at 1¾ inches, 1¼ inches, and ¾ inch	optional	Section E	none
Scrolls (7)	40	1	optional	around wings	quilling needle
Tear drops (3)	82	1	optional	around wings	quilling needle
Open tear drops (6)	6	3, marked at ¾ inch	optional	around wings	quilling needle

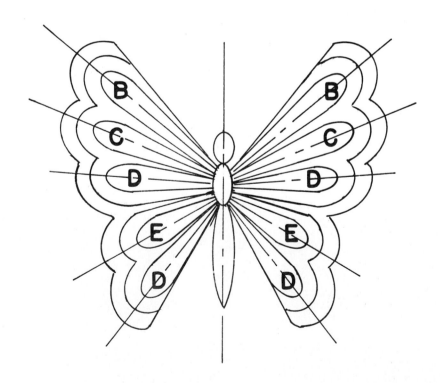

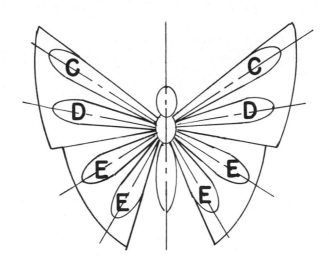

Small Butterfly

Shape and Shape Number	Amount	Strip Length (in inches)	Color	Use	Tool
Triple loops (23)	2	6¾; marked at 2¾ inches, 2¼ inches, and 1¾ inches	optional	Section C	none
Triple loops (23)	2	5¼; marked at 2¼ inches, 1¾ inches, and 1¼ inches	optional	Section D	none
Triple loops (23)	4	3¾; marked at 1¾ inches, 1¼ inches, and ¾ inch	optional	Section E	none
Scrolls (7)	32	1	optional	around wings	quilling needle
S shapes (12)	2	1	optional	on top of wings	quilling needle
Open tear drops (6)	16	2, marked at ¾ inch	optional	around wings	quilling needle

6. Place triple loops over butterfly patterns on appropriate sections. Put a small amount of white glue between adjacent triple loops at the points of contact, but do not glue them to body. Pin in place. (See Photograph 1-43.)

7. Refer to butterfly photograph below . Fill in areas between the triple loops with appropriate shapes. Apply a small amount of white glue at the points of contact, and pin in place on the

pattern. (See Photograph 1-44). The triple loops are held together by the additional quills that are glued between them.

8. Remove pins from one wing and the body section. Take both pieces off quilling board. Apply a small amount of white glue to the inner edge of the pinned-down wing, position the body against it, and pin body in place as you did in Step 4. (See Photograph 1-45.) Allow the glue to dry thoroughly.

9. Remove the glued-together body and wing piece from the pattern. Pin the other wing in its place on the quilling board, and apply white glue

Photograph 1-43

Photograph 1-44

34

to its inner edge. Attach the previously assembled body-wing section to this wing, at the angle you desire. In other words, the wings may be fully open, fully closed, or anywhere in between. Pin the section in place over the pattern. If you angled the wing, place a large hatpin or corsage pin behind it for support. (See Photograph 1-46.)

10. Cut a 2-inch piece of bead wire to make an eye for hanging. Fold the wire in half. Starting at ¼ inch from the folded end, twist the wire three times around. Insert the ¼-inch eye of the wire through the center part of one wing, right next to

the body. Twist the open ends together, under the body, to secure wire. It may be necessary to add another wire for balance. If so, make another one and place it between the body and tail sections, as shown in Photograph 1-47.

11. Paint the body with acrylic paint. Try to match the colors in the wing section.

12. Adhere one seed bead to each side of the head for eyes, using white glue. Measure width of one wing at the widest point. Cut the antennae to this width and shape, as shown in Photograph 1-48. Glue two seed beads to the end of each antenna, as shown.

Photograph 1-45

Photograph 1-47

Photograph 1-46

Photograph 1-48

13. Assemble the mobile according to instructions in the Helpful Hints chapter.

36

Floral Cigarette Canister (See page 47.)

Decorative Shadow Box

The shadow box frame used in this project was made in a frame shop; however, suitable frames are available in craft shops and many paint stores. If this exact size cannot be obtained, the design can be adapted to other sizes. In this project, the shadow box frame was used to display an announcement. You may want to use it to display pictures of the children, wedding and birth announcements, or perhaps, your favorite poem, proverb, or limerick.

Materials

shadow box frame, 8 by 10 inches
2 pieces posterboard, 8 by 10 inches, in white
quilling strips in pastel colors
quilling board
rolling tools
scissors
birth or wedding announcement, invitation, or any other memento of your choice
pencil
ruler
⅓ yard antique satin, in white
white glue
4½ feet bead wire, 26 gauge
wire cutters
2 feet satin cord, #1 rattail, in color of your choice
1 roll floral tape, in light olive green
silicone adhesive
½ yard satin ribbon, ¼ inch wide, in color of your choice
3 sheets notebook paper, in white
X-acto knife
long ¹/₁₆-inch-diameter rolling tool
8 seed beads, #11/0
1 sheet tracing paper
straight pins or corsage pins
1 large hatpin
1 jar acrylic paint, 2-ounce size, in color of your choice

Instructions

1. Place announcement, faceup, on work surface. Draw a faint line, ¼ inch in from the edge, around the entire announcement. Measure the length and width of the box you have just drawn. Cut an opening of this same size in the center of one of the pieces of posterboard. This hole should overlap the announcement by ¼ inch. (See Photograph 1-49.)

2. Place the white antique satin on your work table, dull side down. Apply a very thin coat of white glue over the entire white side of the posterboard. Position posterboard in the center of the satin. Turn over. Press satin tightly to the board, and work out all wrinkles with your hands.

37

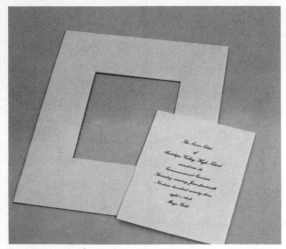

Photograph 1-49

(Make sure that your hands are clean.) Trim off the excess satin around the edge of the poster-board. Allowing about 1 inch from the borders, cut out the center of the silk. Cut the material diagonally to each corner, as shown in Photograph 1-50, being careful to cut right to the corner but no farther. Apply a thin coat of white glue to a 1-inch area on the back side of the posterboard, around the opening. Fold the material over and adhere it in place.

3. Using a piece of bead wire, apply a thin line of white glue around the inside edge of the opening. Adhere satin cord around this edge.

4. Cut two pieces of bead wire to 7½-inch lengths and two pieces to 6-inch lengths. Wrap floral tape around each piece of wire. Twist the two 7½-inch pieces together and the two 6-inch pieces together. Apply two or three dots of silicone adhesive, evenly spaced apart, to the back of each pair of wires. Position the 6-inch pair of wires above the opening of the posterboard and the 7½-inch pair down the left side. Shape wires as shown in Photograph 1-51.

5. See shape numbers on the following Quilling Instructions table. Refer to corresponding shape numbers in preceding Basic Quilling Shapes section and follow directions. Follow table for amount of each shape to make, lengths of quilling strips, colors, use, and tools needed.

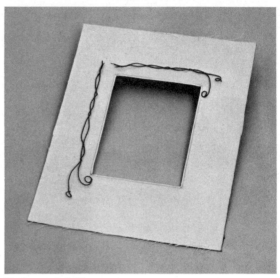

Photograph 1-51

6. Place all the flower quills on your quilling board. Use a tight roll for the center of each flower, and arrange the appropriate quills around the tight rolls, as shown in Photograph 1-52. Assemble two 7-petaled flowers with open tear drops, two 5-petaled flowers with hearts, three 7-petaled flowers with eyes, two 9-petaled flowers with tear drops, and one 5-petaled flower with tight rolls. With white glue, adhere shapes to each other at the points of contact and to the center.

7. Position flowers and double spray leaves around the bead wire vine, as shown in Photo-

Photograph 1-50

38

Photograph 1-52

graph 1-53. Apply drops of silicone adhesive to adhere them in place.

8. Cut the satin ribbon to a 14-inch length. Following directions in the Helpful Hints chapter, make a four-looped bow with the ribbon. Simulate a knot by wrapping a 1½-inch piece of ribbon around the middle of the bow. Adhere it to the back with white glue.

9. Place entire design piece on the white side of the uncut posterboard. Make sure all edges are flush. Trace the outline of the opening onto the

Photograph 1-53

Quilling Instructions

Shape and Shape Number	Amount	Strip Length (in inches)	Color	Use	Tool
Open tear drops (6)	14	1½, marked at ⅝ inch	pastel	flowers	quilling needle
Hearts (8)	10	1½	pastel	flowers	quilling needle
Eyes (4)	21	1½	pastel	flowers	quilling needle
Tear drops (3)	18	1½	pastel	flowers	quilling needle
Tight rolls (1)	15	1	pastel	1 flower and 10 flower centers	quilling needle
Double sprays (25) (3-looped)	14	1¾ for 2-loop side, marked at ½ inch; 1¼ for 1-loop side, marked at ⅝ inch	pastel	leaves	#01 tin can curling tool
Double sprays (25) (5-looped)	6	2¾ for 3-loop side, marked at ⅞ inch; 2¼ for 2-loop side, marked at ⅞ inch	pastel	leaves	#01 tin can curling tool

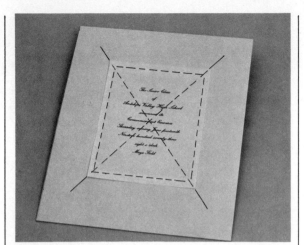

Photograph 1-54

uncut posterboard. Remove piece. Draw diagonals across this outlined section, extending lines 1 or 2 inches beyond each corner. Apply a drop of white glue to each corner of the announcement, align corners with diagonals, and adhere to posterboard. (See Photograph 1-54.) Make sure announcement is perfectly centered. Apply white glue to corners of posterboard, and glue the quilled posterboard piece in place over the announcement. (See Photograph 1-55.)

10. Refer to the Helpful Hints chapter for instructions on how to assemble shadow box frame.

11. Make the small butterfly according to instructions in the Butterfly Mobile project. When completed, glue butterfly to the bottom right corner of the frame with silicone adhesive.

Peacock Shadow Box

This peacock, designed by Lillian Corell of Granada Hills, California, should be displayed in an oval-shaped frame. If you prefer, however, use a rectangular frame of the same height and width. Colored quills can be worked into the tail and wing sections, if you wish.

40

Photograph 1-55

Materials

shadow box frame, oval-shaped, 8 by 10 inches

1 piece posterboard, 8 by 10 inches, in white

quilling strips in white

quilling board

rolling tools

scissors

tracing paper

pencil

straight pins or corsage pins

white glue

1 sheet notebook paper, in white

silicone adhesive

2 feet floral wire, 24 gauge

wire cutters

1 roll floral tape, in white

⅓ yard silk, in color of your choice

Instructions

1. See shape numbers on the following Quilling Instructions table. Refer to corresponding shape numbers in preceding Basic Quilling Shapes section and follow directions. Follow table for amount of each shape to make, lengths of quilling strips, colors, use, and tools needed.

2. Trace the pattern onto a piece of tracing paper. Place tracing paper beneath transparent work surface of your quilling board. Pin the

Photograph 1-57

peacock's head tear drop over the head section of the pattern. Apply white glue to a 1-inch segment in the center of a 12-inch strip. Wrap and adhere strip around tear drop head. Place a straight pin on each side of the outline of the neck, just below the head, to hold the strip in place. Place a pin on each side of the neck outline at the point where the body starts. Continue to place pins at ¼-inch intervals around the complete outline of the body. Arrange the strip so that it lies inside the pins in the body section. Bring the two ends of the strip together at the bottom of the body and down through the vertical line in the tail section, as shown in Photograph 1-56. Glue them together with white glue and pin in place. Keep section pinned until glue has dried.

3. Cut a piece of notebook paper to the size and shape of the tail section. This will be used as a base upon which tail quills will be glued. Remove pins and lift up vertical tail strip. Position the paper cutout over the tail section on the pattern. With white glue, adhere the glued-together tail to the cutout.(See Photograph 1-57.)

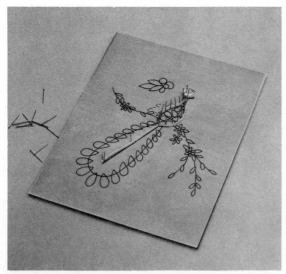

Photograph 1-56

41

Quilling Instructions

Shape and Shape Number	Amount	Strip Length (in inches)	Color	Use	Tool
Tear drops (3)	1	6, marked at 1¼ inches	white	head	quilling needle
Tear drops (3)	8	6, marked at 1¼ inches	white	body	quilling needle
Tight rolls (1)	4	1½	white	neck	quilling needle
Scrolls (7)	122	¾	white	tail	quilling needle
Tear drops (3)	15	12, marked at 1½ inches	white	tail	quilling needle
Tear drops (3)	17	8, marked at 1⅛ inches	white	tail	quilling needle
Tear drops (3)	14	4, marked at ¾ inch	white	tail	quilling needle
Eyes (4)	3	8, marked at 1½ inches	white	wing	quilling needle
Tight rolls (1)	2	3	white	wing	quilling needle
Tear drops (3)	1	6, marked at 1¼ inches	white	wing	quilling needle
Tear drops (3)	1	4, marked at 1 inch	white	wing	quilling needle
Scrolls (7)	6	¾	white	wing	quilling needle
Tear drops (3)	24	1, marked at ½ inch	white	flowers	quilling needle
Tight rolls (1)	4	1	white	flowers	quilling needle

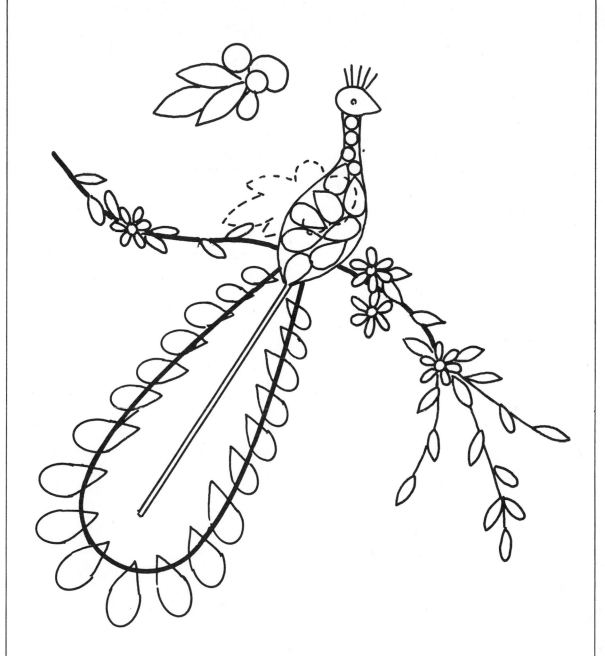

4. Arrange the 8 tear drops to fit the body of the peacock, as shown in Photograph 1-58. Adhere tear drops to each other at the points of contact and to the strip that outlines the body.

5. Adhere in place the 4 tight rolls made for the neck section.

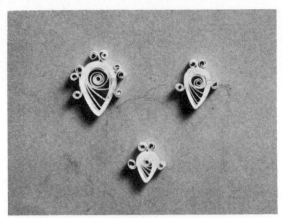

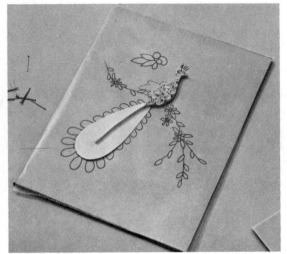

Photograph 1-58

Photograph 1-59

6. Adhere 4 scrolls around one of the 15 tear drops, as shown in Photograph 1-59. Repeat procedure for the remaining 14 tear drops. Take one of the 17 tear drops and adhere 2 scrolls around it, as shown in Photograph 1-59. Repeat for the remaining 16. Adhere 2 scrolls around one of the 14 tear drops, as shown in Photograph 1-59, and repeat for remaining 13.

7. Position these tear drops around the outside of the tail section, over the outlined tear drops on the pattern. The largest tear drops should be at the bottom of the tail and the smallest at the top. Adhere them to paper and to each other, at the points of contact, with white glue. Pin in place.

8. Fill the center of the tail with silicone adhesive. (See Photograph 1-60). Start from the bottom of the tail section and work your way up. Position the largest, then the medium-sized, and finally the smallest, tear drops in overlapping rows, with pointed ends in. (See Photograph 1-61.) The pointed ends should be pressed into the silicone adhesive.

44

Photograph 1-60

Photograph 1-61

9. Adhere 2 scrolls around each of the 3 eyes. Position all wing quills, according to pattern, and adhere them to each other at the points of contact. Pin in place until the glue has dried.

10. Make four ¼-inch-deep slits in a ⅜-inch-long quilling strip. Glue this piece to the top of the peacock head, as shown in Photograph 1-62, for a topknot.

Photograph 1-62

11. With white glue, adhere the wing to the body, following the dotted outline on the pattern. (See Photograph 1-63.)

12. To form the branch that the peacock is sitting on, cut floral wire into three 8-inch pieces. Wrap 2 inches at the end of each piece with floral tape. Place the three pieces of wire, side-by-side, and wrap the bare 6-inch part of all three together with floral tape. You should now have one long

Photograph 1-63

piece that branches out into three pieces at the ends.

13. Assemble 4 tight rolls on your quilling board. Evenly space 6 tear drops around each tight roll, with pointed ends in. Adhere the tear drops to the tight roll and to each other at the points of contact. (See Photograph 1-64A.)

14. Cut 24 leaf-shaped pieces from a quilling strip. Each leaf should be approximately ⅜ inch long and should resemble the leaf in Photograph 1-64B.

Photograph 1-64A   Photograph 1-64B

15. Cut posterboard to fit the oval-shaped shadow box frame. Place the silk on your work surface. Apply a thin coat of white glue over the entire white side of the posterboard. Place posterboard on the silk and press firmly. Turn over and work out any wrinkles with your hands. Trim the excess silk from the edge of the posterboard. Fit the posterboard into the back of the shadow box. Position the branch on the silk and the peacock on the branch. Lightly mark the branch section that the peacock will be sitting on. Remove peacock and branch. Using silicone adhesive, glue leaves and flowers to the branch and glue branch in place on the silk. Apply silicone adhesive to the area of the branch that the peacock will sit on and to the back of the peacock. Place peacock in position. (See Photograph 1-65.)

16. Assemble your shadow box according to instructions in the Helpful Hints chapter.

Photograph 1-65

46

Butterly and Fern Glass Dome (See page 51.)

Floral Cigarette Canister

Designed by Glynn Taylor of Winnetka, Illinois, this interesting cigarette canister will make an ideal piece for a coffee table or bar. For this project, you will be learning a technique of rolling two strips simultaneously on the rolling tool. The result is a fascinating design theme that can be applied to almost any kind of box.

Materials

cigarette canister (The one used in this project is 6½ inches tall, including the handle, and 3 inches in diameter. The ridges are 3⅛ inches in diameter and the base is 3⅜ inches in diameter.)

quilling strips in light olive green, dark olive green, orange, light blue, and medium blue

quilling board

rolling tools

scissors

sandpaper, #400

tack rag

several paintbrushes, ½ inch wide

Treasure Sealer

gold leaf kit

white glue

1 jar acrylic paint, 2-ounce size, in white

antiquing glaze, in burnt umber

lint-free cloth or paper towel

1 can clear vinyl varnish

Instructions

1. Lightly sand the canister, inside and outside, with sandpaper. Wipe it clean with a tack rag. Seal inside and outside of canister with Treasure Sealer.

2. Following directions on the kit, gold leaf the inside, bottom, base, ridges, and handle of canister, as shown in Photograph 1-66.

3. Using a paintbrush, apply a coat of white glue to those parts of the canister that have not been gold leafed. When glue has dried somewhat and is slightly tacky to the touch, apply one coat of white acrylic paint.

4. Allow the paint to dry until the finish crazes and cracks. Go over the entire white area with burnt umber antiquing glaze. Leave the glaze on for 1 or 2 minutes; then wipe off as much as possible with a cloth or paper towel.

5. Allow the piece to dry for 24 hours. Apply one coat of vinyl varnish to the entire canister, inside and outside, with a soft bristle brush.

6. See shape numbers on the following Quilling Instructions table. Refer to corresponding shape numbers in preceding Basic Quilling Shapes sec-

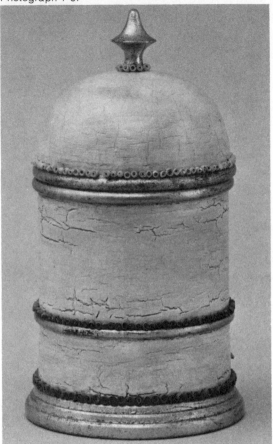

tion and follow directions. Follow table for amount of each shape to make, lengths of quilling strips, colors, use, and tools needed. When making the continuous scroll, the running vines, and the basic fans, work with light and dark olive green quilling strips. Place the light strip on top of the dark one and either roll or loop them, both at the same time. The dark strip will appear on the outside.

7. Use white glue to place the light blue tight rolls, side-by-side, around the base of the handle and above the ridge on the cover. Place the 140 medium blue tight rolls above the center ridge of the canister and the 72 medium blue tight rolls above the ridge of the base, in the same manner. (See Photograph 1-67.)

8. With white glue, adhere the 14 eyes to the ridge of the base, just above the 72 tight rolls. (See Photograph 1-68.) Place the continuous

scroll around the canister, above the eyes, in the same manner. (See Photograph 1-69.)

9. Place 5 eyes on your quilling board. Evenly space and arrange them into a circle, with points touching the center. Adhere eyes at the center with white glue. (See Photograph 1-70A.) Evenly space and glue 3 tight rolls on top of the eyes. Center one more tight roll on top of the three and adhere. (See Photograph 1-70B.) Repeat this procedure for eleven more flowers.

10. Evenly space and glue three flowers below the lip of the canister. These should be approximately 3 inches apart. Glue three flowers above the ridge of medium blue tight rolls. Space them evenly apart from each other and midway between the upper flowers. Connect upper and lower flowers with the running vines. Adhere the remaining six flowers around the canister, next to the vine, as shown in Photograph 1-71.

Quilling Instructions

Shape and Shape Number	Amount	Strip Length (in inches)	Color	Use	Tool
Tight rolls (1)	140	1, cut in half lengthwise	light blue	base of handle and ridge of cover	quilling needle
Tight rolls (1)	140	1, cut in half lengthwise	medium blue	center ridge	quilling needle
Tight rolls (1)	72	2, cut in half lengthwise	medium blue	ridge of base	quilling needle
Eyes (4)	14	8, marked at 1½ inches	orange	above 72 tight rolls	quilling needle
Continuous scroll (22)	enough to go around canister	8, cut in half lengthwise	light and dark olive green	above 14 eyes	quilling needle
Eyes (4)	100	2½, cut in half lengthwise, marked at ⅝ inch	orange	flower petals	quilling needle
Tight rolls (1)	56	2, cut in half lengthwise	orange	flower centers	quilling needle
Running vines (21)	6	20, cut in half lengthwise	light and dark olive green	vines	none
Basic fans (14) (5-looped, without tails)	8	4¾, cut in half lengthwise	light and dark olive green	leaves	none

Photograph 1-68

Photograph 1-70A

Photograph 1-70B

Photograph 1-71

Photograph 1-69

50

11. Assemble eight flowers on your quilling board, each with 5 eyes for petals and one tight roll for the center. (See Photograph 1-70A.) Using white glue, randomly place and adhere the flowers to the lid of the canister. Glue a basic fan next to each flower, as shown in Photograph 1-72.

Photograph 1-72

Butterfly and Fern Glass Dome

This charming arrangement can be done in a glass dome, in a shadow box frame, or on a simple wood or metal base. Glass domes look particularly lovely when placed on mantels, credenzas, or console televisions. They also make lovely table centerpieces.

Materials

glass dome, 11 inches high, with wooden base

quilling strips in olive green, light yellow, dark yellow, and turquoise

quilling board

rolling tools

scissors

1¼ yards floral wire, 18 gauge

wire cutters

ruler

white glue

waxed paper

electric drill

floral clay

3 sheets notebook paper, in white

X-acto knife

pencil

long 1/16-inch-diameter rolling tool

8 seed beads, #11/0

15 inches bead wire, 26 gauge

1 sheet tracing paper

straight pins or corsage pins

1 large hatpin

1 jar acrylic paint, 2-ounce size, in yellow

glass-cleaning solution

Instructions

1. See shape numbers on the following Quilling Instructions table. Refer to corresponding shape numbers in preceding Basic Quilling Shapes section and follow directions. Follow table for amount of each shape to make, lengths of quilling strips, colors, use, and tools needed.

2. With the wire cutters, cut the floral wire into a 13-inch length, a 10-inch length, and four 5-inch lengths.

3. Place a thin coat of white glue on each wire. Wrap olive green quilling strips around each one, from end to end. When wrapping, overlap each turn by about one half the width of the strip.

4. Shape the wires and attach the quilled leaves, as shown in the pattern. Follow designations on leaf pairs for the appropriate eye shape to use. A leaf pair marked 9 inches indicates that you should use two eyes made from the 9-inch quilling strips. Work over waxed paper and use white glue to adhere leaves to wire.

5. Drill a ½-inch hole through the center of the wood base of the glass dome. Pack the hole with floral clay. Insert one of the 5-inch wire stems vertically into the floral clay, as shown in Photograph 1-73. Insert the 13-inch stem into the clay, directly in front of the 5-inch stem, and insert the 10-inch stem directly behind the 5-inch stem. (See Photograph 1-74.) Place two of the remaining 5-inch stems in the front and the last remaining fern in the back.

6. Make the medium-sized butterfly according

Quilling Instructions

Shape and Shape Number	Amount	Strip Length (in inches)	Color	Use	Tool
Eyes (4)	22	12, marked at 2 inches	olive green	12-inch leaves	quilling needle
Eyes (4)	22	11, marked at 1¾ inches	olive green	11-inch leaves	quilling needle
Eyes (4)	18	10, marked at 1½ inches	olive green	10-inch leaves	quilling needle
Eyes (4)	16	9, marked at 1¼ inches	olive green	9-inch leaves	quilling needle

9"
9"
10"
10"
10"
11"
11"
11"
11"
11"
12"
12"
12"
12"
12"
12"

9"
9"
10"
10"
11"
11"
12"
12"
12"

9"
10"
11"
12"

13" Wire

10" Wire

5" Wire

Photograph 1-73

Photograph 1-75

to instructions in the Butterfly Mobile project. Make the butterfly with yellow wings and body. Accent the wings with turquoise quills. You will not need a loop for hanging.

7. Using white glue, attach the butterfly to the curved section of the centermost 5-inch stem. (See Photograph 1-75.)

8. Clean the glass dome with glass cleaning solution of your choice. Place dome over arrangement.

54

Photograph 1-74

Tinsel Art

T inseling is a craft technique in which transparent designs are painted in reverse on glass. The designs are outlined in black ink and filled in with transparent oil paints. The backgrounds are completely opaque. A sheet of crumpled aluminum foil is placed behind the design area, so that when light passes through the transparent paint, it will bounce off the foil and form multifaceted reflections.

During the latter part of the eighteenth and the early part of the nineteenth centuries, painting on glass was quite the "in thing" to do in England. Primarily, the technique was used to decorate mirror heads—the most elegant and expensive of which were done in gold or silver leaf. The design outline was applied with a stencil and black paint. When dry, an adhesive surface was added, to which gold or silver leaf adhered. A background of either black or white was painted around the design. English craftsmen who were attracted to the technique but not to its cost experimented and adapted it to their budgets by replacing the expensive gold and silver leaf with the less expensive tinsel.

Meanwhile, painting on glass had become very popular in the United States. During the middle of the nineteenth century, craftsmen started experimenting with transparent paints. Their goal was to imitate the glowing, shimmering effect that was typical of Chinese art. They found that they could very nearly duplicate this effect by simply crushing a sheet of tin foil (then called tinsel) and placing it behind the transparent colors. The tinsel reflected the light that passed through the transparent colors. These early pieces were usually flower and Oriental bird designs. Again, they were outlined in black and usually had opaque black or white backgrounds.

Contemporary tinsel art designs are composed in much the same way as these earlier ones. Today, however, the availability and low cost of materials makes tinsel art a simpler and more enjoyable craft.

Tinsel Art Materials and Tools

Before beginning work on the tinsel art projects, learn about the equipment you will be using. First and foremost, you will need a transparent surface on which to paint the design. Most of the projects in this chapter are done on either glass or acetate surfaces. You can have glass sheets cut for you, or you can cut them yourself with a glass cutter. Acetate sheets (.0075 inch thick) are used when curved surfaces are desired, such as for in the cylindrical lamp base project in this chapter. You will also need a solution with which to clean the glass or acetate. For cleaning glass, experiment with the solutions you already have at home; if they leave streaks, you will not want to use them. For acetate, I have found that alcohol makes a very fine cleaner. Have some lint-free cloths or paper towels nearby, too.

Since you will be tracing design patterns, you will, of course, need tracing paper and a pencil. When transferring the traced designs to the glass or acetate surface, use a technical fountain pen and black waterproof india ink. Technical fountain pens can be bought individually or in sets containing one handle and several different points. The #00 line width is the point you will need for tinsel work.

After the design has been transferred, you will need to apply Treasure Sealer, a product made by the Connoisseur Studio, to fix the ink on the glass. Buy the spray can rather than the container.

Basically, there are four kinds of paint used in tinsel work. Water-base acrylic paints are used for the background areas, since they are opaque. They come in 2-ounce jars, in an assortment of colors. You will be using white more than any other color, however, since most backgrounds are done in white. If you wish, oil-base enamel paints can be used instead of acrylics.

The design sections are done in transparent oil paints. The paints are thinned with a clear vinyl varnish. Many paint colors that are labeled transparent—particularly those that are members of the yellow family—are actually not so. To test them, apply a bit to a piece of glass and hold it up to the light. If you can't see through the paint, it is not transparent and should not be used for tinseling. Basically, I have found that alizarin crimson, Prussian blue, and Winsor and Newton's or Weber's Indian yellow are the only colors I need. From these three, I can mix practically any color I would want; furthermore, I know that they're transparent. You may, of course, purchase as many colors as you wish. I suggest, however, that you test each one for transparency before using.

An iridescent lacquer-base paint, called Liquid Pearl, is used to create special effects in designs and backgrounds. The natural shade is sometimes used to replace white in certain design features, such as in daisies, butterflies, the sails of ships, and fruit. (See Photograph 2-1.) When mixed with an oil paint, the result is an iridescent, "pearly," semitransparent color.

Another way in which to achieve an interesting background is to apply Liquid Leaf. Available in either gold or silver, Liquid Leaf gives a rich, opaque quality to your work.

Although it is always best to have a wide variety of brushes at your disposal, you can manage with only two. A #1 or liner brush is used to paint around the outline of the design and to paint small sections of the design. A larger brush (½ inch or wider) is used to paint large background areas. Sable brushes are best for tinseling. You will also need a palette on which to mix colors. Disposable palette pads are your best bet, since they cut down on cleaning-up time.

Two very important items are aluminum foil and corrugated cardboard. The aluminum foil is, of course, placed behind the glass or acetate surface; the corrugated cardboard is cut into a mask, which traps the edges of the foil and keeps it in place against the glass or acetate.

Additional items needed are an X-acto knife (see Photograph 1-1), sandpaper or garnet paper, a tack rag, a ruler, a pair of scissors, cotton swabs, lacquer thinner, and white glue. The X-acto knife is used to scrape off erroneous lines made on the glass. Sandpaper (#400) and garnet paper (#350) are used to sand wood surfaces, such as the trinket box in this chapter. Tack rags are chemically treated cloths used to wipe surfaces after sanding.

At the end of the book, you will find a list of these tinseling materials and tools and where to locate them.

Basic Tinsel Art Instructions

Although tinseling may be easy and fun to do, it does require patience and accuracy. You will be tracing a design pattern onto tracing paper, transferring it to glass, painting in the opaque background, painting the transparent design, turning the glass around, positioning the aluminum foil against the glass, and masking the piece with corrugated cardboard. Read the following general instructions carefully before beginning a project and then refer to them whenever necessary.

A. **Cutting the glass:** Have the glass cut to the size you want or do it yourself with a glass cutter. Refer to the Helpful Hints chapter for instructions on how to measure and cut glass. Acetate sheets can be cut with a pair of scissors.

B. **Cleaning the glass:** Clean the glass with a cleaning solution of your choice and a soft, lint-free paper towel or cloth. Remove all grease and dirt. Once the glass has been cleaned, handle it by the edges to avoid leaving greasy finger smudges. If you are using acetate sheets, clean them in the same manner. Put glass or acetate aside in a clean, protected spot, until you are ready to use it.

C. **Selecting the design:** In addition to the designs offered in this chapter, there are numerous sources for other designs. Greeting cards,

57

magazines, craft books, wrapping paper, wallpaper, and nature books are all excellent sources. And, of course, there is no reason why you can't create an original design. Since tinsel art resembles Oriental artwork, any Oriental motif would be ideal. Select or compose open, airy types of designs rather than intricate, tightly grouped ones. The reflective effect is often lost when designs are too intricate.

D. Tracing the design: Once the design has been chosen, place a sheet of tracing paper over it and trace the outline of all parts. If necessary, tape the tracing paper in place with masking tape. Some designs will have to be enlarged or reduced in order to fit the glass area of your project. Follow the instructions in the Helpful Hints chapter.

E. Reversing the design: The design is transferred to what will actually be the back side of the work. In other words, after you have painted the design on the glass, you will turn the glass over. The design will be viewed through the unpainted side of the glass. Therefore, if the finished design is to be identical to the original, you will have to reverse the original. This can be done by turning the traced design over, facedown, and working with its back side. The designs in this book have already been reversed, however, so that you won't have to do this. Actually, it is up to the craftsman to decide whether or not he wants to reverse his design. You may like the reversed version better than you do the original. Remember, of course, that when working with a design that contains alphabet letters (mottos, initials, etc.), you will have to reverse the design.

F. Transferring the design onto glass: Place the glass over the traced design. Position the glass so that the design will be exactly where you want it, and tape it down with masking tape. Work on a clean surface. Using the technical fountain pen and india ink, carefully trace the design onto the glass. (See Photograph 2-2.) This is probably the most difficult part of tinseling,

58

Photograph 2-1

Photograph 2-2

since the traced design must be neat and exact. Try to trace an entire line with one continuous stroke of the pen. Stopping and starting again will leave marks that will show up on the finished side of the work. Sometimes, of course, it will be unavoidable. If this does happen, remember that going over the line again will not improve its quality. Instead, wipe off the line with a damp paper towel or cotton swab, and try it again.

If you extend a line too far, allow the ink to dry before trying to correct the mistake. Scrape the extended tip off with an X-acto knife. Check all lines to be sure that they are exact and make all corrections before proceeding. After the ink has dried and all necessary corrections have been made, spray a coat of Treasure Sealer over the entire inked side of the glass. Allow glass to dry.

G. Painting in the background: Although the original tinsels usually had black enamel backgrounds, modern-day tinsel backgrounds are usually done in white. Black backgrounds tend to make the designs look somewhat gaudy. However, this is a matter of personal taste. Any color can be used for the background.

There are three types of backgrounds you may use—plain opaque, Liquid Pearl, or Liquid Leaf.

Plain opaque backgrounds: Use the liner brush to apply paint to the complete outline of the design and to small background areas within the design. I prefer using water-base acrylic paints. They are neat, easy to apply, and easy to clean up. Oil-base enamels can be used, but they require much more drying time. Single line areas in the design, such as stems, can be painted over with the background color. Do not, however, cross into the interior areas of the design with the background color. It will show through when the piece is turned over. After you have painted the entire outline and small background areas, change to a ½-inch (or wider) brush and finish applying the background color. (See Photograph 2-3.) The larger the background area, the wider the brush should be. Allow the paint to dry (about ½ hour for acrylic paint and 24 hours for enamel). Apply

Photograph 2-3

a second coat and allow it to dry. Examine the background for thin areas by holding the glass up to the light. If there are any, apply a third coat of the background color. Remember that the background must be perfectly opaque.

Liquid Pearl backgrounds: A variation of the standard background is the Liquid Pearl or pearly background. This is achieved by applying natural Liquid Pearl to the background before applying the acrylic or enamel paint. The Liquid Pearl gives the background a slightly irridescent quality. First, vigorously shake the Liquid Pearl. Select a starting area and paint around a small part of the outline with a liner brush. Fill in the background of this immediate area with Liquid Pearl. Use a daubing motion of the hand rather than brush stroking. Work quickly. The trick here is to blend the Liquid Pearl background into the outline while it is still wet. The amount of background area that can be painted at one time, therefore, will depend on how fast you can work. Underestimate at first, until you have built up speed. Continue in this manner until the whole background is covered with Liquid Pearl. (See Photograph 2-4.) If you want the background to have an even more pearly quality, apply a second coat of Liquid Pearl in the same manner. Allow

59

Photograph 2-4

Photograph 2-5

the Liquid Pearl 24 hours to dry. The opaque background can now be applied over the Liquid Pearl. (See Photograph 2-5.) If you wish to use acrylic paint, first combine ½ teaspoon of liquid detergent with 2 ounces of paint. This not only gives the acrylic paint better wetting-action but helps it adhere to the Liquid Pearl and prevents cracking in the paint. If you are applying oil-base enamel paint over the Liquid Pearl, you must allow 24 hours drying time between coats.

Liquid Leaf backgrounds: Liquid Leaf is applied in the same manner as Liquid Pearl. Outline a small section of the design at a time. Daub on Liquid Leaf, and while the outline is still wet, blend it into the outline. The result will be a rich, gold background. Allow the Liquid Leaf to dry for about 1 hour; then apply a second coat. Continue applying coats of Liquid Leaf in this manner until the background is completely opaque. Do not apply any other kind of paint over a Liquid Leaf background.

H. Mixing the paints: Before learning how to mix colors, you must know how to control their intensity. Intensity of color—light red as opposed to dark red, for example—will depend on the amount of varnish you have added to the paint. For a light red, add quite a bit of varnish to alizarin crimson; for a medium red, add less; and for a dark red, add just a drop. To make pink, simply add a lot of varnish to alizarin crimson. By controlling the amount of varnish added to alizarin crimson, Indian yellow, Prussian blue, or any other color, you can create a variety of shades.

Mixing paints to achieve specific colors requires patient experimentation, practice, and the learning of a few basic color formulas. You are probably already familiar with most of them. In any case, the following list should be of help to you. Refer to it when following the Color Suggestions chart that appears after each design pattern in this chapter. Whether or not you wish to use the same colors as I have, you will still need to be familiar with these basic formulas.

Color	Formula
green	Indian yellow + Prussian blue
orange	Indian yellow + alizarin crimson
purple	Prussian blue + alizarin crimson
brown	Indian yellow + Prussian blue + alizarin crimson
fleshtone	Indian yellow + small amount of alizarin crimson + touch of Prussian blue

Tan is a lighter version of brown, and lavender is a lighter version of purple. Add more varnish to brown or purple to achieve these shades. To create a pearly variation of a color, mix Liquid Pearl with the color. Do not thin the color with varnish. If thinning is necessary, add lacquer thinner to the mixture.

In any of these color combinations, varying the amount of one color component will determine the end result. For example, to achieve more of a yellow quality in a green, add more Indian yellow. To achieve more of a blue quality, add more Prussian blue. It's as simple as that.

I. Painting the design: Arrange your paints on a palette, and place a small container of varnish next to it. Dip the brush into the varnish and then into the edge of the paint. For the first coat, use paint that has been mixed with a lot of varnish. Apply subsequent coats, experimenting with the amount of varnish added, until you have reached the desired effect. (See Photograph 2-6.) Crumple a piece of aluminum foil and, with the shiny side up, hold it behind the design. Observe the design area to make sure you like its appearance. Work each section of the design in the same manner. Allow the colors to dry.

J. Shading areas of the design: Add a coat of paint to those specific areas of the design that are to be shaded. Shading colors should be similar but darker than the original colors.

Most of the design patterns that follow will be accompanied by Color Suggestion charts. These will designate colors to be used for each part of

Photograph 2-6

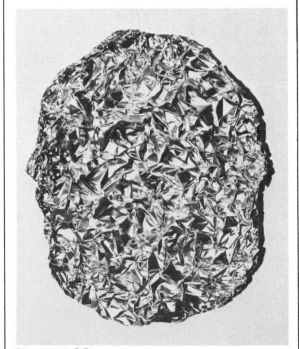

Photograph 2-7

61

Photograph 2-8

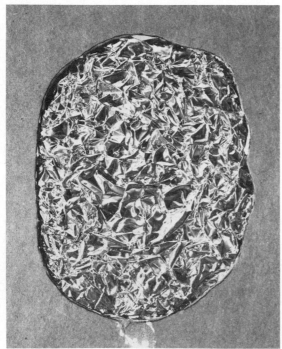

Photograph 2-9

the design and for those areas to be Liquid Pearled or shaded. These are, of course, only suggestions; you may prefer to use your own color scheme.

K. Applying the foil: After the paint has dried, turn the glass over. The painted side is now facing down. Crumple a sheet of aluminum foil so that there are many facets on the shiny side. The foil will be placed, shiny side up, behind the design (see Photograph 2-7), and the facets will reflect the light that passes through the paint. The crumpled sheet of foil must be large enough to cover the entire design area. If necessary, two or more pieces of foil can be used—simply overlap the edges so that there will be no voids in the reflective area.

L. Masking the design: Cut a piece of tracing paper and corrugated cardboard to the same size as the glass. Place tracing paper over the design. Trace roughly around the outside edges of the design area, leaving about a ½-inch margin around it. (See Photograph 2-8.) Transfer the outline of the design from the tracing paper to the corrugated cardboard. The easiest way in which to do this is with carbon paper. Cut this section out of the cardboard. The remaining section of cardboard—the mask—will serve to hold the foil in place behind the transparent design. It will also ensure that the foil will not be crushed, thereby losing its reflective facets. If desired, the mask may be adhered to the glass with a dab of white glue placed at each corner. This might cause the paint to peel, however. The best way to hold the glass, the foil, and the mask together is to place the foil behind the transparent design and place the mask around the foil. Make sure the edges of the foil are trapped in the mask. (See Photograph 2-9.) Then assemble a frame around the mask. All tinsel projects in this chapter that require a mask will also need a frame of some sort. It is the frame—whether it be a picture frame, shadow box frame, a tray bottom, a sconce, or a trinket box—that will hold the pieces together.

Daisy Tinsel Picture

This bright, cheerful design serves as an ideal introduction to tinseling. It's easy to do, and the results are charming. The same instructions apply to Raggedy Ann and Andy, Country Church, and Strawberry Bouquet. Choose the one you like best and have fun.

Materials

picture frame, 6 by 9 inches
1 sheet of glass, 6 by 9 inches
glass-cleaning solution
lint-free cloth or paper towel
tracing paper
pencil
masking tape
technical fountain pen
waterproof india ink, in black
Treasure Sealer
1 jar acrylic paint, 2-ounce size, in white
1 liner brush, or #1 brush
1 paintbrush, ½ inch or wider
Liquid Pearl, in green and natural
transparent oil paints, in alizarin crimson, Indian yellow, and Prussian blue
1 can clear vinyl varnish
palette pad
aluminum foil
1 piece corrugated cardboard, 6 by 9 inches
scissors

Instructions

1. Clean the glass with solution of your choice.
2. Place a sheet of tracing paper over the design pattern and carefully trace design.
3. Place glass on top of tracing paper. Position so that design is centered. Trace the design onto the glass with technical fountain pen and india ink. (See Photograph 2-10.) Allow the ink to dry. Remove tracing paper from beneath the glass. Check all lines on glass against tracing paper to be sure that they are correct. If there are any mistakes, correct them according to directions in step F in Basic Tinsel Art Instructions.
4. Spray the design side of the glass with Treasure Sealer to fix the ink.
5. Paint a plain, opaque background, following directions in step G of Basic Instructions. Paint background with white acrylic paint. Check to make sure that all areas are well covered. If there are thin spots, apply a second or third coat to the

63

Photograph 2-10

background. Remember that it must be completely opaque.

6. Squeeze small amounts of alizarin crimson, Indian yellow, and Prussian blue onto your palette, and place a small container of varnish beside it. See design pattern and Color Suggestions chart. Refer to steps H and I in Basic Instructions for directions on how to mix colors and paint design.

Photograph 2-11

7. Allow the paint to dry and turn glass over so that design will be facedown. Crumple and shape the aluminum foil, as shown in Photograph 2-11, so that it will fit behind the design.

8. According to directions in step L of Basic Instructions, cut the center out of the corrugated cardboard to form a mask. (See Photograph 2-12.) The mask should be sized so that it will barely trap the edges of the foil.

9. Place the foil, shiny side facing the design, against the glass. Position mask around the foil.

Assemble and position frame against the cardboard mask.

The following three design patterns can be used as alternates to the Daisy design. Follow the same procedures for Raggedy Ann and Andy, Country Church, and Strawberry Bouquet.

Photograph 2-12

Color Suggestions

Liquid Pearl

Part	Color
daisy leaves	green
daisy petals	natural

Transparent Oil Paints

Part	Color
flower centers	medium yellow
large leaves, large stems, and calyx	light green
small leaves	medium green
3 flowers (above and to left of center daisy) and small buds	medium pink
forget-me-nots	medium blue
violets (below center daisy)	medium lavender

Shade

Part	Color
Large leaves and calyx	dark green

64

Strawberry Bouquet Color Suggestions
Liquid Pearl (2 coats)

Part	Color
flower petals	natural

Transparent Oil Paints

Part	Color
strawberries	medium red
leaves	medium green
flower centers	medium yellow

Shade

Part	Color
strawberries	dark red
leaves	dark green
flower centers	light brown

Raggedy Ann and Andy Color Suggestions
Liquid Pearl (2 coats)

Part	Color
apron, shirt background, alternate stocking stripes, pantalettes, buttons, and dress flowers	natural

Transparent Oil Paints

Part	Color
pants, tie, eyes, and dress background	light blue
alternate stocking stripes, lips, and polka dots	medium red
hair	dark orange
hands and faces	fleshtone
cheeks	medium pink
flowers and butterfly	medium yellow
leaves and grass blades	medium green

Shade

Part	Color
pants and dress	medium blue

Country Church Color Suggestions

Liquid Pearl (2 coats)

Part	Color
church sides	natural

Transparent Oil Paints

Part	Color
roofs	light blue
windows	medium yellow
leaves and ground	medium green
tree trunks	medium brown
shaded door and window areas	light red

Shade

Part	Color
leaves and ground	dark green

Springtime Serving Tray

The tray used for this project was 13¾ by 19½ inches. The design pattern can be adapted to any size square or rectangle, however. Metal trays can also be used, but in that case the strips of wood will have to be secured with clear epoxy glue rather than white glue.

Materials

large tray, unfinished wood, in size of your choice
garnet paper, #350
Treasure Sealer
sandpaper, #400
tack rag
2 jars acrylic paint, 2-ounce size, in white and olive green
1 paintbrush, ½ inch or wider
lint-free cloth or paper towel
gold leaf kit
metallic braid, ¹/₁₆ inch wide, long enough to go around outside edge of tray twice, in gold
1 can satin varnish, ½-pint size
4 soft pinewood strips, ⅛ by ⅛ inch, long enough to fit each side of inside perimeter of tray
white glue
1 sheet of glass, large enough to fit inside perimeter of tray
glass-cleaning solution
tracing paper
pencil
masking tape
technical fountain pen
waterproof india ink, in black
Liquid Pearl, in natural
1 liner brush, or #1 brush
transparent oil paints, in alizarin crimson, Indian yellow, and Prussian blue
1 can clear vinyl varnish
palette pad
aluminum foil
1 piece corrugated cardboard, ⅛-inch thick, same size as glass
scissors
4 soft pinewood strips, ⅛ by ¼ inch, approximately same lengths as ⅛-inch strips
1 sheet of paper, large enough to cover tray
1 broadcloth square, 6 by 6 inches (Use a scrap from an old cotton shirt, blouse, or sheet.)
2 dozen sequin pins, ⅜ inch long
screwdriver

Instructions

1. With #350 garnet paper, sand tray until it is smooth. Be careful not to round off the corners, or it will be difficult to apply braid.

2. Spray a coat of Treasure Sealer over the entire tray. Allow to dry for about ½ hour. Sand lightly with #400 sandpaper and then wipe surface with tack rag.

3. Paint the entire tray with a coat of white acrylic paint. Allow to dry for about 1 hour. Apply a second coat and allow to dry. Sand lightly with #400 sandpaper and wipe with tack rag. Mix a small amount of olive green acrylic into white acrylic to make a light olive green. Apply two coats of light olive green to all parts of the tray except for the top flat area. Allow 1 hour between coats and 1 hour after final coat for drying. (See Photograph 2-13.)

Photograph 2-13

4. Follow instructions on the gold leaf kit and gold-leaf the top flat edge of the tray. Glue metallic braid around rim. (See Photograph 2-14.)

5. Apply a coat of satin varnish to entire tray. Allow to dry for 24 hours; then apply a second coat. Allow to dry.

6. Fit the four ⅛- by ⅛-inch strips of wood around the sides of the top flat area. Adhere in place with white glue, as shown in Photograph 2-15.

7. Clean the glass with solution of your choice.

The glass must fit firmly over the strips and be as close as is possible to the inside edge of the tray.

8. Following instructions for enlarging patterns in the Helpful Hints chapter, enlarge design pattern by 55 percent. If you are using the grid method of enlarging, each square should measure 1 inch. Trace enlarged pattern onto a piece of tracing paper.

9. Place glass on top of the tracing paper. Position so that design is centered. Trace the design onto the glass with technical fountain pen and india ink. Allow the ink to dry. Remove tracing paper from beneath the glass. Check all lines on glass against tracing paper to be sure that they are correct. If there are any mistakes, correct them according to directions in step F of Basic Instructions.

10. Spray the design side of glass with Treasure Sealer to fix the ink.

11. Paint a Liquid Pearl background as described in step G of Basic Instructions. Use natural Liquid Pearl and two coats of white acrylic paint. Allow to dry for 24 hours. Remember that the background must be completely opaque.

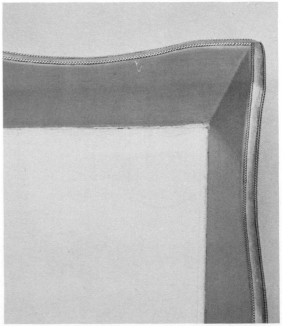

Photograph 2-14

70

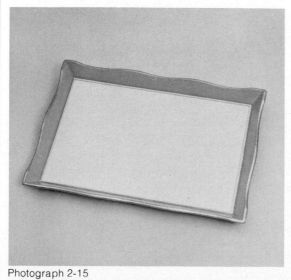

Photograph 2-15

Photograph 2-16

71

12. Squeeze small amounts of alizarin crimson, Indian yellow, and Prussian blue onto your palette, and place a small container of varnish beside it. See design pattern and Color Suggestions chart. Steps H and I in Basic Instructions explain how to mix colors and paint design.

Color Suggestions

Liquid Pearl (2 coats)

Part	Color
flower petals and buds	natural

Transparent Oil Paints

Part	Color
small leaves, calyxes; head and bottom wing feathers of left bird; top wing feathers of right bird	medium green
large leaves	light green
dotted front and alternate tail feathers of left bird; back of right bird	medium yellow
breast, middle wing feather, and alternate tail feathers of left bird; dotted front, bottom wing, and tail feathers of right bird	reddish orange
bird bills	medium red
stems	medium brown
flowers and buds	light orange
flower centers	light green

Shade

Part	Color
leaves	medium green

13. Allow the paint to dry; then turn glass over so that design will be facedown. Crumple and shape the aluminum foil so that it will fit behind the design.

14. Cut out the center of the corrugated cardboard to form a mask. Refer to step L in Basic Instructions. The mask should be sized so that it will barely trap the edges of the foil.

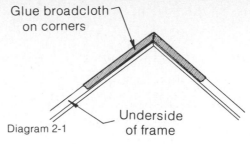

Glue broadcloth on corners

Diagram 2-1   Underside of frame

15. Place the foil, shiny side up, against the mask, with the edges of the foil resting on the mask. Position the cardboard mask in the bottom of the tray. (See Photograph 2-16.) Position the glass, design side down, over the mask. The glass should rest on the ⅛- by ⅛-inch strips of wood.

16. From the ⅛- by ¼-inch strips, make a frame to fit over the glass and hold it in place. To determine the exact size the frame should be, place a large sheet of paper over the glass. Crease edges of paper all along the line where the glass and the tray meet. Remove paper and cut along the creased lines. Place the wood on the paper, with its ¼-inch side up. Cut strips to lengths of creased lines. Miter the corners according to instructions in the Helpful Hints chapter. Adhere the frame together with white glue. Allow the glue to dry.

17. Cut pieces of broadcloth to fit around each corner of frame. Adhere to underside of frame with white glue. (See Diagram 2-1.) After the glue has dried, trim away excess material.

18. Spray Treasure Sealer over frame. Apply two coats of light olive green acrylic paint. Allow 1 hour between coats and after the second coat for drying. With white glue, adhere braid to pinewood-strip frame.

19. Put frame in position on top of the glass. Secure frame to tray with sequin pins, as shown in Photograph 2-17. The pins can be pressed in with the flat edge of a screwdriver.

Photograph 2-17

Glass Top Trinket Box

An ordinary box can be made into a shadow box simply by turning its lid upside down. Make sure that the box you use has a lid that is deep enough to hold both the aluminum foil and the glass. This particular design pattern is best suited for octagonal or hexagonal boxes. If you prefer to use a square or rectangular box, you can easily adapt one of the other design patterns in this chapter or, perhaps, design your own. Paint the outside of the box, and either gold-leaf or line the inside.

Materials

octagonal box, unfinished wood, 3½ by 7¼ by 7¼ inches

garnet paper, #350

screwdriver

1 pair of brass hinges, ⅝ by ¾ inch

Treasure Sealer

sandpaper, #400

tack rag

2 jars acrylic paint, 2-ounce size, in white and light blue

1 paintbrush, ½ inch or wider

lint-free cloth or paper towel

1 can satin varnish, ½-pint size

1 sheet of glass, large enough to fit inside lid

12 or 16 soft pinewood strips, ⅛ by ⅛ inch, long enough to fit each side of box

ruler

pencil

white glue

glass-cleaning solution

tracing paper

technical fountain pen

waterproof india ink, in black

1 liner brush, or #1 brush

transparent oil paints, in alizarin crimson, Indian yellow, and Prussian blue

1 can clear vinyl varnish

aluminum foil

paper towels

metallic braid, ⅛ inch wide, long enough to trim perimeter of box, in gold

X-acto knife

grosgrain ribbon, ⅝ inch wide, long enough to surround perimeter of box plus 12 inches, in green

Instructions

1. With #350 garnet paper, sand the entire box until it is smooth. Be careful not to round the corners or edges, or you will have trouble fitting the inverted lid.

2. Remove hinges with screwdriver. Invert the lid of the box and position it over the bottom part. Follow the instructions in the Helpful

Hints chapter. Mark the inside of the box, and fit the hinges so that the lid will cover the box perfectly. (See Photograph 2-18. The top of the lid is now the bottom, and the bottom is now the top.) Place hinges aside for safekeeping.

3. Spray a coat of Treasure Sealer over entire box. Allow about 20 minutes drying time and then sand lightly with #400 sandpaper. Wipe surface with tack rag.

4. Paint entire box with two coats of white acrylic paint. Allow 1 hour drying time between coats and after the last coat. Sand lightly and wipe clean with a lint-free cloth. Apply two coats of light blue acrylic paint to the outside of box and lid, and to lip of lid. Paint carefully so that no brush marks will show. Allow the paint to dry for 1 hour between coats and after the final coat. Apply two coats of satin varnish, allowing 24 hours drying time between coats.

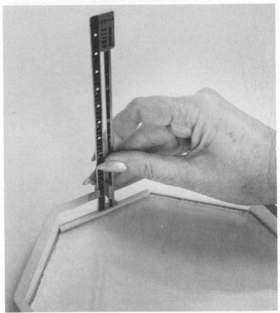

Photograph 2-19

5. Place the glass inside the lid, making sure that it fits firmly and lies flat against the bottom. Place one of the wood strips on top of the glass. Measure from the top of the strip to the top edge of the lid, as shown in Photograph 2-19. Make a note of this measurement. Remove the glass, and measure from the bottom of the lid up to the recorded measurement. (See Photograph 2-20.) Draw a line around the inner sides of the lid at this measurement.

6. Using white glue, adhere six or eight of the pinewood strips around inside of lid so that the tops of the strips barely touch the drawn line. (See Photograph 2-21.) The distance above the sticks should be equal to the thickness of the glass plus ⅛ inch.

7. Clean the glass with solution of your choice.

8. Place a sheet of tracing paper over the design pattern and carefully trace design.

9. Place the glass on top of tracing paper. Position so that design will be centered. Trace the design onto the glass with technical fountain pen and india ink. After the ink has dried, remove tracing paper from beneath the glass. Check all lines on the glass against tracing paper to be sure

Photograph 2-18

75

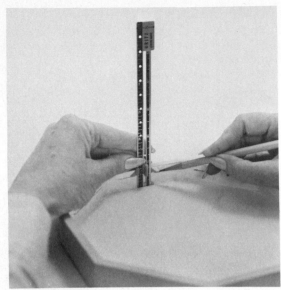

Photograph 2-20

Photograph 2-21

that they are accurate. Correct any mistakes you find, according to directions in step F in Basic Instructions.

10. Spray the design side of the glass with Treasure Sealer to fix the ink.

11. Paint a Liquid Pearl background, following directions in step G of Basic Instructions. Use natural Liquid Pearl and two coats of white acrylic paint. Allow to dry for 24 hours. Remember that the background must be completely opaque.

12. Squeeze small amounts of alizarin crimson, Indian yellow, and Prussian blue onto your palette, and place a small container of varnish beside it. See design pattern and Color Suggestions chart. Directions for mixing colors and painting design are given in steps H and I in Basic Instructions.

Color Suggestions

Liquid Pearl

Part	Color
small leaves	natural (light coat)
dogwood petals	natural (2 coats)

Transparent Oil Paints

Part	Color
stems and edges of dogwood	reddish brown
dogwood centers and large leaves	light green
small flower petals	medium blue
small leaves	medium green
small flower centers	medium yellow

Shade

Part	Color
large leaves	dark green
dogwood petals	light tan

13. Allow the paint to dry for 24 hours; then turn glass over so that design will be facedown. Crumple and shape the aluminum foil so that it will fit behind the design. It should be large enough to cover the design with a generous margin. Line the inside of the lid with crumpled

76

paper towels, using enough towels to hold the foil tightly against the glass. These towels will serve as your mask. Place the foil, shiny side up, on top of the towels. Place the glass, design side down, over the foil.

14. Miter ends of the remaining wood strips, according to directions in the Helpful Hints chapter. Apply two coats of light blue acrylic paint to each strip. Allow 1 hour drying time between coats and after the last coat. Use white glue to adhere the strips to inside of lid, on top of the glass. (See Photograph 2-22.)

15. Use white glue to adhere the metallic braid to the strips. (See Photograph 2-23.) Miter at joints and press down with X-acto knife.

16. Attach hinges to the inside of lid, and reassemble the box.

17. Using white glue, adhere grosgrain ribbon around box just below the lid. Begin wrapping the ribbon from the middle of one of the front panels. Wrap around once completely.

18. Cut a 6½-inch length, a 4-inch length, and a 1-inch length of grosgrain ribbon. Following Diagram 2-2, make a tailored bow. Bring points A and B to center and adhere with white glue. Simulate a knot with the 1-inch piece. Fold the 4-inch piece in half, and glue one side to back of bow. Slip other side over starting point of ribbon on box and glue in place.

Photograph 2-23

Photograph 2-22

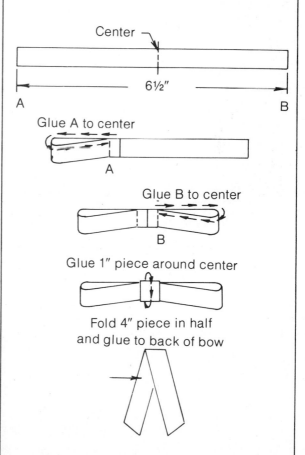

Diagram 2-2

Flower Bells Lamp Base (See page 93.)

Daisies and Violets Sconce

The easiest way to approach this project is to purchase a ready-made shadow box sconce from a decoupage studio. Regular wood sconces can be purchased, but it would then be necessary to make, or have made, a shadow box frame for it. A third alternative is to make the entire unit yourself. See Diagram 2-3 at the end of the project if you wish to build your own shadow box sconce. The sconce can also be wired so that electric candles or other types of decorative lights can be used.

Materials

shadow box sconce, unfinished wood, in size of your choice
glass-cleaning solution
lint-free cloth or paper towel
tracing paper
pencil
masking tape
technical fountain pen
waterproof india ink, in black
Treasure Sealer
Liquid Pearl, in natural
2 jars acrylic paint, 2-ounce size, in white and olive green
1 liner brush, or #1 brush
1 paintbrush, ½ inch or wider
transparent oil paints, in alizarin crimson, Indian yellow, and Prussian blue
1 can clear vinyl varnish
aluminum foil
1 piece corrugated cardboard, same size and shape as glass in shadow box frame
sandpaper, #400
tack rag
gold leaf kit
white glue
metallic braid, $^1/_{16}$ inch wide, long enough to trim perimeter of glass, in gold
6 glazier points

Instructions

1. Remove glass from sconce, and clean it with your choice of solution. Following instructions for enlarging patterns in the Helpful Hints chapter, enlarge design pattern by 10 percent. If you are using the grid method of enlarging, each square should measure 1 inch. Trace enlarged pattern onto a piece of tracing paper.

2. Place glass on top of tracing paper, and proceed to trace the design onto glass with technical fountain pen and india ink. Allow the ink to dry. Remove tracing paper from beneath the glass. Check all lines on glass against tracing paper to be sure that they are correct. If you see any

mistakes, correct them according to directions in step F in Basic Instructions.

3. Spray the design side of the glass with Treasure Sealer to fix the ink.

4. Refer to step G of Basic Instructions for directions on painting a Liquid Pearl background. Use natural Liquid Pearl and two coats of white acrylic paint. Allow to dry for 24 hours. Be sure that the background is completely opaque.

5. Squeeze small amounts of alizarin crimson, Indian yellow, and Prussian blue onto your palette, and place a small container of varnish beside it. See design pattern and Color Suggestions chart. Mix colors and paint design, according to steps H and I in Basic Instructions.

Color Suggestions

Liquid Pearl

Part	Color
small leaves	natural (light coat)
daisy petals	natural (2 coats)

Transparent Oil Paints

Part	Color
flower centers	medium yellow
violets	medium lavender
large leaves and stems	light or yellow green
7 flowers and small buds	medium pink
small leaves	medium green

Shade

Part	Color
daisy centers	light reddish brown
large leaves	medium to dark green
daisy petals	very light reddish brown

6. Allow the paint 24 hours drying time; then turn glass over so that design will be facedown.

Crumple and shape the aluminum foil so that it will fit behind the design.

7. Cut out the center of the corrugated cardboard to form a mask. Refer to step L in Basic Instructions. The mask should be sized so that it will barely trap the edges of the aluminum foil.

8. With #400 sandpaper, lightly sand all the wooden parts of the sconce. Wipe clean with a tack rag.

9. Apply two or three coats of white acrylic paint. Allow 1 hour drying time between coats and after the final coat. Paint the outer and inner edges of sconce with two coats of olive green paint. Allow 1 hour drying time between coats and after the final coat.

10. If the sconce has a sculptured edge around the glass of the shadow box frame, follow the instructions that accompany the gold leaf and apply it to the sculptured part. Use white glue to attach metallic braid to the gold-leafed edge.

11. Assemble the sconce. Place the aluminum foil, shiny side facing design, against the glass. Position mask behind foil. Secure entire piece with screws or glazier points.

The following design pattern can be used as an alternate for the Daisies and Violets. Follow the same procedures for Hanging Fruits.

Hanging Fruits Color Suggestions

Transparent Oil Paints

Part	Color
leaves and quince	medium green
cherries and strawberry	medium red
2 apples	dark red
orange	medium orange
plum and berries	medium purple
lemon, pear, and peach	medium yellow

Shade

Part	Color
leaves	dark green
lemon	light green
pear (right side) and peach	medium orange

Diagram 2-3

Front view   Side view

Back view

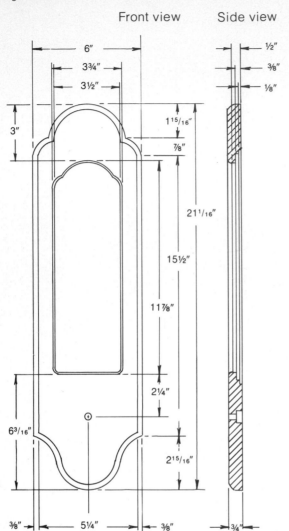

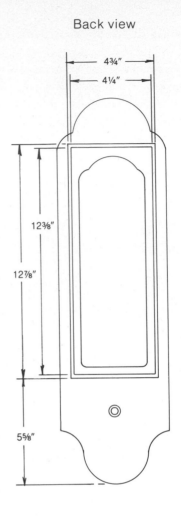

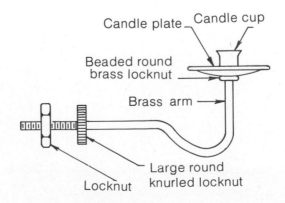

Candle plate — Candle cup

Beaded round
brass locknut

Brass arm →

Large round
knurled locknut

Locknut

Twelve Days of Christmas Ornaments

Clear plastic domes are available in many different sizes and shapes. I prefer circle and oval shapes for Christmas ornaments. The following design patterns represent each of the twelve days of Christmas, in accordance with the famous carol. It might be a fun idea to decorate your tree this Christmas with one partridge, two love birds, three French hens, and so on, all the way up to twelve drummers drumming.

Materials

clear plastic domes, oval-shaped, with plastic backings, 3½ by 5 inches, 2 for each ornament
glass-cleaning solution
lint-free cloth or paper towel
tracing paper
pencil
scissors
masking tape
technical fountain pen
waterproof india ink, in black
Treasure Sealer
Liquid Pearl, in natural
several jars acrylic paint, 2-ounce size, in assorted colors
1 liner brush, or #1 brush
1 paintbrush, ½ inch or wider
transparent oil paints, in alizarin crimson, Indian yellow, and Prussian blue
1 can clear vinyl varnish
scissors
cardboard squares, slightly larger than the domes, 1 for each ornament
white glue
approximately 3½ feet metallic braid, ¼ inch wide, in gold, for each ornament
1 spool beige thread, #50
aluminum foil
1 box facial tissue
14½ inches cord, ¹/₁₆ inch wide, in gold, for each ornament
1 tassel, in gold, for each ornament
embroidery needle, #7

Instructions

1. Clean both plastic domes, inside and outside, with solution of your choice.

2. Place a sheet of tracing paper over the selected design pattern and trace design. These patterns are already the proper size. Cut off excess tracing paper around the design so that it can be taped in place on the dome.

3. Place the traced design on the outer surface of the plastic dome, with the design facing out. (See Photograph 2-24.) Observe the placement of the

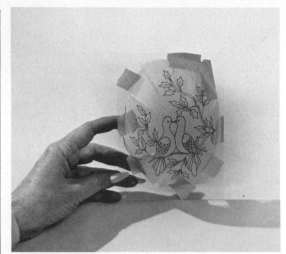

Photograph 2-24

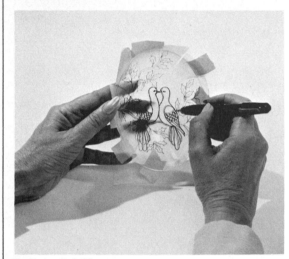

Photograph 2-25

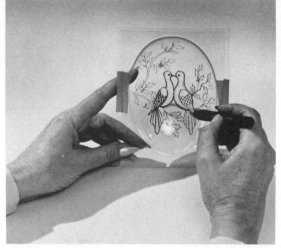

Photograph 2-26

design through the inner surface of the dome, position as desired, and secure in place with masking tape. In order to fit the paper to the curvature of the dome, you may need to slit the edges of the paper in a few places. Make ¾-inch slits if necessary.

4. With the technical fountain pen and india ink, trace the design onto the inner surface of the plastic dome. (See Photograph 2-25.) Remove tracing paper from the dome.

5. Wipe the second plastic dome. When the ink on the first dome is completely dry, place the second dome inside it and secure with masking tape. Carefully trace the design onto the second dome. (See Photograph 2-26.)

6. Allow the ink on the second dome to dry. Check all lines on both domes against tracing paper to be sure that they are correct. If there are any mistakes, correct them according to directions in step F in Basic Instructions.

7. Spray the design side of both domes with Treasure Sealer to fix the ink.

8. Squeeze small amounts of alizarin crimson, Indian yellow, and Prussian blue onto your palette pad, and place a small container of varnish beside it. See design patterns and Color Suggestion charts. Refer to steps H and I in Basic Instructions for directions on how to paint backgrounds, mix colors, and paint designs.

Partridge in a Pear Tree Color Suggestions

For background: Apply two coats of natural Liquid
Pearl and then two coats of white acrylic paint.

Liquid Pearl

Part	Color
throat	natural (2 coats)

Transparent Oil Paints

Part	Color
body, head, and pears	pearly light orange
wing design	light orange
throat outline	light red
wings and tail	pearly dark pink
stems	medium brown
leaves	light green

Turtle Doves Color Suggestions

For background: Apply two coats of natural Liquid
Pearl and then two coats of yellow acrylic paint.

Liquid Pearl

Part	Color
body and tail	natural (2 coats)

Transparent Oil Paints

Part	Color
wings	medium blue
bills	medium yellow
leaves and branches	medium green
berries	medium red

French Hen Color Suggestions

For background: Apply two coats of natural Liquid Pearl and then two coats of yellow acrylic paint.

Transparent Oil Paints

Part	Color
body and wing	pearly brown
leaves	medium green
comb, beak, and wattle	medium red
nest	medium yellow

Calling Bird Color Suggestions

For background: Apply two coats of natural Liquid Pearl and then two coats of white acrylic paint.

Liquid Pearl

Part	Color
body and tail	natural (2 coats)

Transparent Oil Paints

Part	Color
wings	pearly blue
bill	medium yellow
ribbon	medium pink
leaves	medium green
berries	medium red

Gold Ring Color Suggestions

For background: Apply two coats of natural Liquid Pearl and then two coats of pink acrylic paint.

Liquid Pearl

Part	Color
pillow	natural (2 coats)

Transparent Oil Paints

Part	Color
leaves	light green
stems	light brown
ribbon	light red
ring	medium yellow

Drummer Drumming Color Suggestions

For background: Apply two coats of natural Liquid Pearl and then two coats of light orange acrylic paint.

Liquid Pearl

Part	Color
drum skin and bottom drum triangles	natural (2 coats)

Transparent Oil Paints

Part	Color
face and hands	fleshtone
upper drum triangles	medium red
collar, shoulder pads, and drumsticks	light pearly red
coat and pants	medium pearly blue

Goose A'Laying Color Suggestions

For background: Apply two coats of natural Liquid Pearl and then two coats of light green acrylic paint.

Liquid Pearl

Part	Color
goose	natural (2 coats)

Transparent Oil Paints

Part	Color
eggs	medium blue
nest	pearly yellow
leaves	medium green
beak	medium orange

Maid A'Milking Color Suggestions

For background: Apply two coats of natural Liquid Pearl and then two coats of light blue acrylic paint.

Liquid Pearl

Part	Color
bodice and apron	natural (2 coats)
pail	natural (1 light coat)

Transparent Oil Paints

Part	Color
face, neck, and hands	fleshtone
skirt, sleeves, shoe, and bow	pearly medium pink
flowers and hair	medium yellow
grass	medium green

Acrylic Paint

Part	Color
milk	white (2 coats)

Lady Dancing Color Suggestions

For background: Apply two coats of natural Liquid
Pearl and then two coats of pink acrylic paint.

Transparent Oil Paints

Part	Color
face, neck, and hands	fleshtone
garland	medium green
dress	dark pearly pink
hair	medium yellow

Piper Piping Color Suggestions

For background: Apply two coats of natural Liquid
Pearl and then two coats of light green acrylic paint.

Transparent Oil Paints

Part	Color
face and hands	fleshtone
horn	medium yellow
tunic, tights, sleeves, shoes, and hat	pearly medium green
leaves and grass	medium green

Lord A'Leaping Color Suggestions

For background: Apply two coats of natural Liquid Pearl and then two coats of white acrylic paint.

Liquid Pearl

Part	Color
collar	natural (2 coats)

Transparent Oil Paints

Part	Color
face and hands	fleshtone
garment background, tights, and hat	pearly red
trim on garment, lower sleeves, and undergarment	medium yellow
leaves and grass	medium green

Swan A'Swimming Color Suggestions

For background: Apply two coats of natural Liquid Pearl and then two coats of yellow acrylic paint.

Liquid Pearl

Part	Color
body	natural (2 coats)

Transparent Oil Paints

Part	Color
leaves	medium green
water	medium blue
bill	medium yellow

9. Cut the plastic backings off each of the plastic domes, as shown in Photograph 2-27. Cut flush to the edge where the raised section begins. Lay one of the plastic domes on a piece of cardboard, and trace outline with pencil, as shown in Photograph 2-28. Cut about ¹/₁₆ inch in from the drawn line, and place the cardboard oval shape aside for later use.

Photograph 2-27

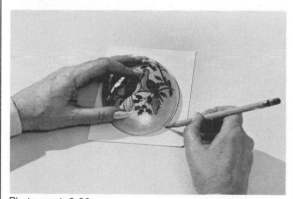

Photograph 2-28

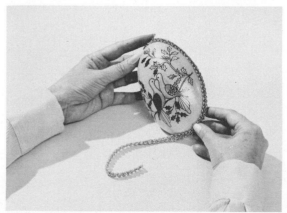

Photograph 2-29

10. With white glue, adhere metallic braid to circumference of each plastic dome. (See Photograph 2-29.) Position the braid so that it will overlap the edge by about ¹/₁₆ inch. Allow the glue about 1 hour to dry. With a needle and beige thread, make running stitches through braid and dome. Stitches should be about ¹/₈ inch long with ¹/₄-inch spaces between.

Photograph 2-30

11. Crumple a sheet of aluminum foil for each dome and place it inside, shiny side up, directly against the design. Trim the edges of the foil to allow a perfect fit.

12. Fill the inside of each dome with crumpled facial tissues. They will serve as a mask to keep the foil in place against the design.

13. Fold the 14½-inch length of cord in half to form a loop. Tie a knot 2 inches from each end. With white glue, adhere the ends of the loop to the top center of the cardboard oval. Slip the knot

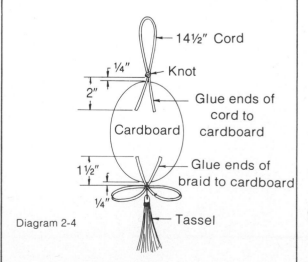

Diagram 2-4

14½" Cord
Knot
¼"
2"
Glue ends of cord to cardboard
Cardboard
Glue ends of braid to cardboard
1½"
¼"
Tassel

91

so that it is ¼ inch above the cardboard. (See Diagram 2-4.) Fold an 11-inch-long piece of gold braid in half to locate the center. Bring each end of the braid across the center to form loops on either side. Extend the ends, 1½ inches beyond the center, as shown in Diagram 2-4. Adhere braid at the point where it crosses to form a bow. Allow to dry for about 15 minutes. Slide the loop of a tassel over one end of the bow so that it will hang from the center of the bow. Glue ends of braid to the cardboard oval so that the center of the bow will hang ¼ inch below the bottom of the cardboard.

14. Place the two plastic domes together, with the cardboard between. (See Photograph 2-30.) Be sure that the tassel is at the bottom of the ornament. With needle and beige thread, stitch the overlapping edges of the metallic gold braid together, as shown in Photograph 2-31.

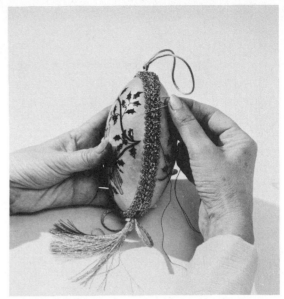

Photograph 2-31

Twelve Days of Christmas Ornaments (See page 83.)

Flower Bells Lamp Base

Lamp hardware is available at specialty lamp supply stores or at shops where lamps are built. The following list of materials includes all the parts needed to assemble the lamp base. I suggest that you go to a lamp supply store and ask for assistance, as you will want to be sure that the hardware pieces fit together properly. Sources for individual parts are listed in the back of the book. The design can be adapted to almost any size cylinder.

Materials

Lamp Hardware:

1 glass cylinder, 16 inches high, 5 inches in diameter

2 check plates, 5 inches in diameter

1 lamp base, 5 inches in diameter, with opening through side for lamp cord

1 IPS pipe, 22 inches long, ⅛ inch in diameter, threaded on both ends

1 top step, 4½ to 5 inches in diameter

1 break, 2½ inches

1 top break, 1½ inches high, 3⅝ inches in bottom diameter, ⅞ inch in top diameter

4 large, round, knurled locknuts, ¾ inch in outside diameter

1 socket, 3-way

1 harp, size will depend on shade

1 lamp cord, 6 feet long, with plug

lampshade of your choice

1 sheet of acetate, .0075 inch thick, same height as lamp cylinder but 1 inch wider

pencil

technical fountain pen

waterproof india ink, in black

tracing paper

masking tape

glass-cleaning solution

lint-free cloth or paper towel

Treasure Sealer

1 jar acrylic paint, 2-ounce size, in white

1 paintbrush, ½ inch or wider

1 liner brush, or #1 brush

transparent oil paints, in alizarin crimson, Indian yellow, and Prussian blue

1 can clear vinyl varnish

Liquid Pearl, in natural

aluminum foil

1 felt circle, same diameter as lamp base, in color of your choice

white glue

Instructions

1. Place and hold the acetate sheet snugly against the inside surface of the cylinder. Make a

94

mark at each end of the acetate at point where it overlaps. (See Photograph 2-32.) Remove the acetate sheet from the cylinder and connect the marks with technical fountain pen. This line will serve as the index around which the design is to be drawn. The line will be removed later.

2. Following instructions for enlarging patterns in the Helpful Hints chapter, enlarge design pattern by 55 percent. If you are using the grid method of enlarging, each square should measure 1 inch. Trace the enlarged pattern onto a large piece of tracing paper, making sure to include dotted line.

3. Turn the acetate sheet over. Clean glass and acetate with solution of your choice.

4. Place acetate on top of the tracing paper, matching drawn line with dotted line. Attach with masking tape. Using technical fountain pen and india ink, trace the part of the design that lies on the right side of the line. (See Photograph 2-33.) Untape the acetate sheet. Slide it directly across the design, aligning the edge of the sheet with the dotted line, as shown in Photograph 2-34. Tape in place. Use the technical fountain pen and india ink to trace the part of the design that lies on the left side of the dotted line. Untape

Photograph 2-33

the acetate sheet. Position it over the design so that the design will be midway between the two traced parts. (See Photograph 2-35.) Tape the sheet of acetate in place, and trace the entire design with the technical fountain pen. After the ink has dried, remove tracing paper from beneath the acetate. Check all lines on the acetate against tracing paper to be sure that they are correct. Any mistakes you might find can be corrected, according to directions in step F in Basic Instructions.

5. Spray the design side of acetate with Treasure Sealer to fix the ink. Turn the sheet of acetate

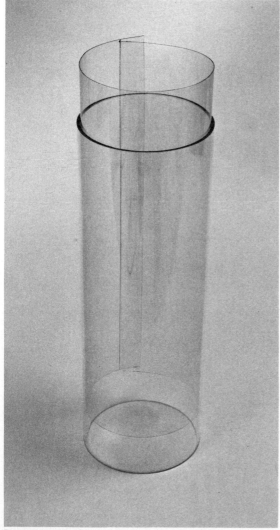

Photograph 2-32

over, and wash away the drawn line with a damp paper towel.

6. Paint a plain, opaque background, following directions in step G of Basic Instructions. Use two coats of white acrylic paint. Allow 1 hour drying time between coats and 1 hour after the last coat. Remember that the background must be completely opaque. If necessary, apply a third coat of white acrylic paint to background.

Photograph 2-34

Photograph 2-36

Photograph 2-35

96

7. Squeeze small amounts of alizarin crimson, Indian yellow, and Prussian blue onto your palette, and place a small container of varnish beside it. See color photograph for color suggestions. Directions on how to mix colors and paint design are given in steps H and I in Basic Instructions. The design was painted with light purple, yellow red, medium blue, light blue, rose pink, medium rose pink, medium green, medium brown, reddish brown, orange brown, medium orange, and yellow brown. In addition to these colors, I also used pearly light blue, pearly medium blue, and pearly medium rose pink in certain areas. I shaded light yellow with brown orange in spots and medium green with reddish brown on the stems.

8. Allow the paint to dry for 24 hours; then place acetate inside cylinder with design side in, and position. Crumple and shape aluminum foil so that it will fit behind the design. Mold foil around the inside of the cylinder, with its shiny side against the acetate. (See Photograph 2-36.)

9. Assemble the ⅛-inch IPS pipe into the lamp base and bottom check plate, and secure with locknuts. Place the cylinder on the check plate with the pipe extending upward through the center. Stuff aluminum foil around the pipe in the cylinder. This extra aluminum foil will serve as a mask to hold design in place. (See Photograph 2-37.)

10. Put the top check plate, top step, and breaks in place, and secure them with locknuts. Mount the socket base to the end of the ⅛-inch IPS pipe, and push the lamp cord up through the pipe to the socket base. Wire the socket, according to instructions in the Helpful Hints chapter.

11. Attach a piece of felt with white glue to the bottom of the lamp base.

Photograph 2-37

97

Glass Top Trinket Box (See page 73.)

Shell Art

Shell art, as we know it today, originated during the Victorian era, but the existence of shells has been traced back some 600 million years. Actual fossil shells have been found not only among the remains of Cro-Magnon man in France but also at archaeological sites in South America. Some of these are thought to date as far back as 3000 B.C.

Some of the earliest cooking utensils, dishes, and cups were made with shells. Shells were also used as a medium of trade and an expression of wealth by a number of early civilizations, such as the Aztecs, the Mayas, the Arabs, the Africans, and the North American Indians. The ancient Greeks attributed mythological significance to the shell, and African tribesmen used shells in their rituals.

The modern-day interest in shells is twofold. The collector displays shells for their intrinsic beauty, while the artist or craftsman prefers to arrange them into elaborate designs. The contemporary style of shell arranging originated in Victorian Europe. The ladies of the day created decorative pictures, shell flowers, arrangements under glass domes, and mosaic patterns. It was also at this time that the sailor's valentine made its appearance. Basically, this was a double shadow box sort of affair that was hinged and usually octagonal in shape. When opened, each side displayed an intricate shell design. It took its name from the fact that seafaring men would while away idle hours aboard ship making them for their loved ones back home.

The popularity of shell art has increased tremendously in modern times. The instructions, photographs, and diagrams in this chapter will acquaint you with the basic techniques. Read them carefully before you begin the projects.

Shell Art Materials and Tools

For those who live by the sea, collecting shells can be a major part of the fun. For those who don't, however, packages or individual shells are available at craft stores and shell shops; they can also be ordered through the mail. (See list of suppliers at the end of the book.) Acquaint yourself with the many different types of shells and choose your favorites. Most of the shells that were used in the following projects are shown in Photographs 3-1A and B.

One of the advantages to buying shells is that you will not have to clean them. If you are collecting your own, however, you can remove most stains with a mild solution of household bleach and water. Mineral oil can be rubbed over the shells to enhance their natural luster. If you wish to paint your shells, you will need transparent oil paints, turpentine, and clear acrylic spray. Acrylic spray protects the painted shells against moisture and dust.

Since shell art is really an art of gluing and arranging, you will need a strong gluing agent. Fast-drying cements are used to adhere shells to each other and to other surfaces. I use Bond #527 All-Purpose Cement or Shellcraft for my work. You will also need white glue for adhering fabric, paper, and wood surfaces. Silicone adhesive —General Electric Silicone Seal, Dow Corning Rubber Silicone Sealer, or Dow Corning Silicone Adhesive—is needed for gluing shells to plastic surfaces and to coral. A plastic adhesive, called Plasti-tak, is useful for holding tiny shells in place before they have been glued. Larger shells should be held down with masking tape.

Since handling tiny shells can often be a troublesome task, you will need a pair of tweezers. The serrated type is best. The flexible blade of a palette knife comes in handy for lifting cemented shell flowers off glass or waxed paper surfaces.

To make shell flowers, you will need floral wire, absorbent cotton, cardboard, and a surface upon which to work. A glass sheet or waxed paper surface is best. Cardboard disks and small pieces of absorbent cotton serve as foundations for the flowers. Stems are made with green-covered floral wire. Gauges 18, 24, and 26 will be used repeatedly in the projects. Wire cutters and

Pyramid top shell

Coral

Top shell

Large scallop shell

Top shell

Small scallop shell

Mushroom coral shell

Top shell

Toenail shell Moon snail shell Cat's eye shell Purple sailor snail shell Turban shell

Venetian pearls

Pikaki shells

Rice shells

Lucine cup shells

Californian wedge

Job's tears

Florida Cerithium

Purple olive

Gar scales

Tiny whelk shells

needle-nose pliers make cutting and bending wires much easier. You will also need green floral tape to wrap around the wires.

Additional pieces of equipment needed are curved manicure scissors for cutting cardboard disks, ordinary straight scissors, paper towels, paintbrushes, a ruler, and a pencil.

At the end of the book you will find a list of where to find shell art materials and tools.

Shell Art Hints and Techniques

The following list of hints and techniques will be of great help to you in your shell work.

Segregate shells according to type and size. This will save time later.

Do not collect shells that have oil or tar stains on them. These stains are almost impossible to remove.

Remove minor blemishes from the surface of shells by soaking them in a solution of bleach and water. Mix 2 ounces of bleach into 1 quart of water, and place shells in the solution. Check shells after a few minutes. If the blemishes are gone, rinse the shells with fresh water and dry them with paper towels. For severe blemishes, you may have to soak the shells for 2 or 3 hours.

If you choose to paint your shells, the best kind of paint to use is transparent oil paint. Place a small amount of paint in a container. Add a bit of turpentine and mix well. Place the shells in the container, and agitate them slightly with a spoon or spatula. Remove the shells from the solution and place them on a paper towel. Allow to dry for at least 24 hours before handling.

Spray painted shells with a coat of acrylic spray after they have dried. This will protect them against moisture when the finished piece is cleaned or washed. If you prefer, you can apply acrylic spray to the entire design piece.

To enhance the natural luster of shells, apply a small amount of mineral oil.

If you are working on a glass surface, apply a small amount of petroleum jelly to the glass.

This will facilitate the removal of cemented shells.

■ When you are assembling a shell flower, it is a good idea to have a live sample from which to copy. If this is impossible, however, a picture or a good imitation will do.

■ Shells used for assembling shell flowers should resemble the petals of the flowers you wish to duplicate. Try to use shells that are approximately the same size and shape.

Shell Flowers

The following instructions, diagrams, and photographs will teach you how to assemble four-teen different flower shapes. Practically any flower can be duplicated with shells. It is simply a matter of following a few basic principles of construction and using your imagination. Once you have learned how to assemble shell flowers, you may want to create your own design pieces. This section will give you a good head start.

Begin by saturating a small piece of cotton —about ¼ inch in diameter—with cement and placing it on your work surface. If you are assembling a large flower, place saturated cotton on a small cardboard disk. Cut the disk to a size that will be slightly smaller than the finished flower. Arrange shells on the cotton, using tweezers to handle them. Start with the outer-most ring of petals and work toward the center or innermost ring. Press shells firmly into cotton. Allow 2 or 3 minutes drying time for each ring. After the cement has dried, lift the flower off the work surface with a palette knife or spatula.

Flower stems are made with green-covered floral wire. Make sure that the wire is strong enough to support the flower. Use 26-gauge wire

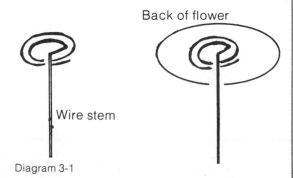

Back of flower

Wire stem

Diagram 3-1

for small flowers, 22- or 24-gauge wire for medium-sized flowers, and 18- or 20-gauge wire for large flowers. Coil one end of the wire, as shown in Diagram 3-1. Adhere it to the back of the flower with cement. For more support, slip the stem through a round piece of paper and glue it to the back of the flower.

Now that you have learned the basic procedure for assembling shell flowers, practice the following shapes. Follow instructions for positioning of shells on the cotton. *Hinge end* refers to the end that would normally connect a shell to its accompanying shell; *cup side* refers to the concave side of the shell. Use suggested shells for each flower or choose your own.

1. Double rose: With hinge ends in and cup sides up, place 7 small cup shells, slightly overlapping each other, in a circle on the cotton. With shells in same positions, place 5 around, and on top of, the bottom row; place 3 around, and on top of, the second row. Glue cup sides of 2 shells together and place them in the center.

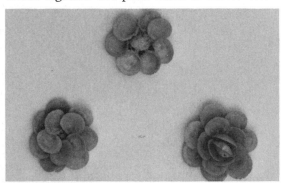

Photograph 3-2

2. Wild rose: With hinge ends in and cup sides up, place 5 medium-sized cup shells, slightly overlapping each other, in a circle on the cotton. Place 5 or 6 tiny whelk shells, points down, in the center of the flower.

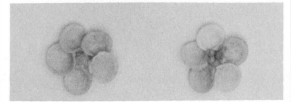

Photograph 3-3

3. Daisy: With pointed ends in, openings facing in the same direction, and sides touching, place 12 rice shells in a circle on the cotton. Place 5 tiny whelk shells, points up, in the center.

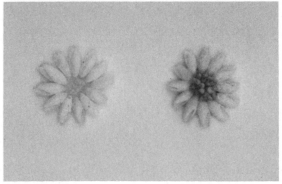

Photograph 3-4

4. Dogwood: With hinge ends out and cup sides up, place 4 toenail shells or dogwood clam cups, slightly tilted and overlapped, in a circle on the cotton. Place 3 brown pikaki shells in the center of the flower. Dab a bit of brown oil paint on hinge ends of shells.

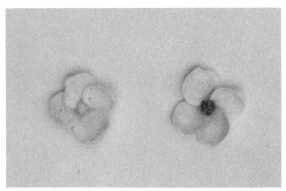

Photograph 3-5

5. Pansy: Cement together hinge ends of two ½-inch-wide lucine cup shells. Place them, cup sides up, on the cotton. Cement 2 smaller lucine cups together in the same position. Place them on the cotton so that they will overlap half of the larger pair. Adhere hinge end of one smaller-sized lucine cup, cup side up, to the center of the smaller pair. With a narrow paintbrush and lavender oil paint, apply thin lines of color to the shells, as shown in Photograph 3-6.

104

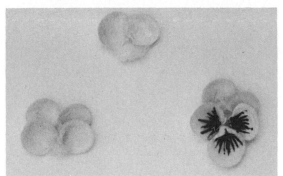

Photograph 3-6

6. **Sweet pea:** With hinge ends out and cup sides down, overlap slightly and cement 2 cup shells together. Place them on the cotton. With cup sides facing one another, tilt 2 cup shells and cement hinge ends to bottom of other pair. Cement cup sides of 2 more shells together, and cement hinge ends between the second pair.

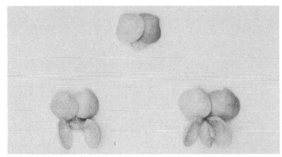

Photograph 3-7

7. **Apple blossom:** With hinge ends in and cup sides up, place 5 cup shells, slightly overlapping each other, in a circle on the cotton. Adhere a tiny cotton puff to the center.

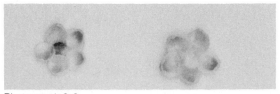

Photograph 3-8

8. **Grape hyacinth:** Wrap the end of a piece of floral wire with cotton, and saturate cotton with cement. With hinge ends up and cup sides in, place 2 tiny cup shells around tip of cotton. With hinge ends up and cup sides out, place 4 more

shells around cotton, below the top pair. Adhere 1 shell to each of the shells in this row. Cup sides should be in; hinge ends should be placed slightly below the accompanying hinge end. Add two rows of 5 pairs, one row of 4 pairs, and one row of 3 pairs of shells to the flower in the same manner.

Photograph 3-9

9. **Poinsettia:** With pointed ends out, equally space seven ¾-inch-long gar scales in a circle on the cotton. With gar scales in the same position, place 5 smaller gar scales around, and on top of, the first row; place 3 tiny gar scales around, and on top of, the second row. Apply a small amount of cement between shells to secure. Break some tiny yellow shells into pieces, and adhere them to center of flower.

Photograph 3-10

10. **Camellia:** With hinge ends out and cup sides down, place 7 lucine cups in a circle, on the edge of the cotton. With cup sides facing in and hinge ends down, place 7 lucine cups at a 45-degree angle, slightly overlapped, in a circle within the outer circle. Make an inner circle of 5 shells and then an inner circle of 3 shells in the same manner. With cup sides facing one another and hinge ends in, place 2 shells in the center.

105

Photograph 3-11

11. Gardenia: With hinge ends out and cup sides down, place 7 lucine cups in a circle, on the edge of the cotton. With hinge ends up and cup sides facing in, place 7 lucine cups at a 45-degree angle, slightly overlapped, in a circle within the outer circle. Make an inner circle of 5 shells and then an inner circle of 3 shells in the same manner. With cup sides facing one another and hinge ends out, place 2 shells in the center.

Photograph 3-12

12. Chrysanthemum: With pointed ends in and cup sides up, place 14 Job's tears in a circle around edge of cotton. With pointed ends up, place 11 Job's tears at an angle, in a circle within the outer circle. Continue to assemble inner circles of shells, reducing each circle by 2 shells. Finish with 1 pair of glued-together shells in the center. Apply cement between shells to secure.

Photograph 3-13

13. Leaf: Wrap 26-gauge wire with cotton, and saturate it with cement. Place 1 green gar scale in a vertical position on the end of the cotton. Place another gar scale to the right of, and slightly overlapping, the first one. Place another one on the left side. Continue in this manner until the leaf is the length you desire.

Photograph 3-14

14. Bud: Insert a 1½-inch-piece of floral wire into a small cotton puff. Saturate it with cement. With cup sides facing and hinge ends in, place 2 tiny cup-shaped shells on cotton.

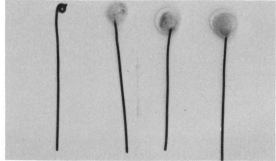

Photograph 3-15

Climbing Coral
Lamp Base

When purchasing lamp hardware for this project, ask your lamp supply dealer for help. Select hardware pieces that will fit properly together and appeal to your taste. The Helpful Hints chapter will give you more details on how to assemble your lamp.

Materials

Lamp Hardware:

1 hurricane lamp glass cylinder, 15½ inches high, 5½ inches in diameter

2 check plates, 5½ inches in diameter

1 lamp base, 5½ inches in diameter, in antique brass

1 IPS pipe, 20 inches long, ⅛ inch in diameter, threaded on both ends

1 break, 2½ inches high, ¾ inch in bottom diameter, ¾ inch in top diameter

2 hexagon locknuts

2 round, knurled locknuts

1 lamp cap, 5½ inches in diameter, in antique brass

1 lamp cord, 6 feet long, with plug

1 socket, 3-way

1 harp, to fit lampshade

3 pieces coral, each approximately 6 inches in diameter

assorted turban shells, chambered Nautiluses, moon snail shells, and mushroom coral; or any other assortment of your choice

ruler

white glue

1 paintbrush, ½ inch wide

pearl flakes

1 can clear vinyl varnish

1 cardboard tube, to cover IPS pipe (Tubes that come with hangers from the dry cleaners are perfect.)

scissors

masking tape

small hammer

2 tubes silicone adhesive, 3-ounce size

tweezers

bead wire, 26 gauge

wire cutters

glass-cleaning solution

lint-free cloth or paper towel

vacuum cleaner

Instructions

1. Place the bottom check plate on top of the lamp base, aligning center holes. Measure height of combined check plate and base. Add ⅛ inch to

107

this measurement and record figure. Measure up from one end of IPS pipe to this recorded figure. Place a round locknut at this point on the pipe. Insert this end of the pipe through the aligned holes from the top side. Place a hexagon locknut on protruding end of pipe, directly under base. Tighten locknut.

2. Brush a coat of white glue on the surface of the bottom check plate. Sprinkle pearl flakes over the glue so that they will completely cover the surface. Allow the glue to dry for 24 hours. Apply one coat of vinyl varnish over the pearl flakes. (See Photograph 3-16.)

Photograph 3-16

3. Cut the cardboard tube to the same length as the glass hurricane cylinder. Cut tube open, place it around the IPS pipe, and close the slit with masking tape.

4. Break the coral into smaller pieces by striking them with a small hammer. Render sharp blows to the underside, near the center. Do not worry if a few of the polyps, or spiny sections, break. This will not show when the coral is attached to the centerpost of the lamp.

5. Starting at the bottom of the cardboard tube and working your way up, adhere pieces of coral around the tube with silicone adhesive. Wrap bead wire around tube to hold pieces in place while the adhesive is setting. Cover the entire cardboard tube in this manner. Arrange the coral pieces so that they will look as though they had

grown out of the centerpost. Remember, however, that the glass cylinder must be able to fit over the centerpost. Check fit several times to make sure. Once the silicone adhesive has dried, remove the wire. (See Photograph 3-17.)

Photograph 3-17

6. Using silicone adhesive, arrange and adhere pieces of mushroom coral over the pearl flakes on the bottom check plate.

7. With silicone adhesive, adhere an assortment of shells around the coral. Start from the bottom and work your way up. (See Photograph 3-18.) I used an assortment of stripped and unstripped chambered Nautiluses, turban shells, and moon snail shells. A stripped shell is one that has had

Photograph 3-18

its external covering—periostracum—removed to reveal a lustrous mother-of-pearl surface underneath. Stripped shells can be purchased at shell shops and craft stores.

8. Clean the glass hurricane cylinder, inside and outside, with glass-cleaning solution of your choice and a lint-free cloth or paper towel. Check to be sure that all shells and coral pieces are secure and will not fall off the tube.

9. Vacuum lightly to remove loose particles and dust. Put the glass hurricane cylinder in place. Assemble the top check plate and break. Secure with round and hexagon locknuts.

10. Put the socket on the lamp. Wire lamp according to directions in the Helpful Hints chapter at the end of the book.

Scallop Swag Lamp

An arrangement of clam shells, moon snail shells, and large scallop shells makes a beautiful shade for a hanging lamp. Ask for help in a lamp supply store to make sure that all the hardware pieces will fit together.

Materials

Lamp Hardware:

swag lamp kit, containing chain, cord, switch, socket, and hooks

1 IPS pipe, 3 inches long, ⅛ inch in diameter, threaded on both ends

2 hexagon nuts

2 flat washers, about 1¼ inches in diameter

ball cap to fit shade and pipe

loop with wireway

half-round plastic lampshade, 16 to 24 inches in diameter, in white

scallop shells, ranging from 3 to 5 inches wide, enough to cover shade

assorted clam shells, moon snail shells, and scallop shells; or any other assortment of small shells

masking tape

waxed paper

6 tubes silicone adhesive, 3-ounce size

tweezers

Instructions

1. Starting at the bottom edge of the lampshade, position the largest scallop shells, approximately 1 inch apart, around shade. Hold them in place with masking tape. Select a group of slightly smaller scallop shells. Tape them around the shade, above the first row, leaving approximately ½ inch between rows and 1 inch between adjacent shells. (See Photograph 3-19.) It took two

Photograph 3-19

rows of scallops to cover my lampshade. Apply as many rows as are needed to cover your shade, using progressively smaller shells for each row.

2. Place the shade over a large piece of waxed paper to protect your work surface. Remove 1 scallop shell from the bottom row. Apply a bead of silicone adhesive around the inner edge of the shell, as shown in Photograph 3-20. Put the shell

Photograph 3-20

back in place and press down firmly. Follow this procedure for each scallop shell.

3. Working on one area at a time, apply and spread silicone adhesive over spaces between scallop shells. Completely cover spaces with moon snail shells and clam shells of assorted sizes. Cover the entire shade in this manner, as shown in Photograph 3-21, leaving room at top for ball cap to rest.

Photograph 3-21

4. Assemble lamp as shown in Diagram 3-2. Screw a nut onto bottom of IPS pipe, ¼ inch from the end. Screw the socket base onto the end of pipe, and tighten the nut down against the base to secure it. Slip a washer onto IPS pipe and insert the pipe up through the hole in the shade. Slip a washer and a nut onto the pipe and secure them over the shade. Place the ball cap on the pipe so that it rests against top of shade. Screw the loop onto the pipe and place against the ball cap. Thread the cord through the chain, going in and out alternate links. Open the bottom link, slip it onto the loop, and close it tightly. Thread the cord through the pipe. Wire the socket according to instructions in the Helpful Hints chapter. Mount hooks for hanging.

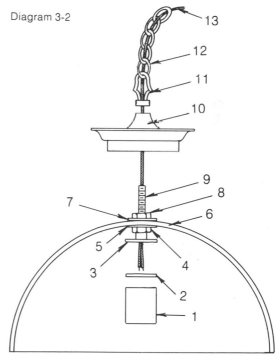

Diagram 3-2

1. Socket   2. Insulator   3. Socket base
4. Nut   5. Washer   6. Lampshade   7. Washer
8. Nut   9. IPS pipe   10. Ball cap
11. Loop with wireway   12. Chain   13. Cord

111

Fancy Flowerpot

Flowerpots of all sizes and shapes are excellent subjects for shell art. Completely cover your pot with randomly placed shells, decorate it with shell flowers, or simply decorate the rim.

Materials

1 ceramic flowerpot, 6 inches in diameter, 4 inches high
assorted rice shells, whelk shells, and green gar scales, or any other assortment of your choice
Treasure Sealer
1 paintbrush, ½ inch wide
1 jar acrylic paint, 2-ounce size, in turquoise
cement
absorbent cotton
ruler
crochet thread, in color of your choice
scissors
white glue
1 can clear vinyl varnish
tweezers

Instructions

1. Apply Treasure Sealer to entire pot. Apply two coats of turquoise acrylic paint and allow to dry.
2. Referring to Shell Flowers section, make 24 daisies (shape number 3) with various sizes of rice shells and tiny whelk shells.
3. Divide the top rim of the pot into quarters, and mark. Drape a double strand of crochet thread between adjacent marks, as shown in Photograph 3-22. With white glue, adhere the

Photograph 3-22

thread to the marked spots on the rim. When dry, apply a coat of vinyl varnish to entire pot.

4. Arrange the flowers on the crochet thread, as shown in Photograph 3-23, and adhere with cement. Adhere green gar scales under the flowers and along the thread.

Photograph 3-23

Shell-rimmed Planter

Here's another example of what can be done with assorted shells and an ordinary flowerpot.

Materials

1 bisque planter, 6 by 6 inches, in natural brown
Treasure Sealer

1 paintbrush, ½ inch wide
1½ yards braid, ⅛ inch wide, in gold
white glue
assorted shells of your choice, ½ to 1 inch wide
tweezers
cement

Instructions

1. Apply Treasure Sealer to planter and allow to dry.

2. With white glue, attach braid to inner and outer edges of rim and around the feet of planter.

3. Adhere shells to rim with cement. (See Photograph 3-24.)

Photograph 3-24

113

Oriental Shell Arrangement

An Oriental snuff bottle makes the perfect vase for this delicate apple blossom arrangement. The height of the piece is approximately 8 inches. If you wish, however, the arrangement can be made larger by using larger shells, a larger vase, and heavier wire.

Materials

Oriental snuff bottle, 2 inches high, 1 inch wide, or vase of your choice
44 Job's tears, ¼-inch long, light green
96 small cup-shaped shells, natural pink
tweezers
absorbent cotton
floral wire, 26 gauge, green-covered
wire cutters
floral tape, in brown
scissors
notebook paper
ruler

Instructions

1. Referring to Shell Flowers section, make 18 apple blossoms (shape number 7) and 3 buds (shape number 14) with the 96 cup-shaped shells. Make a stem for each flower with floral wire. Attach stems to flowers according to instructions in Shell Flowers section.

2. Cut three 7½-inch pieces of floral wire. With ends even, lightly twist wires together, making about 2 turns per inch. Wrap the entire length of the wires with overlapping rows of floral tape. This will become part of the long center branch.

3. Measure 1½ inches from one end of the branch, and position 2 apple blossoms at this point. Hold stems tightly against the branch. Allowing ¼ inch of stems to extend at the top, wrap the stems and branch together with overlapping rows of floral tape. Wrap up to 1½ inches below the apple blossoms. Do not cut the tape. At this point, add a cluster of 4 apple blossoms, allowing ½ inch of each stem to extend and following same wrapping procedure to attach. Mark off 2 inches from bottom of branch and wrap up to that point.

4. Cut three 3½-inch pieces of floral wire to make another branch. With ends even, twist wires together and wrap with overlapping rows of floral tape.

5. Measure 1¼ inches from one end of the branch. At this point, attach a cluster of 5 apple

blossoms and one bud, allowing ¾ inch of each stem to extend. Wrap for a distance of ½ inch below apple blossoms. With bottom ends even, use floral tape to wrap the bottom of both branches together. (See Photograph 3-25.)

Photograph 3-25

6. Twist together and wrap with floral tape three 5½-inch pieces of floral wire to make the right-hand branch.

7. Allowing ½ inch of stem to extend, follow same wrapping procedure to attach 1 apple blossom and 1 bud, 2 inches below the end. Attach 3

apple blossoms, 1¼ inches below the first two. Wrap all the way to the bottom of the branch with floral tape. (See Photograph 3-26.)

Photograph 3-26

8. To make the left-hand branch, twist and wrap with floral tape three 4¾-inch pieces of floral wire. Allowing ½ inch of stems to extend, attach 1 bud 1¾ inches below end of branch. Attach 3 apple blossoms 1 inch below the bud. (See Photograph 3-27.)

9. Put a small amount of cement on the hinge ends of approximately 43 Job's tears; attach to branches. Follow Photographs 3-25, 3-26, and 3-27 for placement. Shape the branches and arrange in vase.

Photograph 3-27

115

Victorian Shell Wreath

The wreath is made from any assortment of shell flowers. It can be made larger or smaller by simply adjusting the number of flower spray arrangements. Although this wreath was made in a shadow box frame, smaller wreaths can be displayed under a glass dome, as well.

Materials

shadow box frame, 14 by 16 inches
1 piece posterboard, 14 by 16 inches, in white
assorted clam shells, Job's tears, rice shells, whelk shells, lucine cups, and small green gar scales; or any other assortment of your choice
cement
absorbent cotton
floral wire, 24 gauge, green-covered
wire cutters
tweezers
floral tape, in brown
floral wire, 18 gauge, green-covered
1 yard satin ribbon, ¼ inch wide, in beige
white glue
½ yard antique satin drapery material, in off-white
1 paintbrush, ½ inch wide
scissors
4 strips balsa wood, each ³/₁₆ inch thick, 1³/₁₆ inches wide, by 16 inches long
handsaw
4 dozen sequin pins, each ½ inch long
hammer
6 feet satin cord, #1 rattail, in white
awl or ice pick
6 brads, each 1 inch long

Instructions

1. Following instructions in the Shell Flowers section, make an assortment of about 120 flowers and 60 leaves. Make 2-inch stems for each with 24-gauge wire. For my wreath, I made double roses, wild roses, daisies, dogwoods, apple blossoms, grape hyacinths, camellias, and chrysanthemums. Paint shells if you wish.

2. Make a flower arrangement by assembling 12 flowers and 6 leaves. Arrange so that the flower portion of the spray will be about 3 inches long and 2 inches wide. Twist all stems together and wrap with floral tape to secure. (See Photograph 3-28.) Make nine more flower arrangements in the same manner.

3. Make a wreath form from a 31-inch length of 18-gauge floral wire. Overlap the ends by 3

Photograph 3-28

inches and twist them together, as shown in Photograph 3-29.

4. Place the stems of each flower arrangement against the wreath form, as shown in Photograph 3-30. In two or three places, wrap a piece of 24-gauge floral wire around stems and wreath form and twist. Cover the entire wreath form in this manner.

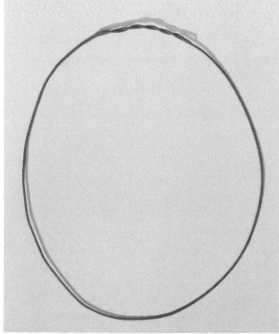
Photograph 3-29

Photograph 3-30

5. Follow directions in the Helpful Hints chapter to make a six-looped bow with a 33-inch length of satin ribbon. Fold a 6½-inch length of floral wire in half to locate the center. Place wire around the center of the bow, keeping ends even in the back. Twist three times to secure. The wire will be used to attach the bow to the wreath. To simulate a knot and cover the wire, wrap a 1½-inch length of ribbon around the middle of the bow. Fasten it on the back side of the bow with white glue.

6. Cut posterboard to fit inside shadow box frame. Cut antique satin to a rectangle, 1 inch larger than posterboard in width and length. Place antique satin, dull side down, on your work surface. Apply a very thin coat of white glue to the white side of posterboard. Position the glued side onto center of satin and press firmly. Turn over and work out any wrinkles with your hands. Trim excess satin from the edges of posterboard. Place the shadow box frame, facedown, on the work surface.

7. Cut two balsa strips, with their $^3/_{16}$-inch-

117

118

Oriental Shell Arrangement (See page 114.)

Victorian Shell Wreath (See page 116.)

sides up, to fit inside of right and left sides of shadow box frame. Place them inside the frame. Cut two balsa strips to make top and bottom sides for an inner balsa frame. (See Photograph 3-31.) Remove the strips of wood.

Photograph 3-31

8. Cut four strips of antique satin to the same lengths as, but 1½ inches wider than, balsa strips. Apply a thin coat of white glue to one side of each balsa strip. Place a satin strip, dull side down, on your work surface. Center and adhere a balsa strip to satin. Repeat procedure for remaining three strips. Put a thin coat of white glue on the back of each balsa strip. Bring satin around the edges of the strips and adhere to the back. (See Photograph 3-32.)

9. Apply white glue to top and bottom end of each strip. Adhere top and bottom strips to two side strips. Hammer a sequin pin through each corner, as shown in Photograph 3-33. You now have a satin-covered frame that will fit inside the shadow box frame.

10. Place posterboard, satin side down, on top of satin frame. Place sequin pins all the way around the frame, spacing them 1½ inches apart. (See Photograph 3-34.)

11. Turn frame over. With white glue, adhere a short piece of satin cord over each corner joint of the frame. Adhere satin cord all around poster-

120

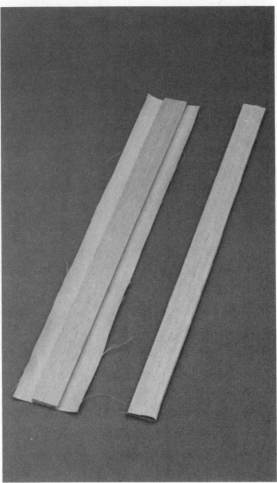
Photograph 3-32

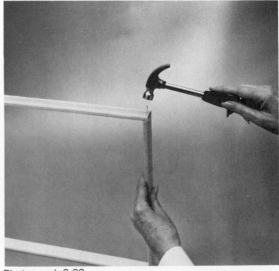
Photograph 3-33

Photograph 3-34

Photograph 3-36

board, starting and finishing at the same corner. (See Photograph 3-35.)

12. Place front of the wreath down on the work surface. Cut four 4-inch lengths of 24-gauge floral wire. Wrap one piece around top of wreath, one at bottom, and one at each side. Twist wire together in back of the wreath. (See Photograph

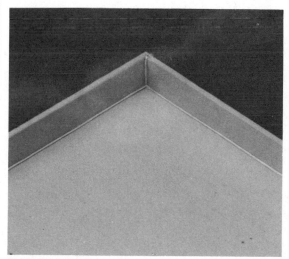

Photograph 3-35

3-36.) These wires will be used to secure the wreath to the satin frame.

13. Attach the bow to top center of wreath. Position it so that the streamers will hang in the

center of the wreath. Slip the wires of the bow between the flowers; twist several times in the back. (See Photograph 3-37.)

14. Center wreath on satin frame. Using an awl or ice pick, punch eight holes through poster-board to match each wire attachment on the

Photograph 3-37

121

Photograph 3-38

wreath. (See Photograph 3-38.) Insert the wires through the holes, and twist four or five times in the back.

15. Assemble glass and satin frame into shadow box frame. Drive brads into frame to secure, placing one at the top, one at the bottom, and two at each side. Put a paper backing on the shadow box frame, according to instructions given in the Helpful Hints chapter.

Shell-bordered Mirror

Adding a border of shells and shell flowers is a graceful way to decorate an ordinary mirror. Two new flower shapes were used to decorate this mirror. Use the same flower shapes I did, design your own, or choose your favorites from among those given in the Shell Flowers section.

Materials

1 piece Masonite, 4 inches larger than mirror in length and width

1 mirror, 1 by 1½ feet

1 frame, ⅜ inch wide, to fit around Masonite

450 California wedge shells, each ½ to ¾ inch wide

200 olive shells, each ⅝ inch long, purple

40 Florida Cerithium shells, each ½ to ¾ inch wide

40 Venetian pearl shells, yellow

40 Venetian pearl shells, natural

1 picture hanger

ruler
pencil
1 paintbrush, ½ inch wide
silicone adhesive
2 yards metallic cord, ⅛ inch wide, in gold
white glue
scissors
cardboard
absorbent cotton
tweezers
cement
10 glazier points

Instructions

1. Center and mount the picture hanger to the back of the Masonite, about 1 inch from the top. The shorter sides of the Masonite are the top and bottom sides.

2. Measure 2 inches from each side of the Masonite and draw an inner rectangle. This marks where the mirror will be placed. (See Diagram 3-3.)

Photograph 3-39

3. Apply an even coat of silicone adhesive over the drawn rectangle. Position the mirror and press firmly in place. Allow to dry for 24 hours. (See Photograph 3-39.)

4. Attach metallic cord around edge of mirror with white glue. (See Photograph 3-40.)

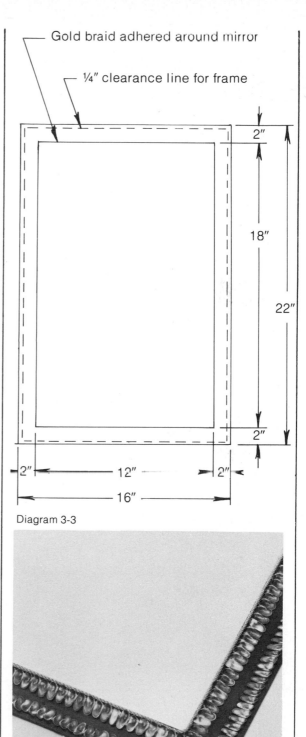

Gold braid adhered around mirror

¼″ clearance line for frame

2″

18″

22″

2″

2″   12″   2″

16″

Diagram 3-3

Photograph 3-40

123

5. Draw a line around four sides of Masonite, ¼ inch in from the edge. (See Diagram 3-3.) This is the allowance for the frame.

6. With white glue, attach a row of California wedge shells around edge of mirror so that they overlap slightly and tilt in the same direction. Leave a bare area of 5 inches to the right of and below the top left-hand corner. Attach a row of California wedge shells along the line drawn for the frame, overlapping and tilting shells in the opposite direction. Leave a bare area of 3 inches to the right of and below the top left-hand corner. (See Photograph 3-41.)

Photograph 3-43

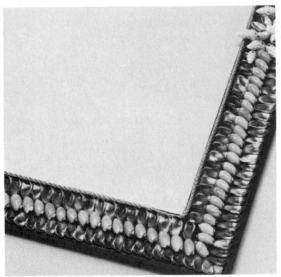
Photograph 3-41

7. Use white glue to adhere a row of olive shells between the two rows of wedges. Position shells at a slight angle, with pointed ends toward the mirror and open sides down. (See Photograph 3-41.)

8. Referring to the Shell Flowers section, make 2 chrysanthemums (shape number 12) using California wedge shells. Assemble the flowers on 1-inch-diameter disks for support. After the fifth row of shells has been assembled on the flower, put a cluster of 7 yellow Venetian pearl shells in the center. (See Photograph 3-42.)

Photograph 3-42

Photograph 3-44

Shell-bordered Mirror (See page 122.)

Photograph 3-45

9. Saturate a piece of cotton with cement, and place it on a ⅞-inch-diameter disk. Position 7 purple olive shells in a circle on the cotton. Pointed ends should face in and open sides should be up. Leave a ½-inch opening in the center. Place a cluster of 8 natural Venetian pearls in the center and press in place. (See Photograph 3-43.) Make 5 flowers in this manner.

10. Saturate a piece of cotton with cement and place it on a ¾-inch disk. Place a circle of 7 California wedge shells on the cotton, cup sides up, pointed ends toward the center. Place a second row of 5 California wedge shells around cotton in the same manner. Place 3 shells, cup sides facing center, on top of the flower. Position so that they will stand up, leaving about ¼ inch of space in the center. Place a cluster of yellow Venetian pearls in the center. (See Photograph 3-44.)

11. Assemble frame around Masonite and attach in place with glazier points. Place three at each side and two each at the top and bottom. Arrange the flowers on top left-hand corner, as shown in Photograph 3-45, and adhere in place with white glue. Fill in spaces around the flowers with Florida Cerithium shells.

Pod and Cone Art

Although Englishmen had discovered the art of decorating with pods, cones, seeds, and nuts early in the nineteenth century, it was not until the 1870s that the craft became popular. At that time, mainly as a result of American enthusiasm for the craft, pod and cone art broke out as one of the rages of the era in England and throughout Europe. Baskets, thermometer and calendar frames, flower stands, hanging baskets, fan and glove boxes, hand mirrors, lambrequins, wall pockets, lamp mats, place mats, and picture frames were popular projects of that time. These pieces were popularly decorated with pine cone scales and mixed with other treasures of the forest, such as acorns, beechnut hulls, oak apples, nuts, and seeds.

Our ancestors used a knife to strip the pine cone scales from the cones. Since the tip of a pine cone has an interesting rosette shape, it was usually cut off and used as a flower or a design centerpiece. There were two methods of attaching pine cones to surfaces. One was to apply a thin coat of putty over the surface and to place the cones on the putty. The other was to cover pasteboard with brown silk or paper and to sew on the scales, either by casting loops of brown thread over the tail sections of the scales or by passing them through small drilled holes. The pasteboards were then adhered to the surface with a gum or resin glue. When the designs were finished, they were given a coat of varnish. This was done not only to protect the design and provide a lustrous finish but also to give the work an elegant, carved-wood look.

Part of the fun of pod and cone art is collecting the pods and cones. The trees and shrubs around your home, as well as those in nearby parks, national forests, and open mountain and wooded areas, offer an endless supply of materials. Take a look around your neighborhood in late summer and all during the autumn, particularly in October—in North America, the best time for collecting. You will be pleasantly surprised by the wealth of berries, cones, nuts, leaves, and pods available. Of course, remember to obtain the proper permission first. State and national parks do not allow collecting, but city parks and national forests usually do. Ask the city parks department or forest ranger for permission. If you wish to collect on private property, obtain permission first from the caretaker, custodian, or owner. Most times you will find that permission is enthusiastically granted. If you prefer to buy your pods and cones, they are available at craft stores and at some floral distributors.

Pod and Cone Art Materials and Tools

Become familiar with the wide variety of pods, cones, seeds, and nuts that are available to you, and choose your favorites. Some of the many different types of pods and cones are shown in Photographs 4-1A and 4-1B. Have fun collecting an assortment or purchase pods and cones at craft stores.

Most of the tools that you will need to complete the projects in this chapter are shown in Photograph 4-2. Going from right to left on the bottom row of the photograph are a pair of wire cutters, long-nose pliers, an awl, two pairs of clippers (large and small), and a small electric drill. Since pine cones are attached with gauges 18 and 24 green-covered floral wire, wire cutters and pliers will be needed to cut and bend the wires into shape. Pliers are also used occasionally to pull scales off cones, but it is usually better to use clippers. If you have a large and a small pair, use the large pair to strip scales off large cones and the small pair to strip small cones. Clippers are also useful for trimming scales. Awls or ice picks are used to punch small holes through soft surfaces. The electric drill is used for harder surfaces and will produce a neater hole.

Pod and cone art involves a great deal of gluing. A fast-drying white glue, such as Slomons Velverette Craft Glue or Aleene's Tacky White Glue, is best for adhering cones and for assembling pine cone flowers. Also needed to assemble flowers are absorbent cotton and small disks cut

Jeffrey pine cone

Sugar pine cone

Aleppo pine cone

Wide open piñon pine cone

Baby hemlock cone

Hemlock cone

Closed piñon pine cone

Sequoia cone

Jack pine cone

Deodar rose cone

Douglas fir cone

Longleaf pine cone

White pine cone

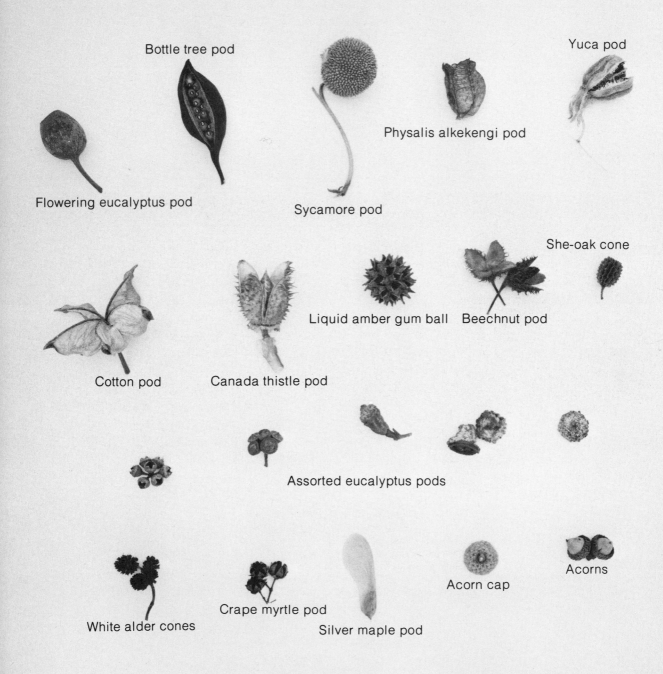

Bottle tree pod

Yuca pod

Physalis alkekengi pod

Flowering eucalyptus pod

Sycamore pod

She-oak cone

Liquid amber gum ball   Beechnut pod

Cotton pod

Canada thistle pod

Assorted eucalyptus pods

Acorns

Acorn cap

White alder cones

Crape myrtle pod

Silver maple pod

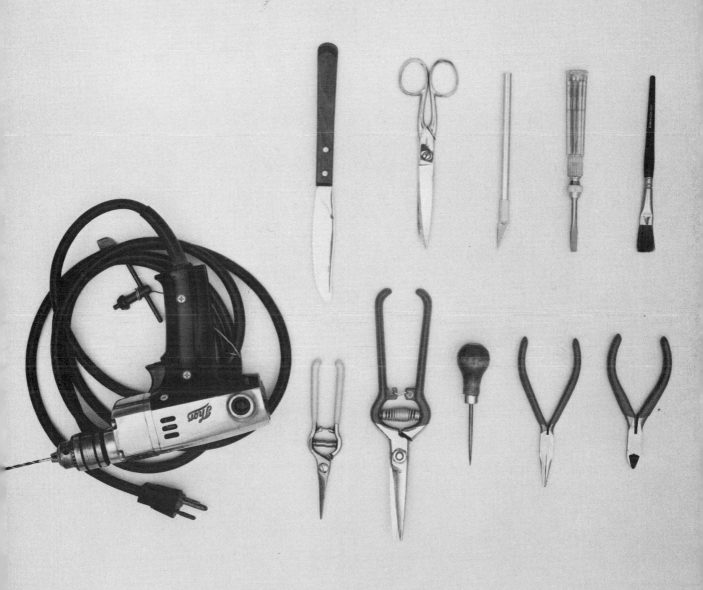

from notebook paper. A large cardboard box will provide a good work surface for assembling pine cone flowers.

In addition to acrylic paints, which are used to paint Styrofoam, unfinished wood, and other surfaces, you will need Treasure Gold and Treasure Jewels. These are metallic wax colors that are wonderful for highlighting pods and cones. Treasure Jewels are often used with turpentine and are applied with a 3- by 3-inch polyurethane sponge rather than a paintbrush. By this method, the four corners of the sponge are held together with the fingers so that a ball shape is formed. The "ball" is then dipped into turpentine, and then rubbed into the Treasure Jewels. After the paint has been applied, #0000 steel wool is rubbed over the surface. To seal Treasure Gold, Treasure Jewels, and unfinished wood, use Treasure Sealer. To give stained wooden pieces a durable, waterproof finish, satin varnish is used.

In addition to these materials, you will need #400 sandpaper, #350 garnet paper, 1-inch-wide and ½-inch-wide sable paintbrushes, lint-free cloths, curved manicure scissors, paper towels, a ruler, a compass, a pencil, a screwdriver, an X-acto knife, ordinary straight scissors, and a serrated knife. (See top row of Photograph 4-2.)

Pod and Cone Art Hints and Techniques

Following is a list of hints and techniques that will help you in your pod and cone work.

■ Try to collect cones and pods when they are closed. This ensures that they are good and fresh. To open them, place them in a container and allow the container to stand in the sun. Another method is to place the cones in the oven. Spread the cones out on a tray, and place the tray in a 150- to 200-degree oven. The amount of heat they receive will determine the degree to which they will open.

■ The best place to look for pods and cones is under a tree. Avoid damp areas, however, as

moisture tends to ruin them for decorative purposes. The color fades and they tend to crack.

■ Always be sure that all pods and cones are thoroughly dry before storing. If not, they will mold.

■ Always store dried cones and pods in a cool, dry place, and keep them away from light. If they are placed in containers, these containers should be ventilated.

■ Interesting color effects can be achieved with cones and pods that are still green. Spread them out in a dark place, and allow them to dry for several weeks. Drying in a dark place will enable them to retain their green color. The green pods and cones should then be exposed to strong sunlight for one or two days. After they have taken on a reddish tan color, remove them from the sunlight and store in ventilated boxes.

■ Separate and store your pods and cones according to size. This will make your work much easier.

■ Before you start stripping the scales from a pine cone, cut off the tip of the cone, just below the second or third row of scales. (See Photograph 4-3.) Do this with clippers or a knife. Save the

Photograph 4-3

rosette portion. It can be used as a flower or as a flower center.

■ When stripping scales, start at the point from which the tip was cut off. Cut as near to the axis or stem of the cone as possible. Work around the cone, taking scales off row-by-row with clippers. Separate and store the scales according to size and type.

■ When removing scales from a cone, examine the base or stem end. They often make excellent bases for decorating.

Pine Cone Flowers

The assembling of pine cone flowers is a basic part of pod and cone art. Scales are stripped from cones and glued together to form flower shapes. These flowers have a carved-wood effect when viewed from a distance. Flower arrangements in vases or baskets look particularly lovely when placed in rustic- or Victorian-style rooms.

Basically, all pine cone flower shapes are assembled in the same way. The number of rows and type of center will vary among shapes, but the method of construction will usually be the same. The following photographs, diagrams, and instructions will teach you the basic technique.

Pine cone flowers are constructed on small paper disks. Use a compass to draw a 1-inch-diameter circle on a piece of notebook paper. Draw an inner ½-inch-diameter circle and cut out the outer circle with curved manicure scissors. (See Diagram 4-1.) The inner circle will serve as a guide for positioning scales.

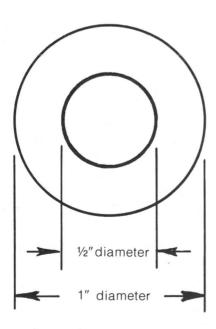

½" diameter

1" diameter

Diagram 4-1

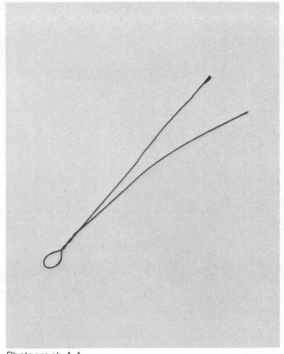

Photograph 4-4

If you wish to make a stem for your flower, cut a 14-inch length of 24-gauge green-covered floral wire. Fold the wire in half. Twist two or three times, about ¼ inch below the fold, as shown in Photograph 4-4. You now have a 7-inch-length stem. Vary the length of wire for a longer or shorter stem.

Make a small hole in the center of the paper disk. Insert the ends of the stem through the hole, and slip the disk up to the base of the loop. Bend the loop over so that it will lie flat on the paper disk.

Turn a 6-inch-high cardboard box upside down. With an awl, poke a hole in the bottom of the box. Insert the ends of the wire through the hole in the box and pull down. The paper disk should be resting on the bottom of the box. If necessary, adjust the stem so that the disk will lie flat. (See Photograph 4-5.)

Cut off the tip of a cone, just below the second or third row of scales. Cut off scales with clippers, cutting as close to the axis as possible. Work around the cone, row-by-row.

Photograph 4-5

Place a bead of white glue between the inner circle and the outer edge of the disk. Adhere a row of uniformly-sized scales to this area, with the ends of the scales touching the inner circle. Position the scales side-by-side, as shown in Photograph 4-6.

Photograph 4-7

Photograph 4-8

Photograph 4-6

Saturate a small piece of cotton (about ½ inch in diameter) with white glue, and place it in the center of the flower, as shown in Photograph 4-7. Place a second row of pine cone scales on top of the first row. Press the cut ends of the scales into the saturated cotton, allowing ¼ inch of the outer ends of the first row to extend. (See Photo-graph 4-8.) Place a row of pods, seeds, or nuts in the center of the flower, with the stem ends pressed into the cotton. Place another pod, seed, or nut in a vertical position in the center of the row. (See Photograph 4-9.)

134

Photograph 4-9

The sixteen flower shapes that follow are examples of the many different effects that can be achieved by varying the types of cone, the number of rows, and the type of center.

1. **Flower A:** Adhere a row of Aleppo pine cone scales to the paper disk. Use the cutoff base end of a closed Aleppo cone for the center, and glue it to cotton.

Photograph 4-10

2. **Flower B:** Adhere a row of mountain pine cone scales to the paper disk. Glue a baby hemlock cone to the center.

Photograph 4-11

3. **Flower C:** Adhere a row of Jeffrey pine cone scales to the disk. Glue a cluster of small bell-shaped eucalyptus pods to the center.

Photograph 4-12

4. **Flower D:** Adhere a row of piñon cone scales to the disk. Glue a pod from a soapbark tree in the center.

Photograph 4-13

5. **Flower E:** Adhere a row of Jeffrey pine cone scales to the disk. Use a ring of berry-shaped eucalyptus pods and an acorn for the center.

Photograph 4-14

6. **Flower F:** Adhere a row of mountain pine cone scales to the paper disk. Add a center of eucalyptus pods.

Photograph 4-15

135

7. **Flower G:** Adhere a row of mountain pine cone scales to the disk. Use three baby hemlocks for the center.

Photograph 4-16

8. **Flower H:** Adhere a row of Aleppo pine cone scales to the disk. Adhere black peppercorns to center. Surround peppercorns with wheat kernels and adhere to center.

Photograph 4-17

9. **Flower I:** Adhere two rows of small Jeffrey pine cone scales to the disk, and add a cluster of bell-shaped eucalyptus pods for the center.

Photograph 4-18

10. **Flower J:** Adhere two rows of small Jeffrey pine cone scales to the disk and a large inverted eucalyptus pod for the center.

Photograph 4-19

11. **Flower K:** Adhere two rows of small Jeffrey pine cone scales to the disk. Use a ring of mullein pods and a she-oak cone for the center.

Photograph 4-20

12. **Flower L:** Adhere three rows of Aleppo pine cone scales to the disk and the tip of a small cone to the center.

Photograph 4-21

13. **Flower M:** Adhere two rows of medium-sized hemlock scales to the disk. Use a baby hemlock for the center.

Photograph 4-22

14. **Flower N:** Adhere several rows of large hemlock scales, at an angle, to the disk. Glue the last two scales vertically in the center, cup sides facing one another.

Photograph 4-23

15. **Flower O:** Adhere four rows of hemlock scales in overlapping rows. Each successive row should have fewer scales than the preceding one. Place a baby hemlock cone in the center.

Photograph 4-24

16. **Flower P:** Adhere ten rows of Aleppo pine cone scales to the disk. Starting with the fourth row, use progressively smaller and fewer scales per row.

Photograph 4-25

Pine Cone
Candle Holder

This charming candle holder makes a fine piece for a living room mantel, a family room coffee table, or a dining room table centerpiece.

Materials

wooden lamp base, walnut finish, of size to support a 4½-inch-diameter cylinder
1 candle, 3 by 6 inches, in color of your choice
20 she-oak cones, medium-sized
assorted hemlock cones and Jeffrey and sugar pine cones; or any other assortment of your choice
assorted materials for flower centers, such as small Aleppo or lodgepole pine cone tops, whole black peppercorns, unpopped popcorn kernels, dried corn kernels, and eucalyptus pods; or any other assortment of your choice
clippers
cardboard box, 6 inches high
notebook paper
curved manicure scissors
absorbent cotton
white glue
floral wire, 24 gauge, green-covered
1 roll floral tape, in brown
bead wire, 32 gauge
turpentine
3 jars Treasure Jewels, small size, in onyxite, rose quartz, and renaissance
1 paintbrush, ½ inch wide
paper towels
6 yards satin ribbon, in brown
20 inches floral wire, 18 gauge, green-covered

Instructions

1. Choose the flowers you wish to make from the Pine Cone Flowers section and assemble them, following directions given there, on cardboard box work surface. Make each stem with an 8-inch length of 24-gauge floral wire, folded in half. Each flower should be 2 to 2½ inches in diameter. (For my flower petals, I used scales from Jeffrey pine cones, sugar pine cones, and large hemlock cones. For centers, I used small Aleppo and lodgepole pine cone tops, dried corn kernels, unpopped popcorn kernels, whole black peppercorns, and small eucalyptus pods.) Wrap the stem of the finished flower with floral tape. Make ten flowers or as many as are needed to fit around lamp base.

2. Place the she-oak cones on your work surface. Use an 8-inch length of 32-gauge bead wire for stems. Fold wire in half to locate center. Wrap the two legs of the wire around the short stem at the base four times. Cut ends even. Wrap the entire stem with floral tape. (See Photograph 4-26.)

Photograph 4-26

3. Place two small containers of turpentine next to the jar of onyxite Treasure Jewels. Dip the tip of the paintbrush into one container; blot the brush lightly on a paper towel and fill it with onyxite Treasure Jewels. Paint she-oak cones, flower petals, and flower centers. Allow the Treasure Jewels to dry for 1 hour. Dip the brush into the second container of turpentine to clean it and wipe dry with a paper towel. Dip the tip of the brush into first container of turpentine, blot lightly, and fill the brush with rose quartz Treasure Jewels. Apply this color to flower petals. Allow to dry for about 1 hour. Using a brush or your finger dipped in renaissance Treasure Jewels, highlight the edges of petals, centers of flowers, and she-oak cones. (See Photograph 4-27.)

4. Make twenty spears, each with a 9-inch length of ribbon and a 6-inch length of 24-gauge floral wire. Starting at one end of the ribbon, cast a 1½-inch-long loop around top of wire. Wrap 32-gauge bead wire around ribbon three or four

Photograph 4-27

times. Cast another 1½-inch loop to the right of the first loop, and wrap with wire; cast another loop to the left, and secure with wire. (See Diagram 4-2.) Starting from the point at which the ribbon loops are secured with wire, wrap the entire stem with floral tape.

5. Make ten sprays, each containing one pine cone flower, two she-oak cones, and two ribbon spears. Position the cones and ribbon spears around the flower. Twist the stems of all pieces

Photograph 4-28

together to secure, and wrap with floral tape. (See Photograph 4-28.)

6. With floral tape, wrap a 20-inch length of 18-gauge floral wire. Shape the wire into a circle, overlapping the ends by 2 inches. Twist the ends

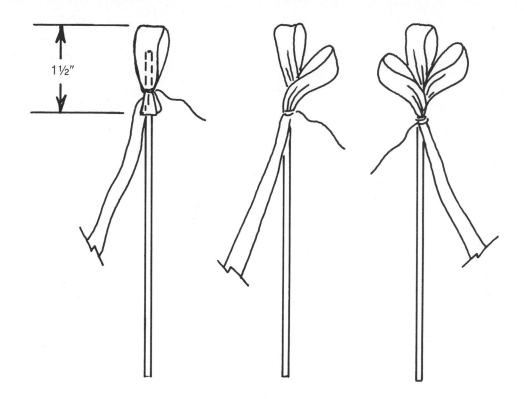

Diagram 4-2

around the wire to secure. (See Photograph 4-29.)

7. Arrange the sprays around the wire form. (See

Photograph 4-30

Photograph 4-30.) Twist the stem of each spray around wire form to attach, and wrap with floral tape.

8. Place the flower wreath on the lamp base. Position candle in the center of the base. If you wish, melt a bit of candlewax on the base to secure the candle.

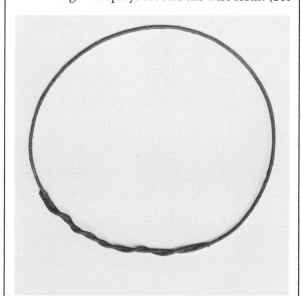

Photograph 4-29

139

140

Victorian Christmas Bell (See page 150.)

Springtime Basket Purse

This flowered basket purse makes an attractive accessory for casual spring outfits. Choose the flowers you like best from the Pine Cone Flowers section. Vary the trim, colors, and size of flowers, if you wish, to make the purse truly your own.

Materials

basket purse, 4-paneled, 5⅛ by 7½ by 7½ inches
assorted hemlock cones, Jeffrey, sugar, Aleppo, and
    lodgepole pine cones; in large, medium, and small
    sizes; or any other assortment of your choice
assorted materials for flower centers, such as whole
    black peppercorns, pine cone ends, and eucalyptus
    pods; or any other assortment of your choice
1 pair hinges, ¾ inch long, ⅝ inch wide
garnet paper, #350
emery boards
lint-free cloth or paper towel
turpentine
1 jar Treasure Jewels, in sapphire
several polyurethane sponges, 3 by 3 inches
steel wool, #0000
Treasure Sealer
1 can satin varnish, ¼-pint size
1 paintbrush, ½ inch wide
white glue
3 yards velvet ribbon, ⅝ inch wide, to match sapphire
    Treasure Jewels
clippers
cardboard box, 6 inches high
notebook paper
curved manicure scissors
absorbent cotton
floral wire, 24 gauge, green-covered
1 jar Treasure Gold, in yellow diamond
1 roll floral tape, in dark brown

Instructions

1. If basket comes already fitted with hinges, examine them to see if they are durable. If not, fit new hinges to the basket. Follow directions given in the Helpful Hints chapter and mark their placement on the basket. Then remove them, as well as the handle, and set aside.

2. Sand the entire basket with #350 garnet paper. Use emery boards to sand rough areas between panels, as shown in Photograph 4-31. Wipe basket with a lint-free cloth or paper towel.

3. Fill a small container with turpentine, and place the jar of Treasure Jewels next to it. Gather

Photograph 4-31

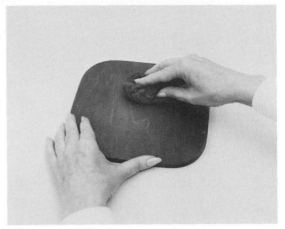

Photograph 4-33

the four corners of a polyurethane sponge with your fingers, and hold it so that the center of the sponge will form a ball shape. Dip the ball-shaped section of the sponge into the turpentine and blot lightly on a paper towel. Rub the sponge into the Treasure Jewels until it is heavily coated with color. Rub sponge briskly over basket parts,

sanding between coats. Allow 1 hour drying time. Apply a second coat of Treasure Jewels to all parts in the same manner, and rub with steel wool. Allow to dry for 4 hours. Cover entire basket with a coat of Treasure Sealer, and allow to dry.

4. Apply four coats of varnish to basket, allowing 24 hours drying time between each coat and after the final coat.

5. Attach the hinges to the lid. Assemble all parts of the basket except for the handle.

6. Apply a small amount of white glue around entire bottom rim of the basket. Starting at the

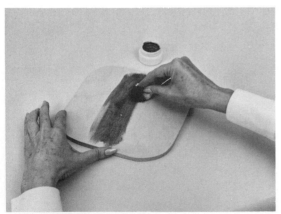

Photograph 4-32

as shown in Photograph 4-32. When the color becomes thin, apply more turpentine and Treasure Jewels to sponge. Paint the outside and lip of the basket and both sides of the lid and handle. Rub surfaces with steel wool while they are still wet. (See Photograph 4-33.) This will blend the color into the wood and eliminate the need for

Photograph 4-34

back center (at the joint in the rim), adhere velvet ribbon around the bottom rim. (See Photograph 4-34.) Overlap ends of ribbon by ½ inch. Put a small amount of white glue on the underside of the overlapping piece of ribbon, and turn it under ¼ inch. Hold the folded overlap between your fingers until the glue sets; glue the overlap in place.

7. Put a small amount of white glue around the entire upper rim of the basket, including the hinges. Starting at one of the handle holes, adhere ribbon around the upper rim. End with a butt joint; do not overlap. (See Photograph 4-35.)

Photograph 4-36

Photograph 4-35

8. Put handle on purse. Apply a thin coat of white glue to the outside of the handle. Starting at one end, just below the screw, adhere ribbon along outside of handle. Bring the ribbon around to the other end of handle, below the screw. Cut the ribbon. (See Photograph 4-36.)

9. Choose flowers from the Pine Cone Flowers section. Make four 2½-inch-diameter flowers with large Jeffrey or sugar pine cone scales, seven 1-inch-diameter flowers from small hemlock scales, and two 1½-inch-diameter flowers from medium-sized hemlock scales, Aleppo pine cone scales, or lodgepole pine cone scales. Use 12-inch lengths of 24-gauge floral wire for the stems. Use whole black peppercorns, ends of pine cones, or eucalyptus pods for the centers of the large and medium-sized flowers. Use one black peppercorn for the center of each small flower.

10. Place two small containers of turpentine next to the jar of Treasure Jewels. Dip the tip of a paintbrush into one, blot it lightly on a paper towel, and fill the brush with Treasure Jewels. Apply the Treasure Jewels to the petals, centers, and backs of all flowers. Allow the Treasure Jewels to dry for about 1 hour. Clean brush by dipping into second container of turpentine. Highlight all flower centers and selected petals with Treasure Gold. Apply the Treasure Gold with your fingers or a brush. (See Photograph 4-37.) For more luster, allow the Treasure Gold

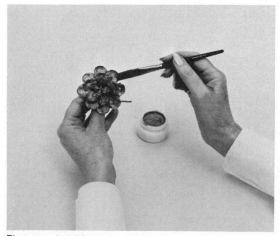

Photograph 4-37

143

to dry for about 1 hour and then buff with a soft, lint-free cloth.

11. Following directions given in the Helpful Hints chapter, make a four-looped bow with a 30-inch length of velvet ribbon.

12. Make a flower spray consisting of four large flowers, one medium-sized flower, and five small flowers. Twist the stems of the flowers together. Cut stems even at the bottom, and wrap bottom 2 inches with floral tape.

13. Make another flower spray consisting of two small flowers and one medium-sized flower. Twist the stems together, and wrap with floral

Photograph 4-38

tape. (See Photograph 4-38.)

14. Position the sprays on the lid, as shown in Photograph 4-39. Attach the sprays to the lid by putting white glue under all stems. Place bow between the large and small sprays, and adhere with white glue.

144

Photograph 4-39

Monogrammed Desk Box

This handsome monogrammed box is ideal for a man's desk or bureau. It can be used to hold cigars, pencils, jewelry, gloves, or anything else he wishes.

Materials

1 box, unfinished wood, 3 by 7 by 10⅜ inches

assorted small hemlock cones, lodgepole, Aleppo and yellow pine cones; or any other assortment of your choice

materials for flower centers, such as eucalyptus pods and whole black peppercorns; or any other assortment of your choice

1 pair brass hinges, ⅞ inch long, ½ inch wide

garnet paper, #350

lint-free cloth or paper towel

turpentine

1 jar Treasure Jewels, in onyxite

several polyurethane sponges, 3 by 3 inches

steel wool, #0000

Treasure Sealer

1 paintbrush, ½ inch or wider

clippers

cardboard box, 6 inches high

notebook paper

curved manicure scissors

absorbent cotton

white glue

Treasure Gold, in classic gold

1 can satin varnish, ¼-pint size

1 tube oil paint, small size, in burnt umber

10 brass corner ornaments, to fit box (As an alternate, use paper gold braid or wooden corner ornaments.)

4 brass feet, to fit box

4 small screws

small hammer

awl

sequin pins, ¼ inch long, in gold

1 package gold monograms or gold card stock paper

Instructions

1. Following instructions given in the Helpful Hints chapter, fit hinges on box and mark placement. Remove hinges and set aside.

2. Use #350 garnet paper to sand the entire box. Wipe with a lint-free cloth or paper towel.

3. Fill a small container with turpentine and place it beside the onyxite Treasure Jewels. Gather the four corners of a polyurethane sponge in your fingers to form a ball shape in the center. Dip the ball part of the sponge into the turpentine and blot lightly on a paper towel. Rub the sponge into the Treasure Jewels until it is covered with a heavy coat of color. Rub sponge briskly over box to apply color, as shown in Photograph 4-40. Cover lip and outside of box and lid in this

Photograph 4-41

manner. While surface is still wet, rub with steel wool. This works the color into the wood and eliminates the need for sanding between coats. (See Photograph 4-41.) Allow to dry for 1 hour. Apply a second coat of Treasure Jewels to the box, and rub with steel wool. Allow to dry for 4 hours. Apply a coat of Treasure Sealer and allow to dry.

4. Follow directions in the Pine Cone Flowers section carefully. Make 5 Flower Ps (shape number 16) from scales of medium-sized Aleppo cones. Make 4 Flower Js (shape number 10) and 4 half Flower Js, using two overlapping rows of Aleppo cones. (See Photograph 4-42.) Use a clus-

Photograph 4-40

Photograph 4-42

145

Pine Cone Floral Arrangement (See page 133.)

Pine Cone Candle Holder (See page 137.)

ter of black peppercorns for the centers. Make 18 leaves by cutting hemlock scales to a point at one end, as shown in photograph.

5. With sponge held in ball-shaped position, dip ball part into turpentine and rub in Treasure Jewels. Rub sponge over all flowers and leaves. (See Photograph 4-43.) Allow to dry for 1 hour.

Photograph 4-43

Using your fingers, accent centers, ends of petals, and ends and tops of leaves with Treasure Gold. Allow to dry for about 1 hour. Apply a coat of Treasure Sealer to flowers and leaves. Let stand for about ½ hour. Apply a coat of satin varnish to the flowers.

6. Pour a tablespoon of varnish into a container. Place a dab of burnt umber oil paint on a piece of paper. Dip the ball-shaped section of a clean polyurethane sponge into the varnish and then the burnt umber. Rub this mixture onto brass hardware to give it an antique finish. (See Photograph 4-44.) At first, use a small amount of burnt umber. Gradually increase the amount until you get the antique effect that pleases you.

7. Apply four coats of satin varnish to the outside of the box. Allow 24 hours drying time between coats and after the final coat.

8. Place the hinges on the lid, and assemble the box. With small screws, attach one foot to each corner of the box. Place the corner ornaments, concave side up, on the work surface. With a small hammer and awl, punch a hole in the top

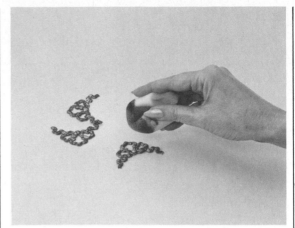

Photograph 4-44

center and bottom corners of each ornament, as shown in Photograph 4-45. Use ¼-inch-long sequin pins to attach two corner ornaments to each lower corner of the box. (See Photograph 4-46.)

Photograph 4-45

148

Photograph 4-46

9. In the same manner, attach a corner ornament to each side of the top of the lid. Center ornaments, and place them ½ inch in from the edge. (See Photograph 4-47.)

10. Arrange the flowers in an oval pattern on the lid, keeping them within the brass ornaments. Position leaves, as shown in Photograph 4-48. When you are satisfied with the design, lift a flower and its accompanying leaf; apply white glue to their backs. Place the leaf and then the flower back in position. Press firmly in place. Repeat procedure until the entire garland of flowers and leaves has been glued in position.

11. Make initials from gold card stock paper or purchase letters for the monogram. With white glue, adhere gold letters to center of the garland.

12. Follow directions given in the Helpful Hints chapter to line the box. Use material of your choice.

Photograph 4-48

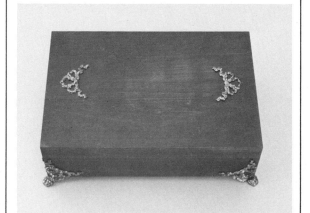

Photograph 4-47

149

Victorian Christmas Bell

This festive Christmas bell is modeled with pine cone scales. It makes an elegant holiday decoration for almost any room.

Materials

1 wicker bell, 6 by 9 inches
2 large Jeffrey or sugar pine cones, approximately 6 by 9 inches
19 small hemlock cones or lodgepole pine cones, approximately 1 by 1½ inches
1 bunch pennycress
10 safflowers
1 bunch strawflowers, in hot pink
clippers
turpentine
1 jar Treasure Jewels, in green amber
1 paintbrush, ½ inch wide
paper towels
white glue
pencil
ruler
bead wire, 26 gauge
awl
2 yards ribbon, ⅝ inch wide, in hot pink
1 roll floral tape, in brown
embroidery needle, #7
thread, in hot pink

Instructions

1. Follow directions in Pod and Cone Art Hints and Techniques to strip the scales from two large pine cones. Approximately 150 to 175 scales are needed.

2. Pour some turpentine into two small containers, and place them next to the jar of Treasure Jewels. Dip the paintbrush into one container, and blot it lightly on a paper towel. Place the brush in Treasure Jewels. Paint each pine cone scale on both sides. (See Photograph 4-49.) Put them aside and allow to dry for 1 hour. Clean brush in other container of turpentine.

3. Starting at the bottom of the bell, adhere a row of scales around it with white glue. Let the scales overlap the bottom of the bell by about ½ inch. Place a second row of scales around the bell, overlapping the first row by about ½ inch; adhere a third row, overlapping the second row by ½ inch. (See Photograph 4-50.)

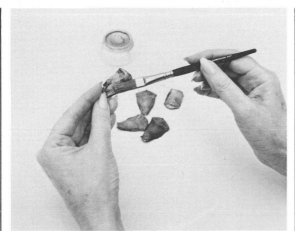

Photograph 4-49

Photograph 4-50

Photograph 4-51

gether three or four times at the base of the cone. (See Photograph 4-52.)

6. Attach a 6-inch-long piece of wire to each of the safflowers. Cut the stem off each safflower, about ⅜ inch below the bottom of the pod. With a sharp awl or needle; punch a hole through the remaining piece of stem, just below the pod. Insert one end of the wire through the hole. Make ends of wire even and twist them together three or four times near the stub of the stem. (See Photograph 4-52.)

7. Make twenty-four sprays consisting of four

4. Measure 2½ inches up from the top of the third row of pine scales. Make a light pencil mark around the bell at this point. Adhere a row of pine scales around the bell so that their bottom edges are even with the line. Adhere overlapping rows around the bell until the entire top part of the bell is covered. Each row should overlap the row below it by ½ inch. Cut short sections off pine cone scales. Place them on top of the bell, under and around the eye hook. (See Photograph 4-51.)

5. Attach a 6-inch length of wire to each of the small pine cones, by slipping one end of the wire between the bottom two rows of scales. Wrap around three-quarters of the cone with the wire. Slip wire through adjacent scales at the bottom of the cone. With wire ends even, twist them to-

Photograph 4-52

151

sprigs of pennycress and five strawflowers each. Place the stems of the pieces together. Arrange so that the foliage part of the spray will be about 1½ inches long. Wrap a 6-inch length of wire three or four times around the stems. Make all ends of wire even. (See Photograph 4-53.)

Photograph 4-53

8. Following directions given in the Helpful Hints chapter, make five 2-looped bows with 10-inch lengths of velvet ribbon. Tie at the centers with a 6-inch piece of wire. With ends even, twist the wire at the center of the bow to secure.

9. Attach sprays to the center section of the bell, as shown in Photograph 4-54, by inserting the

Photograph 4-54

wires through bell. Twist the ends together inside of the bell.

10. In the same way, attach groupings of safflowers, pine cones, and bows around the sprays. (See Photograph 4-55.)

11. Shape a grouping of safflowers, sprays, and small pine cones into a ball, as shown in Photograph 4-56. Twist the wires together, wrap them with floral tape, and bend them over to form a loop for hanging. This will be the clapper of the bell.

12. With white glue, attach the clapper to the tongue of the bell. Place an 18-inch length of ribbon through the eye at the top of the bell. Overlap the ends by ½ inch, and stitch together with embroidery needle and thread.

Photograph 4-55

Photograph 4-56

Pod and Cone Wreath

This beautiful wreath, designed and made by Vivian West of Seattle, Washington, is an outstanding example of what can be done with pods and cones. A beautiful assortment of cones, pods, and nuts are glued to a hardboard wreath form. Hardboard is a Masonitelike material with one rough side. The wreath makes a lovely decoration to hang above the fireplace.

Materials

1 piece hardboard, 2 by 2 feet

5 large Jeffrey or sugar pine cones

42 lodgepole pine cones, or cones of your choice, approximately 2½ by 3½ inches

31 lodgepole pine cones, or cones of your choice, approximately 1½ by 2½ inches

assorted pine cones, pods, and nuts in open, partly open, and closed positions

yardstick compass

saber or jig saw

small electric drill

sandpaper, #350

lint-free cloth or paper towel

picture hanger, heavy-duty

1 can satin varnish, ½-pint size

clippers

white glue

Instructions

1. Using a yardstick compass, draw a 24-inch-diameter circle and an inner 13-inch-diameter circle on the hardboard.

2. Cut out the outer circle with a saber or jig saw. Drill a hole in the center of the inner circle that will be large enough for the blade to fit through. Insert the blade through the hole and cut out the inner circle. Bear in mind that it is rather difficult and somewhat dangerous to cut along curved lines on hard surfaces. If you are not used to working with this type of saw, have the job done for you.

3. Lightly sand inner and outer edges of hardboard. Wipe with a lint-free cloth or paper towel. Drill two holes at top of circle, and mount the picture hanger on the smooth side.

4. Follow instructions given in Pod and Cone Art Hints and Techniques section for stripping scales off cones. Strip scales from five Jeffrey or sugar pine cones. Using white glue, adhere an inner and outer row of scales, cup sides down, to the rough side of the hardboard. Overlap the inner and outer edges of the circle by about ½ inch. (See Photograph 4-57.)

153

Photograph 4-57

5. Place white glue on the stem end of the forty-two pine cones. Place them around the outer edge of hardboard so that they partially cover the scales. In the same manner, adhere a row of thirty-one smaller pine cones around the inner edge. (See Photograph 4-58.)

Photograph 4-59

Photograph 4-58

6. Position clusters of assorted cones, pods, and nuts in the area between the two rows. (I used lodgepole pine cones, sequoia cones, hemlock cones, Aleppo pine cones, Douglas fir cones, yellow pine cones, Sitka spruce cones, acorns, bottle tree pods, walnuts, chestnuts, dried bachelor's button blossoms, and moss.) Alternate positions of cones so that some will be placed with tips up and some will be placed with tips down. Once you have a design that pleases you, remove each piece and glue it in place. (See Photograph 4-59.)

7. Apply a coat of satin varnish to the wreath, using a paintbrush or spray gun.

Hummingbird Mobile

This mobile of dainty hummingbirds is an attractive piece to hang in your kitchen, child's room, or anywhere else in your home. Place the mobile in an area that receives a gentle flow of air so that the birds will be in motion.

Materials

1 large hemlock cone or cone of similar shape

3 small hemlock cones or lodgepole pine cones

6 silver maple pods or silver construction paper

2 slices of white bread

knife

bowl

white glue

waxed paper

cornstarch

glycerin, fabric-softener, or white-colored liquid detergent

monofilament fish line, 6- or 8-pound test

3 straight pins, 1 inch long

1 paintbrush, ½ inch wide

clippers

3 jars acrylic paint, 2-ounce size, in green, red, and white

small jar Treasure Jewels, in emerald

6 beads, size 11/0

steel wire, 22 gauge

wire cutters

long-nosed pliers

Instructions

1. Cut the crust off two slices of white bread, break bread into small pieces, and place pieces in a bowl. If the bread is fresh or very soft, allow to sit for 2 or 3 hours before proceeding.

2. Place 2 tablespoons of white glue in bowl. (It is a good idea to apply hand lotion to your hands before mixing.) Mix bread and glue together with your fingers until thoroughly blended. Roll the mixture into a ball.

3. Place waxed paper over your work surface, and sprinkle lightly with cornstarch. Place the ball on the waxed paper. With the palms of your hands, knead the bread dough until it is no longer sticky. Add ½ teaspoon of glycerin, fabric-softener, or liquid detergent to dough. Mix until smooth and pliable.

4. About ¼ inch below the heads, tie a 6-inch-long piece of monofilament fish line around each of the three straight pins.

5. Make three ½- to ⁹/₁₆-inch-diameter balls out of bread dough. Push each pin through the center of one of the dough balls. Position so that the heads of the pins will be below the surface of the dough and the monofilament fish lines will come through the back top center of the dough. Shape balls to form heads of birds. The pins will become the beaks. (See Photograph 4-60.)

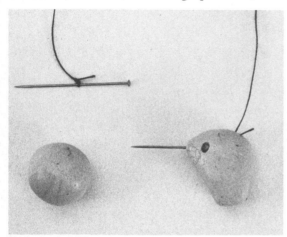

Photograph 4-60

6. Put a light coat of white glue on the stem end of each of the three small cones. Adhere a dough head to each of the cones. Press the neck section of each dough head firmly around the stem section of the cone. (See Photograph 4-61.) Set the

156

Photograph 4-61

pieces aside, and allow to dry for about 2 hours. Prepare a solution containing equal parts of white glue and water. Brush a thin coat of solution onto each dough head. This will prevent the dough from cracking. It takes about 48 hours for the bread dough to dry completely.

7. Cut six silver maple pods to shape shown in Photograph 4-62. If you prefer, use pattern and make wings with silver construction paper.

Photograph 4-62

Adhere a pair of wings to each cone body in back and to either side of the neck. (See Photograph 4-63.)

Photograph 4-63

8. Clip three large scales off large hemlock cone. Adhere scales, cup sides down, between rows of scales at the back lower tip of each pine cone body. (See Photograph 4-64.)

9. Apply a coat of green paint to the entire surface of each bird. Make sure to paint between scales. Allow the green paint to dry for about 1 hour. Starting underneath the bill, apply red paint to the throat of each bird. Apply a

Photograph 4-64

½-inch-wide white strip to the underside center section of bodies. Paint a white triangular section on the underside of tails. (See Photograph 4-65.)

10. With your finger, accent all green areas of the birds with Treasure Jewels.

11. With white glue, attach two beads to each head for eyes.

12. Cut two lengths of wire, each 5½ inches and 4½ inches long. With long-nosed pliers, bend wire to make a small eye on each end of wires. These are the beams for the mobile. Assemble and balance the mobile according to instructions given in the Helpful Hints chapter.

Photograph 4-65

Pine Cone Wind Chimes

This decorative wind chime piece, made from an assortment of pine cones and sea urchin spines, makes an exceptionally lovely decoration for a patio or family room. If you wish, glass or metal chimes may be used in place of the sea urchin spines.

Materials

1 Styrofoam ball, 4 inches in diameter

3 pine cones, approximately 2½ by 3 inches

48 pine cones, approximately ¾ by ¾ inch

21 sea urchin spines, with drilled hole in each

21 plastic matrix stones, with drilled hole in each

serrated knife

knitting needle, #5

12 inches floral wire, 18 gauge, green-covered

wire cutters

1 jar acrylic paint, 2-ounce size, in brown

liquid detergent

1 paintbrush, ½ inch wide

small electric drill and $^3/_{32}$-inch-diameter drill bit

3 feet floral wire, 24 gauge, green-covered

1 roll floral tape, in brown

pencil

white glue

9 yards monofilament fish line, 6- or 8-pound test

21 bead caps, in gold

21 beads, in gold

21 beads, 3-millimeter, in gold

½ yard satin cord, #1 rattail, in color of your choice

Instructions

1. With serrated knife, cut three pieces off Styrofoam ball, as shown in Photograph 4-66.

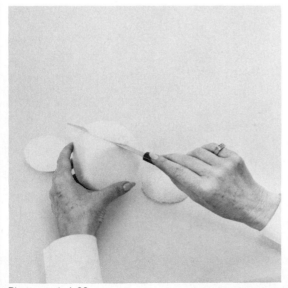

Photograph 4-66

2. Use the tip of the serrated knife to contour each side into a concave shape. The base ends of the three pine cones must be able to fit snugly against each side.

3. With knitting needle, put a hole through the center of the triangle shape at the bottom of the ball, between concave sections.

4. Make a 1-inch-long loop at one end of a 12-inch piece of 18-gauge floral wire. Twist three times to secure. Insert other end of wire through the bottom of hole. Pull the wire up through the hole so that the loop is directly below the ball. (See Photograph 4-67.)

Photograph 4-67

5. Place ½ ounce of brown acrylic paint in a container. Mix in 1 teaspoon of liquid detergent. Apply paint over entire Styrofoam ball, and allow to dry for 1 hour.

6. Drill a $^3/_{32}$-inch-diameter hole across each of

158

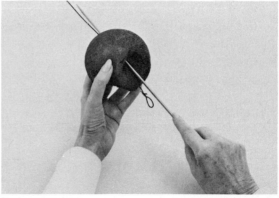

9. Place a 12-inch-piece of 24-gauge floral wire through each cross hole and around pine cones. Let the end extend through the hole about 1½ inches. Twist the wires together over the center of the base to secure. (See Photograph 4-71.)

Photograph 4-71

10. Starting at the cutout side of the Styrofoam ball, insert one of the pine cone wires through each hole. Pull each wire so that the base of the pine cone will lie snugly in the concave cutout section. Twist the 24-gauge wire around the 18-gauge wire to secure. Wrap the four wires with floral tape for 2 inches above the ball. Cut the wires at this point. Bend the ends back to form a 1-inch loop at the top of the ball. Turn the pine cones so that the scales with the holes will face the ball. (See Photograph 4-72.)

11. Starting at the top and working your way down, use the eraser of a pencil to dent Styrofoam ball all over. Small cones must be able to fit vertically in these spots. Use white glue to adhere small pine cones over entire surface of ball. Place

Photograph 4-68

the 3 pine cones, about ¼ inch from the bottom. (See Photograph 4-68.)

7. Randomly select six scales from a 1-inch-wide section between the base and tip of each cone. Drill a $^3/_{32}$-inch-diameter hole through each scale, about $^1/_{16}$ inch from its tip. (See Photograph 4-69.)

8. Starting at the center of each concave area of the ball and using a knitting needle, poke holes through to top center of ball. The holes should be as close as possible to the wire in the ball. (See Photograph 4-70.)

Photograph 4-69

159

Photograph 4-72

Photograph 4-73

cones as close together as possible. (See Photograph 4-73.)

12. To make the chimes, cut pieces of monofilament line that range between 5 and 9 inches long. These lengths are varied so that the chimes will hang at different lengths. Insert the line through the hole in each sea urchin spine. Make the ends of the line even, and tie a knot just above the sea urchin spine. Put a bead cap on the line, and place it on top of the spine. Tie a knot 1 inch above the spine, string on a gold bead, and place a plastic matrix stone on top. Thread the ends of the line through one of the holes in a pine cone scale, and place a 3-millimeter bead on top. Make a knot around bead to secure. (See Diagram 4-3.) Make a chime for each hole in the pine cone scales, using a different length of monofilament fish line for each one.

13. Make three more chimes like this without the top bead. Vary the lengths of the monofilament lines. Tie these three chimes to the center loop at the top of the ball.

14. String an 18-inch piece of satin cord through the top loop. Tie a knot just above it.

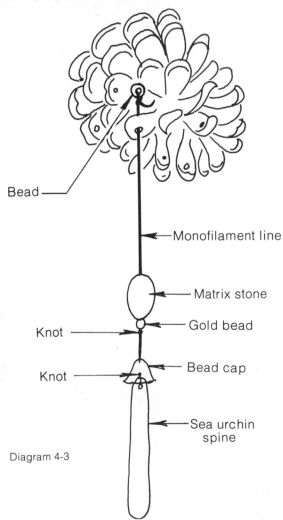

Bead

Monofilament line

Matrix stone

Gold bead

Knot

Bead cap

Knot

Sea urchin spine

Diagram 4-3

160

Pierced
and Cut
Paper

The art of creating designs by making cuts and piercing holes in paper is actually a combination of two separate art forms—paper cutting and pinpricking embroidery patterns.

Paper cutting had been practiced during, and probably before, the seventeenth century in both England and Germany. During the Victorian era, lacy paper cuttings, such as the famous paper valentine, came into style. Throughout the years, unique styles of paper cutting, ranging from black-on-white silhouettes to multicolored floral patterns, have emerged in Poland, China, and Mexico, as well as in England and Germany.

Meanwhile, in the middle of the eighteenth century, ladies were discovering that their embroidery stencils, which were intricate pinpricked patterns, made lovely designs in and of themselves. The early pinpricked designs were not easy to do. Before starting, papers had to be placed on boards that were covered with several layers of soft cloth. The eye of the needle or head of the pin had to be embedded in a piece of cork to protect the fingers. Designs were then traced as a series of dots that were small enough to disappear when pierced. Once each dot had been pierced, the design could be mounted on black or gold-painted paper and framed for hanging.

A variation of pierced paper work was an art called repoussé. After the tiny dots had been pierced, areas of the design were selected to be elevated. For each section that was to be raised, the back side of the paper had to be wetted and stretched. Rounded implements, such as the backs of spoons, were used to stretch and curve these areas. After all desired areas were raised and the paper had thoroughly dried, the back side of the paper was sized with a mixture of glue and water. This mixture ensured that the design would maintain its embossed shape. Some designs were then painted with watercolors. The designs were mounted on black or gold-painted paper and framed for hanging.

It was in the early nineteenth century that the marriage of pierced and cut paper occurred. Portions of the design to be cut were traced as fine lines and portions to be pierced were traced as tiny dots. After the entire design had been pierced and cut, the cut sections were raised to add dimension to the piece. Designs were then painted with watercolors or mounted on black or gold paper. Although a fascinating art, its popularity diminished in the latter part of the nineteenth century. Interest was revived in New England during the 1930s and has been maintained in that area ever since. For the most part, however, the craft has never reached a high level of popularity in the United States.

Since the beauty of pierced and cut paper work is best appreciated when light passes through the cut and pierced sections, the most popular present-day application of the craft is for the making of lampshades and light ornaments. This chapter, therefore, will concentrate on lampshades and Christmas lights. If you wish, however, you can mount the designs, frame them, and hang them.

Pierced and Cut Paper Materials and Tools

Many of the tools needed to do pierced and cut paper work are shown in Photograph 5-1. The first two tools, starting at the top right-hand corner, are pounce wheels—the Grumbacher X893 and the Grifhold #12. Pounce wheels have a series of spurlike points that give between 8 and 16 perforations per inch when rolled over paper. (The number of perforations per inch will depend on the model used.) The perforated line serves as a guide for the actual piercing. Although not essential, pounce wheels ensure even spacing and accuracy.

The holes are made with a piercer. (See tool to the left of small pounce wheel in Photograph 5-1.) This is simply a handled needlelike instrument that is inserted in and out of the paper. To vary the size of the holes, the handle or various types of needles can be used. The next tool shown

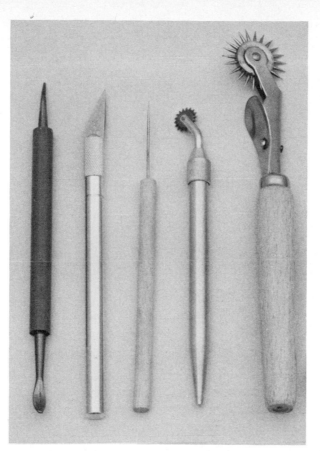

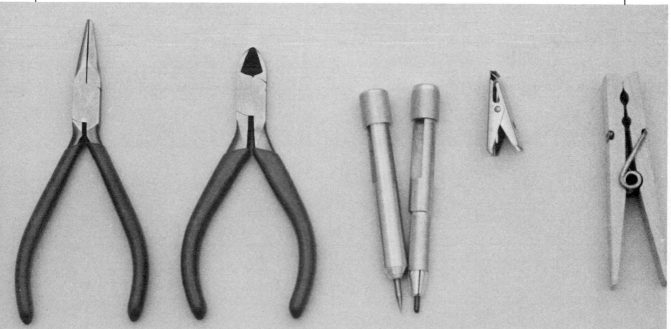

Photograph 5-1

in the photograph is the cutting tool. X-acto knives with #11 blades are best for our purposes.

The last tool on the line is a burnishing tool. It is used to transfer traced designs onto paper-backed foil, metallic embossed paper, or card stock paper.

Shown on the bottom row of tools are a spring-type clothespin, a photographer's clip, a beam compass, a pair of wire cutters, and a pair of long-nose pliers. Clothespins and photographer's clips are used to hold lampshades in place on lampshade rings while the glue is setting. The best kind of glue to use is a fast-drying white glue. A beam compass or a yardstick compass is used to construct tapered lampshade patterns. Ordinary compasses are too small. Since wires of several different gauges are used for many of the following projects, wire cutters and pliers will be needed to cut and bend them into shape.

Several types of paper will be needed for the following projects. In order to make lampshade patterns, you will need large sheets of brown wrapping paper. Sheets of tracing paper in the 8½- by 11-inch size, as well as large sheets, are essential. Purchase large rolls of tracing paper and cut sheets to the size you need.

For the lampshade itself, several types of paper can be used. Basically, you need a large sheet of strong paper, such as Strathmore or heavyweight bond paper. Pierced and cut paper work can also be done on paper-backed foil, card stock paper, and metallic embossed paper.

For most types of paper, watercolors are the best paints to use. Buy a simple set with a few basic colors. Transparent oil paints, in alizarin crimson, Indian yellow, and Prussian blue are used to paint metallic embossed paper or paper-backed foil. Clear vinyl varnish is used as a thinning agent for oil paints.

Essential for the construction of lampshades are lampshade rings. Top and bottom lampshade rings are available in many diameter sizes. Projects will specify which sizes to purchase. Mat acetate sheets are also used in most of the follow-

ing projects. They are available in 1⅔- by 4⅙-foot sheets or can be cut off a roll to the size you want. When attached inside and outside the paper shade, they provide strength, protection, and durability. White paper tape is used to attach acetate sheets to lampshade rings.

Bath towels, sponge rubber kneeling pads, pieces of cardboard, and old magazines are placed over work surfaces for protection. Additional tools and materials needed are ribbons, bias tape, scissors, #2 and #3 pencils, masking tape, paintbrushes in several sizes, a ruler, a yardstick, toothpicks, a carpenter's square or right triangle, and a screwdriver.

Basic Pierced and Cut Paper Instructions for Lampshades

Piercing and cutting paper lampshades can be a relaxing and enjoyable pastime. It is important that it be done neatly and accurately, however, if the end result is to be something you can be proud of. The following instructions, diagrams, and photographs will teach you how to construct, pierce and cut, and assemble paper lampshades onto lampshade rings. Read them carefully before beginning the projects. If you wish to work on the Christmas decoration project, rather than on the lampshades, concentrate primarily on steps C through I.

A. **Making the lampshade pattern:** Basically, there are two types of lampshades—straight and tapered. Straight lampshades are those that have equal diameters at the top and bottom, while tapered lampshades usually have smaller diameters at the top than at the bottom. Since straight lampshade patterns are easier to construct than tapered ones, we will start with them.

Straight lampshade patterns: Decide upon a suitable lampshade diameter for your lamp and purchase a pair of lampshade rings of that size. To decide upon the height of your lampshade, place the top lampshade ring in place at the top of the lamp. Hold the bottom ring at several distances from the top ring until you find the one you

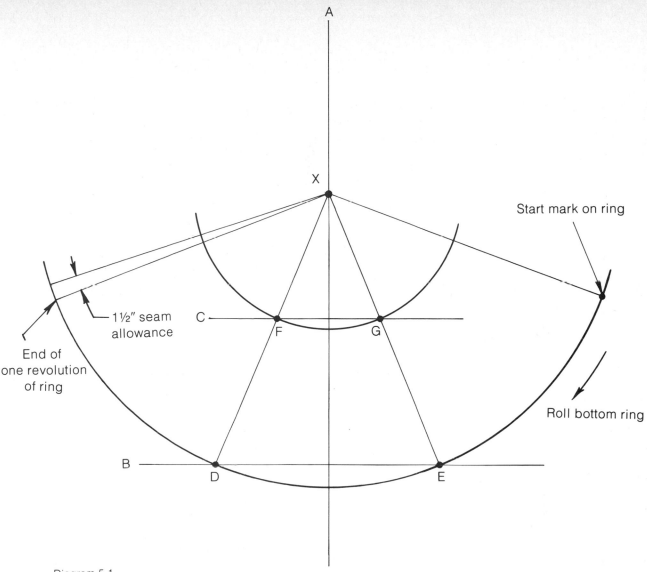

A

X

Start mark on ring

1½″ seam
allowance

C

F G

End of
one revolution
of ring

B

D E

Roll bottom ring

Diagram 5-1

prefer. Measure the distance between the two rings. Cut a piece of brown wrapping paper to a width that is slightly larger than this measurement and a length that is three and one-half times larger than the diameter of the rings. Place the brown wrapping paper across your work surface. Draw a straight line across the top of the paper to the full length of the paper. Measure down from this line to the height you have decided upon; draw a line across the bottom of the paper at this point, parallel to the top line. With pen or pencil, make a mark on one of the lampshade rings and at one end of the top line. With ring held in vertical position over the top line, align the two marks. Roll the ring along the line for one complete revolution, making sure that the ring is directly over the line at all times. Make a mark on the paper, directly below the mark on the ring. Mark off ½ inch beyond this mark for a seam allowance. With a carpenter's square or right triangle, draw perpendiculars from the two outermost marks, connecting top and bottom lines. Cut out brown paper along the lines.

Tapered lampshade patterns: Select lampshade

rings of two different diameters. Decide upon height of lampshade. Place a sheet of brown wrapping paper, 3 feet wide by 5 feet long, across your work surface. Draw a straight line down the center of the paper from top to bottom. (See line A in Diagram 5-1.) Using a carpenter's square or right triangle, draw a line across the paper, 5 inches from the bottom and perpendicular to line A. (This will be line B.) With ruler edge on line A, measure up from line B to the desired height of the shade. Draw a line across the paper at this point, perpendicular to line A and parallel to line B. (This will be line C.) Place ruler across top and bottom lampshade rings and measure their outside diameters. With line A at the midpoint, mark off a distance on line B that is equal to the outside diameter of the bottom ring. Label these points D and E. In the same manner, mark off a distance along line C that is equal to the outside diameter of the upper ring and label points F and G. With a yardstick and pencil, draw a line connecting points D and F and intersecting line A. Repeat procedure for points E and G. The point of intersection on line A should be labelled X. Set a yardstick or beam compass so that the point will be on point X and the pencil point on point D. Swing an arc across the full width of the paper. The arc should pass through both points D and E. Adjust the compass so that the pencil point will be on point F and swing another arc. This arc should pass through points F and G. Draw a line from one end of the bottom arc to point X. Make a mark on the bottom lampshade ring. Stand ring over paper with mark directly on this line. Roll the ring along the bottom arc for one complete revolution. Put a mark on the arc at this point and draw a line connecting it to point X. Measure a ½-inch seam allowance past the mark on the bottom arc and connect this point to point X. Cut out the outer perimeter of the pattern.

B. Making the tracing paper lampshade pattern: Place a large sheet of tracing paper over the lampshade pattern, secure with masking tape, and trace outline. Be sure to include seam allowance line. Cut out the pattern, leaving a 1-inch margin all around.

C. Selecting the design: The designs best suited for pierced and cut paper work are open, airy types, such as flowers, shells, and vine scrolls. Look for appealing designs in greeting cards, magazines, and books. After a while you will develop an eye for picking out those designs that will lend themselves well to pierced and cut paper work. Try to picture the design in its cut and pierced form. Remember that portions of a particular design, rather than the entire design, may be used.

D. Tracing the design: Before you begin to trace, select sections to be cut and sections to be pierced. Attempt to maintain a balance between cut and pierced areas. After you have become somewhat experienced at this craft, you will be able to designate areas for cutting and piercing almost immediately. Although there are no definite rules to follow, flower petals and leaves are usually cut, while flower centers are usually pierced. Large solid sections of leaves or petals are sometimes pierced for emphasis or shading effects, as shown in Diagram 5-2. Long stems and

Diagram 5-2

Pierce to show highlight

166

leaf veins are done either way. If you choose to cut stems, however, make a series of broken cuts, rather than one continuous cut. If you are cutting veins, do not connect them to the main center vein. When tracing, it is important to remember that pieces are never completely cut out; they are always connected to the paper at some point. Flower petals, for example, should be traced with breaks between adjacent petals.

The best way to get a feeling of what the design will look like is to trace a portion of it on a piece of paper and experiment with various patterns of cutting and piercing. Once you have the effect you want, trace the design to reflect this pattern of cutting and piercing. Place a sheet of tracing paper over the design and trace outlines and features with a soft, blunt pencil. Since it would be rather difficult to maneuver the large sheet of tracing paper over the design patterns in this book, you will have to use a smaller sheet of tracing paper and then transfer the smaller tracing to the tracing paper lampshade pattern. Project instructions will tell you how to do this. When working on designs from other sources, you can eliminate this extra step by tracing directly onto the tracing paper lampshade pattern. Trace bold broken lines over areas that will be cut and small dots or circles over areas that will be pierced. Long lines that are going to be pierced should be traced with a dashed line. (See Diagram 5-3.) In the design patterns that follow, areas to be cut and pierced have already been designated. In other words, the patterns appear in their traced form. Trace over these patterns as they are, decide upon your own piercing and cutting scheme, or choose another design and adapt it to the project.

E. Transferring the design: After the design pattern has been traced onto the tracing paper lampshade pattern, the design must be transferred to the Strathmore or bond paper. The design is transferred to the back side of most papers. For metallic embossed paper, card stock paper, paper-backed foil, or papers upon which you will

Diagram 5-3

be painting, however, transfer the design to the front side.

There are three methods of transferring designs. The first method calls for the use of pencil carbon paper. Position the tracing paper lampshade pattern over the back side of the paper, with a piece of carbon paper in between. (See Photograph 5-2.) Partially attach with masking tape. Trace over the outline and entire design. If the design is large, move the carbon around until all areas have been traced. In addition to being somewhat messy, there is another complication to this method of transferring. When you turn the paper over to its front side,

167

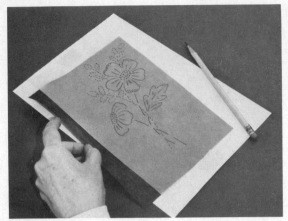

Photograph 5-2

Photograph 5-3

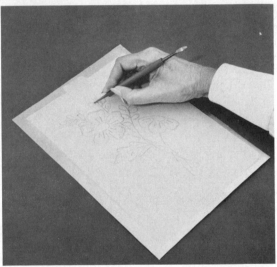

Photograph 5-4

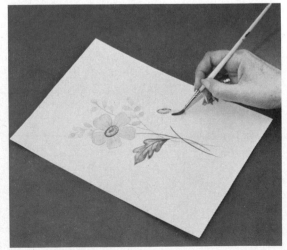

Photograph 5-5

you will actually have the reverse of the original design. It may turn out that you like it better this way. However, if you want to keep the original design, follow the second method of transferring.

The second method of transferring the design involves no carbon paper and is therefore much neater. The tracing paper lampshade pattern is placed, facedown, on the back side of the paper and attached with masking tape. (See Photograph 5-3.) When the lines that show through to the back side of the design are traced over, the lead on the front side transfers to the paper. The outline, the seam allowance line, and the entire design should be traced with a #3 pencil. When you are planning to paint the design, transfer design to the front of the paper.

A third method of transferring is used when you are working with metallic embossed paper, card stock paper, or paper-backed foil. Place the tracing paper lampshade pattern, faceup, on the front side of the paper and secure with masking tape. Trace over lines of design and outline with a #3 pencil or the pointed end of a burnishing tool. (See Photograph 5-4.) This will leave an impression of the design on the paper.

F. Painting the design: Generally speaking, if you wish to paint the design you must do so before you have pierced and cut it. Exceptions to this rule occur, however, such as in step 9 in the pierced and cut Christmas tree project. In this instance the nature of the paper dictates piercing

168

and cutting first. Watercolors work best on paper. Paint the whole design, barely covering the pencil lines with the color. (See Photograph 5-5.) The intensity of watercolors is controlled by the amount of water added.

G. Piercing the design: Piercing is done before cutting to prevent possible tearing of the paper. Work on the side of the paper that the design has been transferred to. If you are using a pounce wheel, place the paper on a piece of cardboard or a magazine and roll the wheel along all lines that are to be pierced. (See Photograph 5-6.) If you wish to vary the distances between holes throughout the design, use several different pounce wheels. To pierce the design, place it on a folded bath towel, a large sponge, or a sponge rubber kneeling pad. Punch holes with the piercer, as shown in Photograph 5-7. You can achieve different effects by using piercing tools of different diameters or by using the point of the tool in some places and the shank of the tool in others.

Photograph 5-6

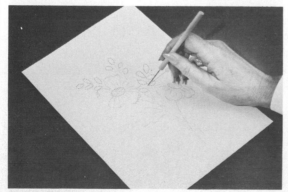
Photograph 5-7

H. Cutting the design: To cut the design, place it on an old magazine or piece of cardboard. Use an X-acto knife with a sharp #11 blade. Start with lines along the perimeter of the design and work your way toward the center. Do the most intricate cuts last. The knife should be held in the same manner as you would hold a pencil. Use the sharp point, rather than the blade, to cut. (See Photograph 5-8.) Since cutting a line

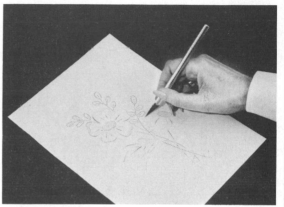
Photograph 5-8

with more than one cut will most likely ruin it, bear down hard enough to cut the paper with one continuous stroke of the knife. If you wander slightly off the line when cutting, gradually bring the knife back onto the line and continue the cut. Do not stop and recut. Remember that pieces are not to be removed from the design. Therefore, cut only to the distance marked and watch out for lines that are too close together. When you are cutting a corner or point, start at the point and cut away from it. This eliminates the possibility of getting crossed cuts. (See Diagram 5-4.) As you cut, position your design so that you will always be able to hold the X-acto knife in an upright position.

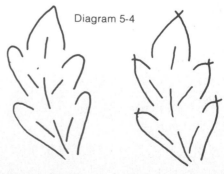
Diagram 5-4

Right way to cut   Wrong way to cut

169

I. Sculpturing the design: To add dimension to the design, contour the edges of selected design areas with your fingers. If you are working on the back side of the paper, pull edges upward. If you are working on the front side, press edges back. Examples of areas that are likely to be sculptured are flower petals, leaves, shells, and scrolls. (See Photograph 5-9.)

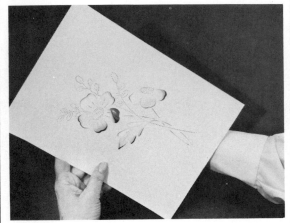

Photograph 5-9

J. Clipping lampshade to wire rings: Starting at the top front center, clip lampshade to top lampshade ring with a clothespin. The edge of the lampshade should be even with the top of the ring. Work in both directions from the center, clipping clothespins every 2 inches along the top edge. Turn the lampshade upside down and repeat procedure for bottom edge and ring. Be sure to keep edges even. (See Photograph 5-10.)

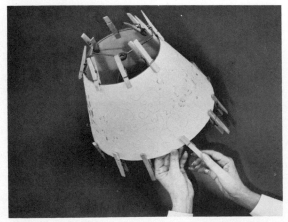

Photograph 5-10

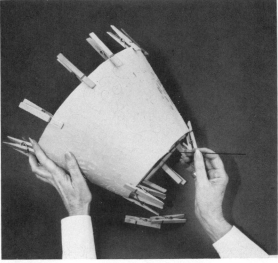

Photograph 5-11

K. Adhering lampshade to wire rings: Starting at the top front center of the lampshade, remove two of the clothespins. With a toothpick or small piece of wire, place a small amount of white glue on the wire ring. Smooth the paper down and put the clothespins back in place. (See Photograph 5-11.) Work around the top ring of the shade, toward the side that does not have the seam allowance. Start at the center again and work toward the opposite side. Do the bottom ring in the same manner, making sure that the paper fits firmly and smoothly on the ring. Finally, put a small amount of white glue on the inside of the seam allowance. Hold shade over this area, from the inside and the outside, for a few minutes. Allow the glue to dry for about 4 hours before removing clothespins.

L. Fireproofing the lampshade: The possibility of your paper lampshade catching on fire is small. Nevertheless, it would be a good idea to fireproof it for safety's sake. Many types of fireproofing products are available. Look under "flameproofing" in your Yellow Pages or contact the State Fire Marshall's Office for advice. Apply the product to the lampshade according to directions on the package.

Scrollwork Lampshade

This lampshade, designed and constructed by Jean Foot of Winnetka, Illinois, is a classic example of pierced and cut paper work. Variations of this type of shade can be made by painting the design or changing color and type of paper.

Materials

1 top lampshade ring, 7 inches in diameter
1 bottom lampshade ring, 12 inches in diameter
yardstick
1 sheet brown wrapping paper, 2 by 2½ feet
2 pencils, #2 and #3
carpenter's square or right triangle
yardstick compass or beam compass
scissors
1 sheet tracing paper, 2 by 2½ feet
masking tape
1 sheet tracing paper, 8½ by 11 inches
1 sheet Strathmore paper, 2 by 2½ feet, in color of
  your choice
folded towel, large sponge, or sponge rubber kneeling
  pad
piercer
old magazine or piece of cardboard
X-acto knife
1 liner brush or #1 brush
white glue
3 dozen clothespins, spring-type
toothpick or small piece of wire
5½ feet grosgrain ribbon, ½ inch wide, in color to
  match Strathmore paper
5½ feet velvet ribbon, ¼ inch wide, in color to match
  Strathmore paper

Instructions

1. Make a tapered lampshade pattern out of brown wrapping paper, according to step A in Basic Pierced and Cut Paper Instructions. Leaving out the seam allowance, fold the pattern in half to locate center.

2. Follow step B in Basic Instructions to make a tracing paper lampshade pattern. Fold the paper in half, not including the seam allowance, to mark off center. Mark spot where center fold and top penciled outline meet.

3. Mark off an area on the top lampshade ring that is equal to one-half of its diameter—3½ inches. (See Photograph 5-12.) Position one of the marks on the ring over the top center mark on the tracing paper lampshade pattern. Roll the

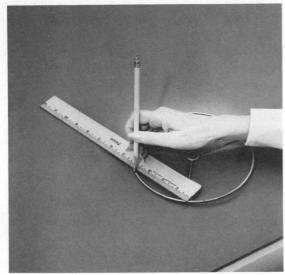

Photograph 5-12

ring along the top line until the second mark on the ring hits the paper. Make a mark on the tracing paper at this point. (See Photograph 5-13.) Position the second mark on the ring over the top center mark on the tracing paper. Roll the ring in the opposite direction until the first mark hits the paper and mark the paper at this point. Make straight folds on the tracing paper at each of the two marks. Disregarding the center fold, you now have a three-paneled tracing paper lampshade pattern.

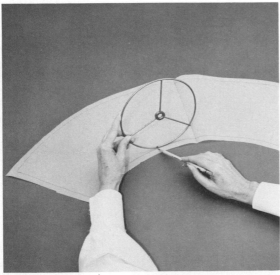

Photograph 5-13

4. Following instructions for enlarging patterns in the Helpful Hints chapter, enlarge design pattern by 20 percent. If you are using the grid method of enlarging, each square should measure 1 inch. Place the small sheet of tracing paper over the enlarged design pattern, secure with masking tape, and trace design with a pencil. Be sure to include the dotted register marks at the top and bottom of the pattern. Remove tracing paper design pattern.

5. Place the tracing paper design pattern on your work surface. Position and center the middle panel of the tracing paper lampshade pattern over it and secure with masking tape. Trace the design onto tracing paper lampshade pattern with a #2 pencil. Repeat procedure for other two panels. (See Photograph 5-14.) Remove tracing paper design pattern.

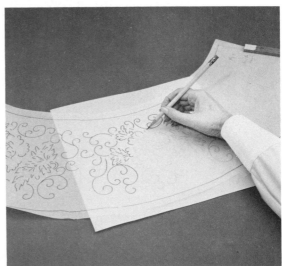

Photograph 5-14

6. Refer to step E in Basic Pierced and Cut Paper Instructions. Following the second method, transfer the design from the three-paneled pattern to Strathmore paper. Remove the tracing paper pattern from the Strathmore paper. Cut out the lampshade outline on the Strathmore paper, making sure to include the ½-inch seam allowance line.

7. Place the Strathmore paper on your work surface. Refer to step G in Basic Instructions and

173

pierce holes, $1/16$ inch apart, along all scrolls in the design pattern. (See Photograph 5-15.) A pounce wheel that gives 16 perforations to the inch would be helpful, but is not essential.

8. Cut along the lines in the flower portion of the design, according to step H in Basic Instructions. (See Photograph 5-16.)

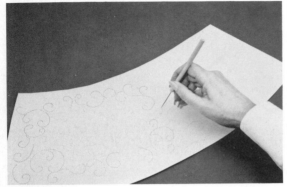

Photograph 5-15

Photograph 5-16

9. Press flower petal and leaf ends upward; contour lightly with your fingers. (See Photograph 5-17.)

10. Place the wrapping paper lampshade pattern over the second large sheet of tracing paper and trace outline. With scissors, cut along the outline, leaving a ½-inch margin all around. This piece of tracing paper will be used for the lining.

11. Place the Strathmore paper on the work surface, penciled side up. With #1 or liner brush, apply a line of white glue along the upper edge and the two sides. Lay the tracing paper

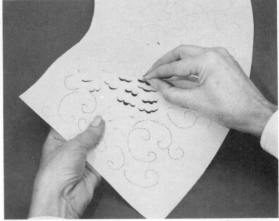

Photograph 5-17

lining over the Strathmore paper. Starting from the top center, smooth down the glued edges. Apply white glue to the bottom edge of the Strathmore. Smooth down the glued edge, making sure that you have accommodated for the space taken up by the contoured flower petal and leaf ends. (See Photograph 5-18.) Trim edges of lining and Strathmore paper even.

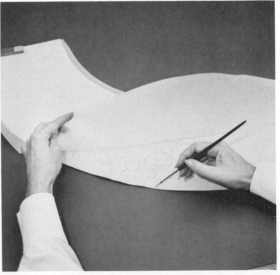

Photograph 5-18

174

12. Follow steps J and K in Basic Instructions to clip and adhere Strathmore paper to lampshade rings.

13. Cut a 23-inch length of grosgrain ribbon. Starting at one end of the ribbon, apply white glue to a 6-inch section. Starting at the seam, attach tape to top edge of shade, with ¼ inch extending above. (See Photograph 5-19.) Place a

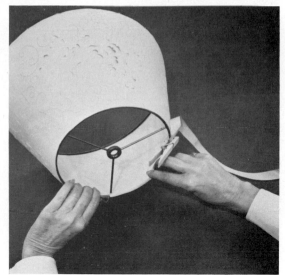

Photograph 5-20

Photograph 5-19

clothespin just beyond the 6-inch area to hold the ribbon. Fold the ribbon firmly over the top edge and adhere to top ring. (See Photograph 5-20.) Continue to glue and clip ribbon around the top edge in this manner. When you come to a spoke, slit the ribbon with the scissors to fit around it. Cut the ribbon, leaving a ¼-inch overlap at the seam. Adhere in place. Turn the shade upside down and adhere ribbon to the bottom edge of the shade in the same manner.

14. Cut a 23-inch length of velvet ribbon. Starting at the seam, adhere ribbon around shade, covering the grosgrain ribbon, on both top and bottom edges of the shade.

176

Floral Lampshade

Floral Lampshade

In this project a new technique is taught. The pierced and cut lampshade is positioned between two sheets of mat acetate. This is a simple and attractive way to protect your shade from wear and tear.

Materials

1 top lampshade ring, 9 inches in diameter
1 bottom lampshade ring, 11 inches in diameter
yardstick
1 sheet brown wrapping paper, 1⅔ by 4¹/₆ feet
2 pencils, #2 and #3
carpenter's square or right triangle
yardstick compass or beam compass
scissors
1 sheet tracing paper, 1⅔ by 4¹/₆ feet
masking tape
1 sheet tracing paper, 8½ by 11 inches
1 sheet Strathmore paper, 1⅔ by 4¹/₆ feet, in color of
    your choice
2 sheets mat acetate, .010 inch thick, 1⅔ by 4¹/₆ feet
folded towel, large sponge, or sponge rubber kneeling
    pad
piercer
old magazine or piece of cardboard
X-acto knife
white paper tape
3 dozen clothespins, spring-type
toothpick or small piece of wire
white glue
2 yards bias tape, ¾ inch wide, in neutral color
2 yards grosgrain ribbon, ⅝ inch wide, in neutral
    color
2 yards grosgrain ribbon, ⅜ inch wide, in color to
    match Strathmore paper

Instructions

1. Refer to step A in Basic Instructions and make a tapered lampshade pattern with brown wrapping paper. Fold the pattern in half, not including the ½-inch seam allowance.
2. Follow step B in Basic Instructions to make a tracing paper lampshade pattern. Mark the center of the pattern.
3. Position a sheet of tracing paper over the design pattern, secure with masking tape, and trace with a pencil. Be sure to include the register marks. Remove tracing paper design pattern.

4. Place the tracing paper design pattern on your work surface, with the tracing paper lampshade pattern over it. Align the center of the lampshade pattern with the vertical register marks on the design and the top outline of the pattern with the horizontal arc at the top of the design. Trace the design onto the center of the lampshade pattern. (See Photograph 5-21.) Working in both direc-

Photograph 5-21

tions from the top center outline of the tracing paper lampshade pattern, measure and mark off every 4 inches. Move tracing paper design pattern to the right, lining up the top vertical register to the 4-inch mark. Trace design onto this section of the pattern. (See Photograph 5-22.)

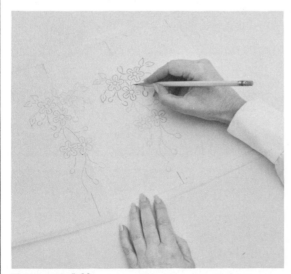

Photograph 5-22

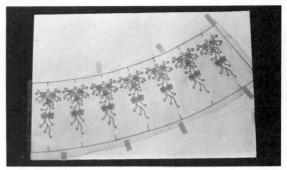

Photograph 5-23

Repeat this procedure until entire pattern is covered with the design. Remove tracing paper design pattern.

5. Using the second method of transferring described in step E of Basic Instructions, transfer design from tracing paper lampshade pattern to Strathmore paper. (See Photograph 5-23.)

6. Place a sheet of acetate, frosted side up, over the pattern. Trace the outline of the pattern onto acetate. Do this very carefully so that the Strathmore paper and the acetate will be the same size. Remove acetate sheet and repeat procedure for second sheet. Remove tracing paper and acetate sheets from Strathmore paper and cut out all outlines. Be sure to include seam allowance lines.

7. Place the Strathmore paper on your work surface. Refer to step G in Basic Instructions and pierce where indicated on pattern. (See Photograph 5-24.)

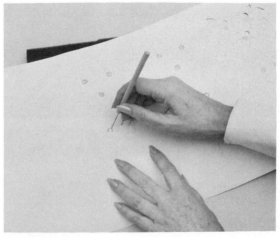

Photograph 5-24

179

8. Refer to step H in Basic Instructions and cut where indicated on the pattern. Make the long flower stem cuts before doing the flower petals. (See Photograph 5-25.)

Photograph 5-25

9. Press tips of leaves and ends of flower petals upward and contour lightly with your fingers.

10. With frosted side in, bring the end of one of the acetate sheets around to the other end, thus forming a tapered lampshade shape. Overlap the ends by about 1 inch and place two pieces of white paper tape across the seam to temporarily hold it. (See Photograph 5-26.)

Photograph 5-26

11. Place the bottom lampshade ring on the work surface and put acetate shade inside it. Working in both directions from the front center of the acetate, attach acetate to inside diameter of ring with ½-inch lengths of white paper tape. (See Photograph 5-27.) When the circular shape

Photograph 5-27

becomes difficult to maneuver, remove paper tape from the seam and finish taping acetate to the bottom ring. Taping must be done neatly.

12. Cut a small notch on the top edge of acetate, directly opposite the seam. Align the top lampshade ring with the top edge of the acetate, placing one of its spokes in the notch. Tape both sides of spoke to acetate. Adhere acetate to top lampshade ring in the same manner as you did the bottom. As you work your way toward the other two spokes, notch the acetate. (See Photograph 5-28.) Attach a piece of white paper tape over the acetate seam from top to bottom, as shown in Photograph 5-29.

13. With cut side in, position the center of the pierced and cut paper around acetate. Align acetate and paper edges and seams as closely as possible. Clip the paper to the outside diameter of the top ring at the center with a clothespin. Following directions in steps J and K of Basic Instructions, clip and adhere Strathmore paper to top and bottom lampshade rings.

14. Place second piece of acetate, frosted side out, over the shade. Align seams and edges. Working in both directions from the front center of the shade, fasten acetate to outside diameter of top ring with ½-inch lengths of white paper tape placed every 3 inches. Turn the shade upside

Photograph 5-28

Photograph 5-29

Photograph 5-30

Photograph 5-31

down and repeat procedure for bottom ring. Cover the entire seam from top to bottom with a strip of paper tape.

15. Cut a 31-inch length of bias tape and apply white glue to a 6-inch section at one end. Adhere tape to the top edge of the shade, allowing ½ inch to extend above the top, as shown in Photograph 5-30. Place a clothespin just beyond the 6-inch area to hold the tape to the shade. Fold the tape over the top edge of the shade and adhere it to the inside of the shade. (See Photograph 5-31.) Continue in this manner until the top edge is covered with bias tape. When you come to a spoke, slit the tape so that it will fit around it,

roll tape over the edge, and adhere. (See Photograph 5-32.) Trim the tape so that you will have a ¼-inch overlap at the seam and glue in place. Cut a 36-inch length of bias tape for the bottom of the shade, turn shade upside down, and repeat procedure.

16. Adhere a piece of the wider ribbon over the paper tape seam covering, as shown in Photograph 5-33. Cut two lengths of the wider ribbon to fit around top and bottom edges of shade. Apply white glue to one side of the ribbon. Starting at the top back seam of the shade, adhere ribbon all around top edge, keeping edges even. When you come to the back seam, cut the end of

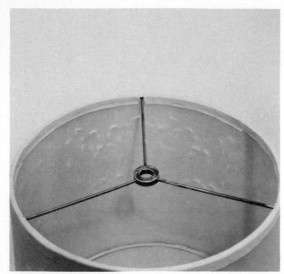

Photograph 5-32

Photograph 5-33

the ribbon leaving a ¼-inch overlap; glue in place. Turn the shade upside down. Adhere the other piece of ribbon to the bottom of the shade in the same manner.

17. Starting at the top back seam, adhere a piece of the narrower ribbon around the shade, overlapping the bottom edge of the top ribbon by $^1/_{16}$ inch. (See Photograph 5-34.) Once you have gone completely around the shade, leave a ¼-inch seam allowance and cut ribbon. Turn lampshade upside down and repeat procedure for bottom edge.

Photograph 5-34

Nursery Lampshade (See page 184.)

Nursery Lampshade

This cheerful lampshade is perfect for a small child's room. Paint animals according to project directions or have fun planning your own color scheme.

Materials

1 top lampshade ring, 9 inches in diameter
1 bottom lampshade ring, 11 inches in diameter
yardstick
1 sheet brown wrapping paper, 1⅔ by 3 feet
2 pencils, #2 and #3
carpenter's square or right triangle
yardstick compass or beam compass
scissors
1 sheet tracing paper, 1⅔ by 3 feet
masking tape
6 sheets tracing paper, 8½ by 11 inches
1 sheet heavyweight bond paper, 1⅔ by 3 feet, in color of your choice
watercolor paint set
watercolor paintbrush
2 sheets mat acetate, .010 inch thick, 1⅔ by 4¹/₆ feet
folded towel, large sponge, or sponge rubber kneeling pad
piercer
old magazine or piece of cardboard
X-acto knife
white paper tape
3 dozen clothespins, spring-type
toothpick or small piece of wire
white glue
2 yards bias tape, ¾ inch wide, in neutral color
2 yards grosgrain ribbon, ⅝ inch wide, in neutral color
2 yards grosgrain ribbon, ⅜ inch wide, in color to match bond paper
2 yards fine lace, ¼ inch wide

Instructions

1. Refer to step A in Basic Pierced and Cut Paper Instructions to make a tapered lampshade pattern with brown wrapping paper.

2. Follow step B in Basic Instructions to make a tracing paper lampshade pattern. Mark the center of the pattern.

3. Follow directions for enlarging patterns in the Helpful Hints chapter and enlarge pattern parts by 10 percent. If you are using the grid method of enlarging, each square should measure

1 inch. Place a small sheet of tracing paper over each enlarged design part and trace. Be sure to include register marks. For my lamp, I traced two rabbits, two chickens, one kitten, and one teddy bear. You may use any combination you prefer, however, as long as there are six parts altogether.

4. Place the six tracing paper design patterns on your work surface, overlapping edges slightly so that register marks will be aligned. Tape together with masking tape. Place tracing paper lampshade pattern over design patterns, with edges even and center aligned with centermost register marks. Attach with masking tape and trace entire design. Remove tracing paper design pattern.

5. Following the second method of transferring described in step E of Basic Instructions, transfer design from tracing paper lampshade pattern to front side of bond paper. The building blocks should be 1¼ inches above the bottom edge.

6. Place a sheet of acetate, frosted side up, over the pattern. Trace the outline onto acetate and bond paper; cut out. Repeat procedure for second acetate sheet. Remove acetate sheet and tracing paper lampshade pattern.

7. Paint the figures and blocks on the bond paper with watercolors and a watercolor paintbrush. Use the following Color Suggestions chart or paint the figures in colors of your choice. Shade the edges of areas that curve, such as ears and feathers.

8. Place the bond paper on your work surface, painted side up. Refer to step G in Basic Instructions and pierce indicated areas on design.

9. Cut indicated areas according to step H in Basic Instructions.

10. Press desired areas to the back of the paper and contour lightly.

11. Follow steps 10 through 17 in the Floral Lampshade project.

12. Use white glue to adhere fine lace over joint between ribbons.

Color Suggestions

Part	Color
bear	light green
kitten	blue
rabbit, chicken's hat, and wagon wheels	pink
chicken	yellow
beak	red
wagon	green
blocks	pink, green, and blue and yellow, green, and blue
kitten's eyes, nose, mouth, and whiskers; teddy bear's eyes, nose, and mouth; chicken's eyes; dotted lines on teddy bear and rabbit; alphabet letters	brown

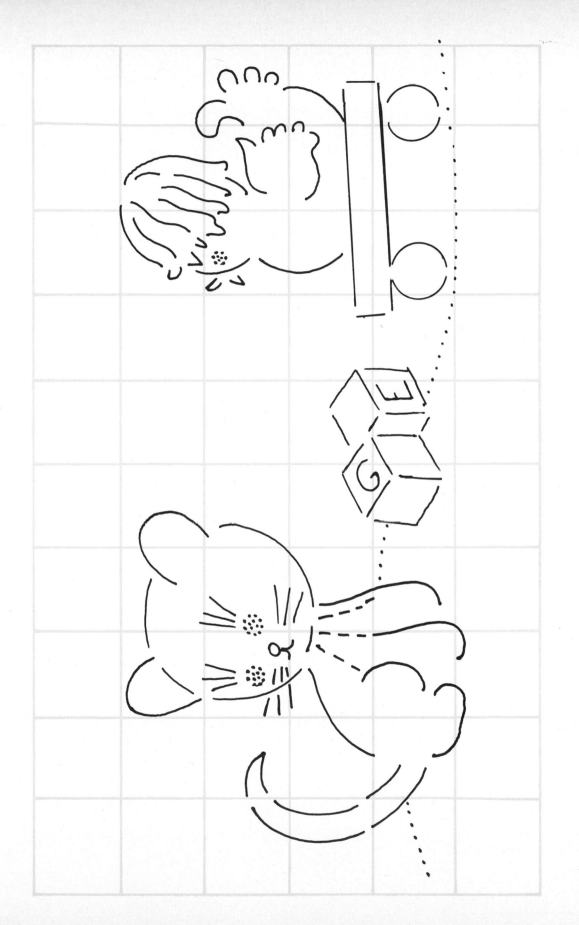

Paper Christmas Tree Lamp

Paper Christmas Tree Lamp

A festive pierced and cut Christmas tree lamp, such as this one, will make a beautiful holiday centerpiece for your dining-room table. It was made out of embossed card stock paper and painted with transparent oil paints. Ask for help when purchasing lamp hardware to make sure pieces fit together properly.

Materials

Lamp Hardware:
2 flat plates, 3 inches in diameter
1 lamp base, 7 inches in diameter
1 IPS pipe, 5 inches long, ⅛ inch in diameter, threaded on both ends
2 lock washers
1 nut
1 socket
base mount-type switch or cord switch
cord, 6 feet, with plug cap
light bulb, 40 watt

yardstick compass or beam compass
1 pencil, #3
2 sheets tracing paper, 23 by 23 inches
1 sheet tracing paper, 8½ by 11 inches
embossed card stock paper, 10 pound weight, 23 by 23 inches, in gold
masking tape
scissors
ruler
pounce wheel, Grumbacher X893
old magazine or piece of cardboard
folded towel, large sponge, or sponge rubber kneeling pad
piercer
X-acto knife
transparent oil paints in alizarin crimson, Indian yellow, and Prussian blue
disposable palette pad or aluminum foil
1 can clear vinyl varnish
1 liner brush or #1 brush
white glue
2 sheets corrugated cardboard, 10 by 10 inches
1 dozen sequin pins, ¾ inch long
Liquid Leaf
1 paintbrush, ½ inch wide
5 chenille stems
20 yards floral ribbon, ⅝ inch wide, in green
1 roll bead wire, 30 gauge
1 beaded spray, in red

Instructions

1. Set the compass to a 23-inch radius and draw

a quarter circle on a large piece of tracing paper. Mark the spot where the point of the compass was located.

2. Follow instructions for enlarging patterns in the Helpful Hints chapter and enlarge design pattern by 40 percent. If you are using the grid method of enlarging, each square should measure 1 inch. Trace the enlarged pattern onto the tracing paper quarter circle, aligning the point of the design cone with the marked-off spot.

3. With point of the compass on one corner of the card stock paper and radius set at 23 inches, draw a quarter circle. (See Photograph 5-35.)

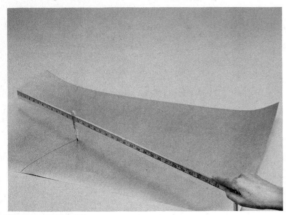

Photograph 5-35

4. Place the tracing paper design pattern over card stock paper, with points and arcs aligned. Fasten in place with masking tape.

5. Trace over outline and design. Press hard enough to leave a good, clear imprint on the gold paper. (See Photograph 5-36.) The design does not cover the full 90 degrees of the quarter circle.

190

Photograph 5-36

The remaining area on the gold paper will serve as a seam allowance.

6. Cut out the card stock paper cone. Place the cone, gold side up, on an old magazine or piece of cardboard. Go over each of the long vertical lines with the pounce wheel, using a ruler as a guide. (See Photograph 5-37.) Each line should be done only once, so bear down hard.

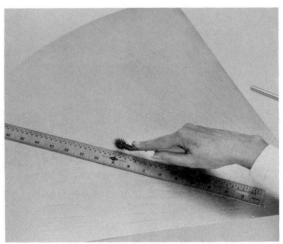

Photograph 5-37

7. Following step G in Basic Pierced and Cut Paper Instructions, pierce holes on vertical lines.

8. Follow step H in Basic Instructions and cut around holly leaves. (See Photograph 5-38.)

9. Dab a bit of each oil paint color onto a palette or sheet of aluminum foil. Place a small container of varnish next to the palette. Mix a small amount of Prussian blue into Indian yellow to

Photograph 5-38

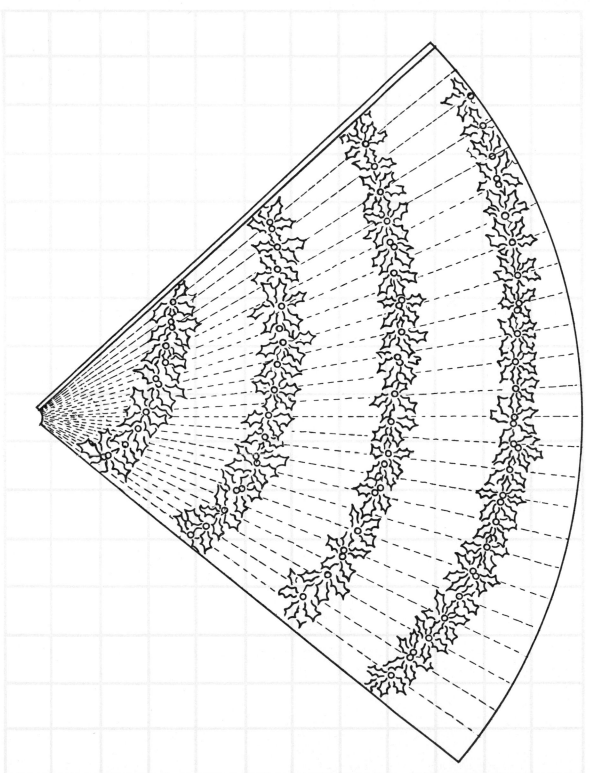

191

make green and thin with varnish. Using a #1 or liner brush, paint the holly leaves green. The level of intensity is controlled by the amount of varnish you add. Thin alizarin crimson with varnish and paint berries. (See Photograph 3-39.)

Photograph 5-39

10. After paint has dried, press tips and edges of leaves to the back side and contour with your fingers. Apply a coat of white glue to the seam allowance of the cone and roll cone into shape. Place a heavy object that can be used as a weight inside the cone, over the lap.

11. Draw and cut out another cone on the second piece of tracing paper. Roll the tracing paper into a cone shape and insert it inside the gold paper cone. Position so that it will fit snugly. Mark along its edge from top to bottom so that you will have a line for gluing. Remove the tracing paper, apply white glue to line, and shape tracing paper into a cone. (See Photograph 5-40.) Apply a

Photograph 5-40

small amount of white glue along the top and bottom edges of the tracing paper cone and adhere to the inside of gold cone.

12. Draw a 10-inch-diameter circle on a piece of corrugated cardboard. Using the same center, draw a 7-inch-diameter circle within it. Cut along circumference of both circles with the X-acto knife. Apply white glue along the outer circumference of the cardboard and place it at the bottom of the cone. (See Photograph 5-41.) Insert ¾-inch-long sequin pins through the cone, into the edge of the cardboard.

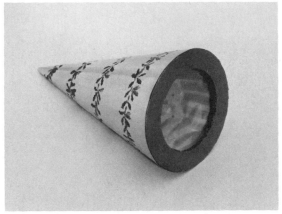

Photograph 5-41

13. Draw a 10-inch-diameter circle on a second piece of corrugated cardboard and cut four holes inside it, as shown in Diagram 5-5. Assemble the lamp hardware and the 10-inch-diameter corrugated cardboard, as shown in Diagram 5-5 (page 193). Apply Liquid Leaf to the bottom of the cardboard.

14. Starting ¾ inch from the top of a chenille stem, cast a loop of ribbon to the right and attach with bead wire. Cast a loop of ribbon to the left and attach with bead wire. Continue casting loops down the stem in this manner, leaving ¾ inch bare at the bottom. (See Diagram 5-6.) Make four ribbon spears in this manner.

Diagram 5-6

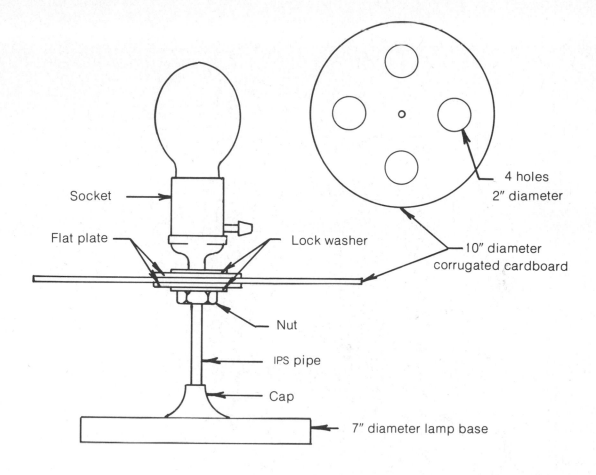

Socket

Flat plate

Lock washer

4 holes
2" diameter

10" diameter
corrugated cardboard

Nut

IPS pipe

Cap

7" diameter lamp base

Diagram 5-5

15. Shape the ribbon spears to fit around the outer edge of the cardboard disk on the lamp base. Put a small amount of white glue around the outer edge of the cardboard and adhere the ribbon spears in place. Insert the ends of the chenille stems into the cardboard. (See Photograph 5-42.)

16. Make a smaller ribbon spear to fit around the top of the cone. Adhere the spear in place with white glue. Insert beaded spray into the top of the cone.

17. Put a light bulb in the socket and place the cone on top of the lamp base. The cone should fit firmly inside the ribbon spear border on the cardboard disk.

Photograph 5-42

Seaweed and Shells Lampshade

This satin-covered lampshade can be seen with its attractive coral lamp base in the Shell Art chapter. Together or separately, both base and shade will make a lovely addition to any room.

Materials

1 top lampshade ring, 15 inches in diameter
1 bottom lampshade ring, 18 inches in diameter
yardstick
1 sheet brown wrapping paper, 2½ by 5½ feet
2 pencils, #2 and #3
carpenter's square or right triangle
yardstick compass or beam compass
scissors
1 sheet tracing paper, 2½ by 5½ feet
1 sheet tracing paper, 8½ by 11 inches
masking tape
1 sheet heavyweight bond paper, 2½ by 5½ feet
1 sheet mat acetate, .010 inch thick, 2½ by 5½ feet
folded towel, large sponge, or sponge rubber kneeling pad
piercer
old magazine or piece of cardboard
X-acto knife
white paper tape
1 yard antique satin, in white
3 dozen clothespins, spring-type
toothpick or small piece of wire
white glue
10 yards bias tape, ¾ inch wide, in neutral color
10 yards grosgrain ribbon, ¾ inch wide, in neutral color
10 yards velvet ribbon, ½ inch wide, in color of your choice
10 yards metallic cord, in gold

Instructions

1. Following step A in Basic Instructions, make a tapered lampshade pattern with brown wrapping paper.
2. Follow step B in Basic Instructions to make a tracing paper lampshade pattern. Mark the center of the pattern.
3. Following directions in the Helpful Hints chapter, enlarge design pattern by 50 percent. If you are using the grid method of enlarging, each square should measure 1 inch. Trace the enlarged design onto a sheet of tracing paper.

Row A   Row B

4. Place the tracing paper design pattern on your work surface with the tracing paper lampshade pattern over it. Trace row A onto tracing paper lampshade pattern to the right and trace row B alongside row A. Continue to alternate and trace designs in this manner until bottom of paper is completely covered.

5. See step E in Basic Pierced and Cut Paper Instructions. Using the second method of transferring, transfer design from tracing paper lampshade pattern to bond paper. Design should be 3¼ inches from the bottom.

6. Place a sheet of acetate, frosted side up, over the pattern. Trace the outline onto bond paper and acetate and cut out. Remove acetate sheet and repeat procedure for second sheet.

7. Position the bond paper on your work surface. Pierce indicated areas of the design according to directions in step G of Basic Instructions.

8. Refer to step H in Basic Instructions and cut designated areas.

9. Sculpture and contour the edges of all shells, according to step I.

10. Follow steps 10 through 12 in the Floral Lampshade project.

11. Pinning across the straight of the antique satin, attach satin to tracing paper lampshade pattern. Cut excess material off satin. Remove the pattern from the material.

12. Place the antique satin, dull side down, on your work surface. Apply white glue to edges of the front side of bond paper. Glue bond paper, front side down, over fabric, making sure that sculptured pieces are facing up. Rub along the edges of paper to secure. Trim the material so that there will be a ¼-inch overlap around each end. Apply a small amount of white glue to the back side of each end of the shade, wrap the overlap around the end, and adhere. Rub out any wrinkles with your hand. Trim top and bottom edges even.

13. Position the satin-covered shade, paper side in, around the acetate. With seams and edges aligned, clip the shade to the outside diameter of the top ring with a clothespin. Follow steps J and K in Basic Pierced and Cut Paper Instructions to clip and glue lampshade to rings.

14. Follow steps 15 through 17 in Floral Lampshade project.

15. Adhere a piece of gold cord over the joint between the velvet and grosgrain ribbons.

Stenciling

Stenciling is the art of applying color to a surface through cutout sections of stiff paper. Although the craft has been practiced for thousands of years by many peoples, the Japanese should be given credit for helping to develop stenciling into a fine art. They are most noted for their intricate silk stenciling work. Basically, we will concern ourselves with two other types of stenciling—bronze stenciling and color stenciling.

Bronze stenciling can also be traced back to the Orient, where Chinese and Japanese craftsmen displayed a high level of expertise in the handling of metal powders. The craft became popular in England and the United States during the early part of the nineteenth century. Famous pieces, such as the Hitchcock Chairs, Boston rockers, Duncan Phyfe-type chairs, and Pennsylvania Balloon Chairs, were designed and created in New England, New York, Pennsylvania, and New Jersey. Trays, commodes, and chests of drawers were also popular projects. In bronze stenciling, bronze powders are applied to surfaces that have been sized with a tacky varnish. The method is simple. The stencil is placed over the surface. A piece of silk-backed velvet is wrapped around the index finger and dipped into the powder. Color is applied to the surface by rubbing the silk over spaces in the stencil.

Color stenciling differs from bronze stenciling in that paints, rather than powders, are used. This type of stenciling was practiced extensively from Ohio to New York and throughout New England. The use of stencils provided a cheap substitute for expensive European wallpapers, Persian carpets, wooden inlaid floors, and painted canvas floor covers. Simple borders in a single color were done with one stencil, while the more intricate multicolored patterns required a stencil for each color. The stencils were made with a heavy paper that had been toughened by oil, paint, and, occasionally, shellac.

In addition to color stenciling on floors, walls, and furniture, the earliest settlers brought with them the technique of stenciling on fabrics. Carpets, counterpanes, and tablecloths were popular projects. The stencils were again made of oil-treated and shellacked paper. Paints and dyes were applied over the stencils, using round blunt-ended brushes. Simple designs were done with one stencil, while more refined and intricate designs were done with a stencil for each color.

Actually, the techniques used in stenciling have changed very little throughout the years. The major change has been in the development of superior materials and tools, which make stenciling easier to do.

Stenciling Materials and Tools

It is important that the equipment used for stencil work be of a good quality. If it isn't, stenciling will become more difficult and tedious than it need be. Scissors, for example, should be clean and sharp.

The best material with which to make a stencil is architects' tracing linen. This is a semitransparent material with a stiff sizing. At one time, starch was used as the sizing agent. Today, synthetic, waterproof linens are available. If you are using the old-fashioned type, however, be sure to keep it away from water. The tiniest drop will cause a distortion in the material and will create wrinkles. For this reason, the synthetic linens are preferable. Acetate sheets (.0075 inch thick) can be used in place of architects' tracing linen but are difficult to cut. Although not required in the following projects, a semitransparent wax-finished paper—stencil paper—can be used for fabric stenciling, and a heavy, stiff material—stencil board—can be used for wall, floor, or furniture stencil work.

Architects' tracing linen is best cut with a pair of straight-bladed, sharp-pointed scissors. Surgical scissors, decoupage scissors, or embroidery scissors are best, although it is possible to use an X-acto knife or scalpel. (See Photograph 6-1.) Whatever you choose to use must be in excellent condition so that the stenciled edges will be sharp

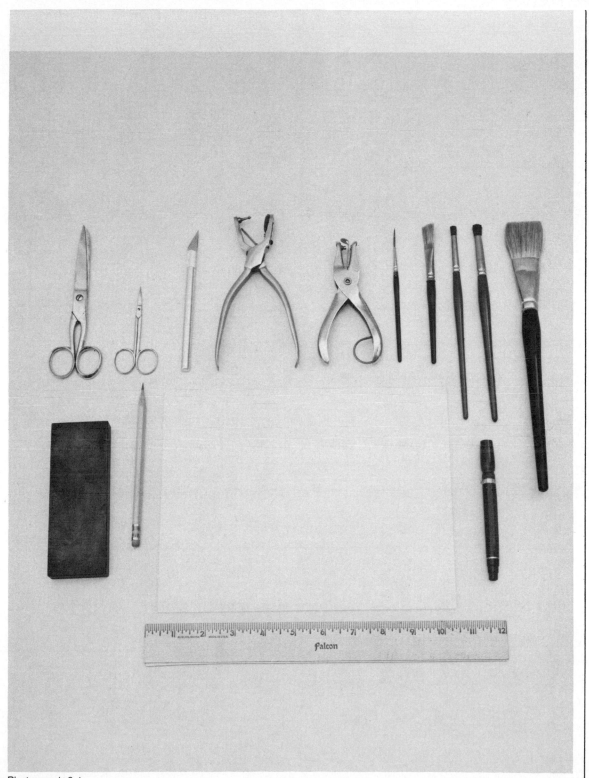

and clean. If using an X-acto knife, work on an 8-by 10-inch sheet of glass. This will provide a firm backing and prevent edges of linen from rolling under. Tape edges of glass so that you will not cut yourself. Dental or paper punches are useful for initiating the cuts in the linen.

Before the stencil is cut the design must be traced onto tracing paper and transferred to the linen. You will need, therefore, small and large sheets of tracing paper. Purchase rolls of tracing paper, and cut sheets to the size you will need. Use a technical fountain pen with a #00 point size to trace designs. India ink provides a heavy line.

For bronze stenciling, you will need varnish, bronze powders, small pieces of velours, and small pieces of silk-backed velvet. Varnish is applied over the surface of the design piece and allowed to dry to a tacky stage. Purchase a slow-drying brand, since the fast-drying types will not remain in the tacky stage long enough for you to do your stenciling. The old-fashioned vegetable gum-type varnish is the best for our purposes. The varnish is also used as a protective covering for finished pieces. Bronze powders, which are finely ground or pulverized metals, are worked into the varnished surface through the cutout sections of the stencil. For this, purchase finely ground aluminum (silver), pale gold, orange gold, copper, and brilliant fire bronze powders. The small pieces of velours are used as palettes. The bronzes stay in place on the velours and are easy to pick up. Pieces of silk-backed velvet, measuring approximately 3 by 3 inches, are wrapped around the index finger and used to rub the bronzes into the varnish. Hem edges of velvet and avoid using synthetics. Raw edges and synthetic velvets tend to shed threads into the varnish. Use a different piece of velvet for each bronze color.

A variety of paints and paintbrushes will be needed for the following projects. Oil paints in alizarin crimson, Indian yellow, and Prussian blue are thinned with clear varnish and applied as a glaze over bronze stencil work. Acrylic paints may be used as a background for stenciled wood pieces. Lamp black oil-base paint is the preferred background color for bronze work. Use disposable palette pads. You will need a minimum of three paintbrushes—a #1 or liner brush, a brush that is ½ inch wide or wider, and a brush that is 1½ inches or wider. The liner brush is used for touch-up work or striping, the ½-inch brush for backgrounds, and the 1½-inch brush for larger backgrounds. For fabric painting, you will need fabric or textile paints. These are mixed with extender to soften the paint and make it go further. Do not use a paint thinner with textile paints.

Additional materials needed are #400 and #600 sandpaper and #350 garnet paper. Lint-free cloths or tack rags are used to rub off sanding residue. Steel wool, #0000, is used to smooth varnish between coats. For appliqué work, you will need a drawing board and pins, thumbtacks, or transparent tape. Stitch Witchery, an iron-on fabric adhesive, is used to attach appliqué pieces. Scissors, pencils, paste wax, lint-free cloths, paper towels, a brush-cleaning solution, mineral spirits, a ruler, masking tape, and white glue should be on hand at all times.

Basic Stenciling Instructions

The following instructions will acquaint you with the basic techniques required in stenciling. Read instructions before starting the projects.

A. Preparing the background: Stenciling can be done on wood, metal, fabric, and many other types of surfaces. Bronze stenciling is usually done on metal or wood, while color stenciling can be done on walls, wood, metal, and fabric.

Bronze stenciling: For work on unfinished wood surfaces, sand to a very smooth finish with #350 garnet paper, followed by #400 sandpaper. Wipe clean with a lint-free cloth or tack rag and seal with Treasure Sealer. After sanding again with #400 sandpaper, apply two coats of lamp black oil-base paint, allowing 24 hours drying time between coats.

For metal surfaces, you will have to watch out for rust. If there is rust on the metal, it must be removed with a rust remover, such as Rust-I-Cide. In any case, to prepare a metal surface, simply prime it with Rustoleum, or any type of metal protector. Sand lightly with #400 sandpaper and wipe clean with a lint-free cloth or tack rag. Apply two coats of lamp black oil-base paint at 24-hour intervals.

Although other colors can be used for backgrounds, black is the most effective. The desired fading-into-shadow illusion is easier to obtain with black than with other colors. If you wish to try a different color, however, dark blue, dark green, vermilion, or dark brown will do nicely. Never use yellows, light oranges, greens, or any other color that reflects light. These give no illusion of the shadow that is essential for bronze stencil work.

Color stenciling: If you are working on a wood or metal surface, follow the same procedure as for bronze stenciling. When stenciling on wood, plaster, wallboard, posterboard, or metal, apply at least one coat of either oil- or water-base paint. Allow the background to dry; sand and wipe again.

If you are color stenciling on fabric, wash and press the fabric.

B. Selecting the design: Almost any design that appeals to you can be used for stenciling. The designs that are most often used are garlands or baskets of flowers, fruits, simple landscapes with and without people, and scenes with people. Once you have become proficient at the craft, designs can be as intricate as you wish.

C. Tracing the design: Place a piece of tracing paper over the design and secure with masking tape. With a technical fountain pen and india ink, trace the entire design. Be sure to trace all details, such as leaf veins and strawberry seeds or other features that you may want to emphasize. (See Photograph 6-2.)

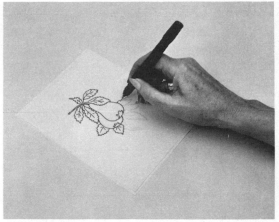
Photograph 6-2

D. Separating the design into units: At this point, the design must be separated into units or groups of units. A unit may be a leaf, a flower, a part of a basket, people, or anything at all. Details, such as leaf veins or strawberry seeds, may also be designated as units. Starting at the center of the traced design, lightly pencil in a #1 in all units that do not touch one another. Go through the design a second time, and pencil in a #2 in units that do not touch one another but may touch #1 units. Continue in this manner until all units of the traced design are marked. (See Diagram 6-1.) You may have to go over the design three, four, or more times. Each of the numbered groups of units will be a separate stencil. Our sample design has two groups of units and will therefore require two stencils. In some cases, you may have one stencil for a single unit. This is usually done when the same unit is repeated several times. For example, a bunch of grapes might very well be done with two stencils of different-sized grapes. For the design patterns that follow, you will not need to designate unit numbers. Units have already been indicated on the pattern. When you are stenciling on your own, however, you will need to do so.

E. Tracing the design onto tracing linen: Position a piece of architects' tracing linen, dull side up, over the traced design. With a technical fountain pen and india ink, trace each of the #1

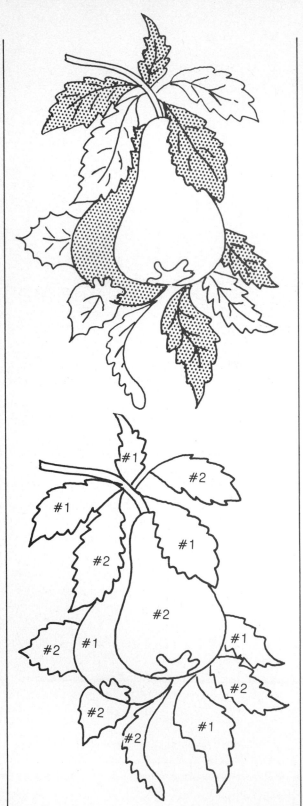

Photograph 6-3

Photograph 6-4

units of the design. (See Photograph 6-3.) Trace accurately, reproducing all the tiny details. Leave a 1-inch margin around the outside of the design so that you will be able to apply color or bronze from the outer edges without dirtying the design portion. Mark the stencil #1. Remove the #1 stencil from the traced design, position a second piece of architects' tracing linen over the traced design, and trace #2 units onto linen. (See Photograph 6-4.) Continue in this manner until all the units of the traced design have been traced onto architects' tracing linen.

Diagram 6-1

F. Cutting the stencil: Make a hole inside one of the #1 units, away from the line on which you are going to cut. Hold the surgical, decoupage, or embroidery scissors with the thumb and third finger in the handles and the blade resting against the index finger. (See Photograph 6-5.) From the underneath side of the linen, insert the blade through the hole. Cut with your hand below the linen so that you will be able to see what you are doing. (See Photograph 6-6.) Except for the opening and closing motion, scissors should be held still. Keeping the scissor blades

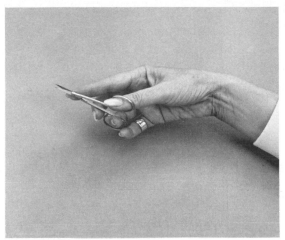

Photograph 6-5

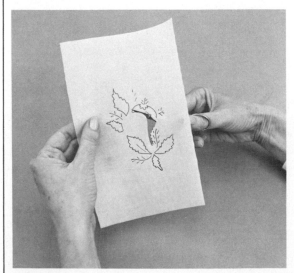

Photograph 6-6

perpendicular to the material ensures a sharp, clean edge. Cut the linen by feeding it into the throat of the scissors. Cut along traced lines of all #1 units. Be careful not to make crossing cuts at **corners or points of angles. When cutting with an X-acto knife, place the linen over a sheet of glass. (See Photograph 6-7.) To begin a cut, punch a hole in the unit with the point of an X-acto knife. You may use the tips of the**

Photograph 6-7

scissors, however, if you prefer. Cutting tiny holes sometimes presents a problem. The easiest method is to punch them with a dental punch, as shown in Photograph 6-8. Another method is to

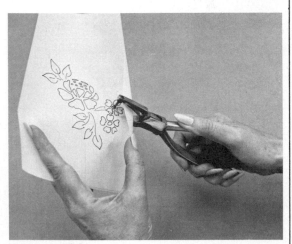

Photograph 6-8

punch through the lines with the tip of an X-acto knife or darning needle, and then to cut out the hole with the tips of scissors, making several short snips. (See Photograph 6-9.) Another way

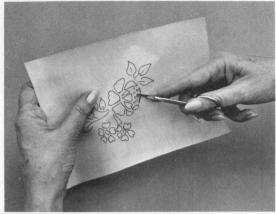

Photograph 6-9

is to punch the holes with a darning needle, turn the linen over, trim off the edges that are pushed through to the other side with scissors, and sand lightly with #400 sandpaper. If the hole is very small, simply punch it with a darning needle, turn over, and sand smooth. (See Photograph 6-10.)

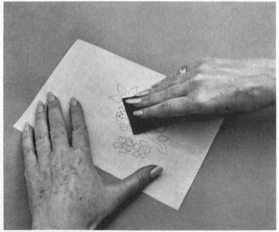

Photograph 6-10

Store your stencils in a flat position, preferably between two sheets of heavy paper. This will keep them flat and clean.

G. Applying the varnish: For bronze stenciling, use a sable or camel hair paintbrush, ½ to 2 inches wide, to apply varnish. Dip about one-third to one-half the length of the bristles into the varnish. Starting at the center of the piece, apply a smooth, even coat. Allow to dry in a

dust-free area until it reaches its tacky stage. Stenciling can be done only when the varnish is in this stage. Test the readiness of your varnish by touching it with your finger. Although it feels tacky, your finger should be clean. The time that it takes the varnish to reach the tacky stage will be dependent on weather conditions. For best results, do not varnish during cold, damp weather. Drying times printed on the can are normally based on 70-degree temperatures and 50-percent relative humidities. Under these conditions, the varnish will probably take from 30 minutes to 3 hours to reach the tacky stage. If you are using one of the old-fashioned gum varnishes, you may want to slow down the drying time and thus increase its tacky period. This can be done by adding linseed oil. Although it may take 2 to 3 days for varnish treated in this way to reach the tacky stage, it will remain in this stage for 12 to 24 hours and may take as long as 5 or 6 days to thoroughly dry. This will give you plenty of time in which to do your stenciling. If you have added linseed oil to the varnish, remember that you do so later on when you are applying the protective coat. If you use a fast-drying varnish instead, the design may crack. With the many synthetic products on the market today, it would be a good idea to check with your paint salesman about slowing-down agents for particular varnishes. Never shake or stir varnish. This produces bubbles of air that are hard to get out.

H. Stenciling: You are now ready to apply color to your design piece. This is done by positioning the stencil over it and applying color over the cutout sections.

Bronze stenciling: Put a small mound of bronze powder on velours palette. Separate each color from the other by 1½ inches. Place the #1 stencil over the varnished piece. (See Photograph 6-11.) The stencil should adhere slightly to the surface. Wrap a piece of silk-backed velvet around your index finger, holding the ends in the palm of your hand. Pick up a few grains of bronze from the edge of the mound onto the velvet. If

Photograph 6-11

you get more than you want, tap the velvet on the velours to remove some. Work from the edge of the stencil toward the center, applying the bronze with a light but brisk oscillating motion. (See Photograph 6-12.) Heavy pressure will tend

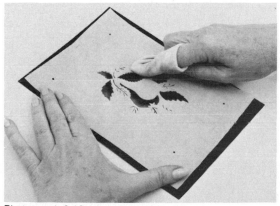

Photograph 6-12

to scar the varnished surface. Keep the finger in contact with the surface while applying the bronze. Never dab it on. Follow the shading in your design as you apply the bronze. Learn how to create the fading-into-shadow effect by practicing. Repeat this procedure for each stencil. (See Photographs 6-13 and 6-14.)

If one of your stencils is a detail stencil, do the detail first. For example, if you are doing leaves, stencil the veins first. (See Photograph 6-15.) Immediately position the open stencil of the leaf around the veins and shadow it in with bronze.

Photograph 6-13

Photograph 6-14

Photograph 6-15

Color stenciling: For color stenciling on walls, wood, or metal, use either oil paints or water-base paints. Hold the stencil down firmly so that it will not move when you are applying the color. Dip the brush into paint and remove the excess by rubbing it across a piece of scrap paper or paper towel. With the brush held in vertical position, apply the paint over the holes in the stencil. Do not stroke back against the edges of the stencil or you will get a heavy color build-up against its edge. If more then one stencil is being used, allow the paint to dry between stencil applications. Follow the color in the design as a guide for shading.

When you are stenciling on fabric, use textile or fabric paints. Follow the instructions that come with the paint to set the color. Cover your work surface entirely with wrapping paper. Your work surface should be large enough for the entire fabric to lie flat. Place a white blotter or a double thickness of paper towels over the wrapping paper surface and place the fabric on top. Fasten the fabric for extra support with masking tape or transparent tape. Do not pin the fabric unless it is to be used as an appliqué piece. Use a palette pad or a doubled sheet of waxed paper for a surface on which to mix colors. Place a tiny dab of each color on the palette and mix colors with your stencil brush, using only the tip of the brush. (A small amount of white is often added to a color mixture when a bright color is desired on a dark fabric. When mixing colors that contain white, add some extender.) Position the stencil on the fabric and hold firmly in place. Dip the tip of the stencil brush into the color and rub it over scrap paper to remove excess. Working off the surface of the stencil into the opening, apply the paint. Brush the paint onto the fabric with light strokes, making more strokes where darker color is desired and fewer strokes for lighter tints. Follow your design for shading. Do not scrub or pound the paint into the fabric; paint should not show through to the opposite side. If you make a mistake or get paint on the fabric where you do not want it, immediately wash out the spot with cold water and soap. Hot water might set the color in and make the spot impossible to remove. Use a different brush for each color you use, or clean them each time you change the color, using dry-cleaning fluid, mineral spirits, paint thinner, or soap and cold water. Then reshape them and allow to dry. When finished stenciling, immediately clean the stencils with dry-cleaning fluid, mineral spirits, or paint thinner.

I. Overlaying design with transparent colors: Interesting and brilliant displays can be achieved by painting over selected areas of the bronze stencil design with oil paints. Place a

small container beside the palette. Varnish controls the intensity of oil paint. For dark colors use a small amount of color; use more for lighter colors. Using a #1 or liner brush, apply paints to selected areas of the design. (See Photograph 6-16.)

Photograph 6-16

J. Varnishing the stenciled design: For protection, at least two coats of varnish should be applied over wood or metal surfaces. For color stenciling, use a clear vinyl varnish. For bronze stenciling, be sure to use the same type of varnish that was used before. In other words, the varnish should take the same amount of time to dry. (Sometimes a slow-drying varnish may be used over a fast-drying varnish, but a fast-drying varnish can never be used over a slow one.) Allow each coat of varnish to thoroughly dry before applying subsequent coats. Between coats, rub over varnish lightly with #0000 steel wool and wipe away all residue with a lint-free cloth. After the final coat of varnish has been applied, rub with steel wool again and wipe away residue. Apply a coat of paste wax for protection.

Bronze Stencil
Clock Plaque

This handsome clock plaque can be placed in almost any room of the house. Although designed for a 14- by 14-inch plaque, the pattern can be adapted to any size or shape.

Materials

1 piece of wood, 1½ inches thick, 14 by 14 inches
electric drill
chisel
small hammer
garnet paper, #350
sandpaper, #400
lint-free cloth or tack rag
Treasure Sealer
1 paintbrush, ½ to 2 inches wide, sable or camel's hair
oil-base paint, in lamp black
2 sheets tracing paper, 8½ by 11 inches
masking tape
technical fountain pen
waterproof india ink, in black
pencil

architects' tracing linen
1 sheet of glass, 8 by 10 inches
surgical, decoupage, or embroidery scissors
X-acto knife
varnish, slow-drying
bronze powders, in pale gold and silver
velours palette
silk-backed velvet pieces
steel wool, #0000
numbers for clock, ⅝ inch high, gold paper braid
Treasure Gold, in classic gold
soft cloth
ruler
white glue
10 feet metallic cord, in gold
paste wax
clock works, Westclox TR-3 Transistor Battery Clock
     Kit or the equivalent
picture hanger

Instructions

1. Make the wooden plaque—or have it made for you—according to Diagram 6-2. If you are making it yourself, cut out the plaque with an electric saw. Use an electric drill to make the center hole and a small hammer and chisel to make the cutout section in the back. Prepare the plaque according to step A in Basic Instructions for Bronze Stenciling.

2. Trace following design pattern onto tracing

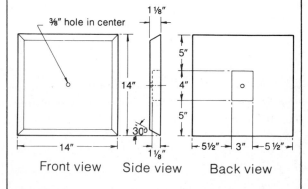

Front view   Side view   Back view

Diagram 6-2

paper with technical fountain pen and india ink. Be sure to include the register lines. (See Photograph 6-17.) Two stencils will be needed for the

Photograph 6-17

outer design, and one stencil will be needed for the center. The shaded areas are #1 units, the unshaded areas are #2 units, and the center design is a #3 unit.

3. Referring to step E in Basic Instructions, trace #1 units onto an 8- by 8-inch piece of architects' tracing linen. The edges of the linen should overlap the tracing paper design by ½ inch. (See Photograph 6-18.) Trace #2 units

Photograph 6-18

onto another 8- by 8-inch piece of linen and #3 units onto a 4- by 4-inch piece in the same manner. (See Photographs 6-19 and 6-20.)

4. Cut out each of the three stencils, following instructions in step F.

Photograph 6-19

Photograph 6-20

5. Apply one coat of varnish to the beveled edge of the plaque, making sure not to get varnish on the face of the plaque. When the varnish has reached the tacky stage, apply a heavy coat of pale gold bronze powder to the beveled edge.

6. Once the beveled edge has dried, apply an even coat of varnish to the front face of the plaque. Set aside in a dust-free area until it has dried to the tacky stage, as described in step G of Basic Instructions.

7. Position stencil #1 over one corner of the plaque, dull side up, with register lines exactly over the corner. Follow directions in step H to apply pale gold bronze powder. Shade from the ends of the flower petals to their centers; that is, make the centers darker. Change velvet fingers and apply silver bronze powder to small flower

Photograph 6-21

Photograph 6-23

petals and scrolls. (See Photograph 6-21.) Do all four corners in the same manner.

8.   Align the register lines of stencil #2 with one corner of the plaque. Repeating the same stenciling procedure, apply pale gold bronze powder to all leaves. The ends of the leaves should be dark, with center veins gradually fading into shadow. Do each corner in this manner. (See Photograph 6-22.)

Photograph 6-22

9.   Center stencil #3 over the hole in the middle of the plaque, with the tips of the design shape pointing at appropriate positions for numbers 12, 2, 4, 6, 8, and 10. (See Photograph 6-23.) In the same manner as before, apply pale gold bronze powder. Lift the stencil and rotate it so that tips will be pointing at positions for numbers 1, 3, 5, 7, 9, and 11. Apply pale gold powder. (See Photograph 6-24.) Allow to dry for at least 24 hours before proceeding.

Photograph 6-24

10.   With sable or camel's hair brush, apply two coats of varnish to the entire plaque, allowing 24 hours between coats. Lightly rub with steel wool, and wipe clean with a lint-free cloth or tack rag.

11.   Paint the clock numbers with lamp black oil-base paint, and allow to dry. Apply Treasure Gold to each number with your fingers, and immediately burnish with a soft cloth.

12.   Place a ruler across the center design, lining up opposite points. Make a mark 3 inches from each tip of the center design, and attach the appropriate clock number over each mark with white glue. (See Photograph 6-25.)

13.   Adhere gold cord to top and bottom beveled plaque edge. (See Photograph 6-26.)

14.   Apply a coat of paste wax to the face of the clock. Assemble the clock works and hands onto the clock, according to directions that come with them. Attach a picture hanger to top back center of the clock.

Bronze Stencil
Wastepaper Basket

An attractive piece to add to a den or Victorian-style bathroom, this wastepaper basket is stenciled with silver powders and then painted with transparent oil paints.

Materials

metal wastepaper basket, oval-shaped, 7 by 10½ by
   13 inches
Rustoleum
sandpaper, #400
line-free cloth or tack rag
1 paintbrush, ½ to 2 inches wide, sable or camel's hair
oil-base paint, in lamp black
2 sheets tracing paper, 11 by 15 inches
masking tape
technical fountain pen
waterproof india ink, in black
pencil
3 sheets architects' tracing linen, 11 by 13 inches
1 sheet of glass, 8 by 10 inches

211

surgical, decoupage, or embroidery scissors

X-acto knife

varnish, slow drying

bronze powder, in silver

velours palette

silk-backed velvet pieces

transparent oil paints, in alizarin crimson, Indian yellow, and Prussian blue

palette pad

#1 or liner brush

5 feet metallic braid, ¼ inch wide, in gold

white glue

steel wool, #0000

paste wax

soft cloth

Instructions

1. Follow step A in Basic Stenciling Instructions to prepare the metal basket for stenciling.

2. Position and center the short end of a sheet of tracing paper over the grape-leaf design. With the technical fountain pen and india ink, carefully trace the design, making sure to include the dotted grapes. (See Photograph 6-27.) Turn the tracing paper, and position over the fruit-grape-leaf design; align dotted grapes over top grapes and leaf over dotted leaf. Carefully trace the fruit-grape-leaf design with the technical foun-

Photograph 6-28

tain pen and india ink. (See Photograph 6-28.) There are three stencil units to this design. Areas of the design that have no shading are #1 units, dotted areas are #2 units, and lined areas are #3 units.

3. Place a piece of architects' tracing linen over tracing paper design, dull side up, overlapping the design by 1 inch on all sides. Following directions in step E of Basic Stenciling Instructions, trace #1 design units onto tracing linen. (See Photograph 6-29.) Trace #3 leaf veins. Re-

Photograph 6-27

212

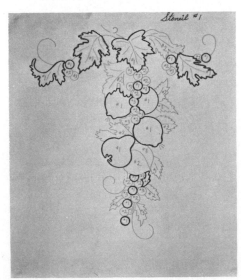

Photograph 6-29

213

move stencil #1 from the design tracing. In the same manner as before, trace #2 units onto a second piece of architects' tracing linen. (See Photograph 6-30.) Remove stencil #2 and tape the third piece of architects' linen over the design. Trace all #3 areas onto linen, as shown in Photograph 6-31. Trace veins of #1 leaves.

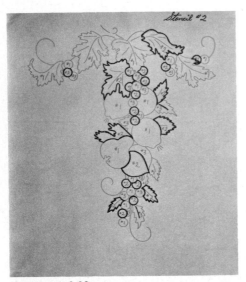

Photograph 6-30

Photograph 6-31

4. According to instructions in step F of Basic Instructions, cut out the three stencils.

5. Apply an even coat of varnish to one side of the wastepaper basket. Set basket aside in a dust-free place until it has dried to the tacky stage.

6. Test the varnish as described in step G of Basic Stenciling Instructions. When it has reached the proper stage, place it on your work surface, varnished surface up. Apply silver bronze powder over stencil #1 on the front center of the wastebasket, following directions in step H. (See Photograph 6-32.) Shade from the edge

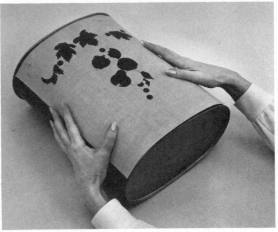

Photograph 6-32

of the opening to the center. Your pattern of shading should be consistent, or, in other words, reflecting the same light source, as shown in Photograph 6-33. Remove stencil #1. Position

Photograph 6-33

214

stencil #2 on basket, using the stenciled forms as a guide for positioning. Apply the silver bronze to #2 units in the same manner. Apply the powder heavily and burnish in areas where strong light is indicated. Gradually fade to black in shadowed parts of the design. (See Photograph 6-34.) Position stencil #3 and apply silver

Photograph 6-34

bronze powder. (See Photograph 6-35.) Allow the pieces to dry for 24 hours. Varnish and stencil the other side of the basket in the same manner, and allow to dry for 24 hours.

Photograph 6-35

7. Place a dab each of alizarin crimson, Indian yellow, and Prussian blue on your palette; set a small container of varnish beside it. Mix colors and apply over design with a #1 or liner brush. The amount of varnish used will determine the intensity level of the color. (See Photograph 6-36.) Allow to dry for 24 hours.

8. Apply two coats of varnish, allowing 24 hours between coats. Place in a dust-free area to dry. After the second coat of varnish has thoroughly dried, use white glue to adhere metallic braid around top and bottom edges of the wastepaper basket. Lightly smooth surface with steel wool, apply a coat of paste wax, and buff.

Photograph 6-36

Bronze Stencil Wastepaper Basket (See page 211.)

Playtime Stool

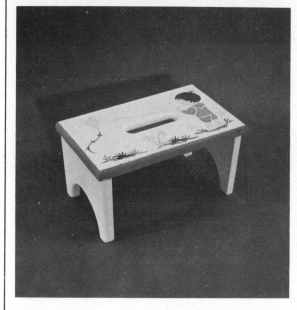

Here is a perfect gift for a toddler and an attractive addition to his room. The stool is stenciled in Dutch style, which is basically the absence of shading. Follow Color Suggestions or choose your own color scheme.

Materials

1 stool, 7 inches high, with 7- by 12-inch top
garnet paper, #350
sandpaper, #400
lint-free cloth or tack rag
Treasure Sealer
1 paintbrush, ½ to 2 inches wide, sable or camel's hair
7 jars acrylic paint, 2-ounce size, in white, light blue, medium green, light yellow, pink, terra cotta, and fleshtone
2 sheets tracing paper, 8½ by 11 inches
masking tape
technical fountain pen
waterproof india ink, in black
pencil
architects' tracing linen
1 sheet of glass, 8 by 10 inches
surgical, decoupage, or embroidery scissors
X-acto knife
paper towels
stencil brushes, #2 and #6
brush-cleaning solution
mineral spirits
#1 or liner brush
1 can clear vinyl varnish

Instructions

1. Prepare the stool according to step A in Basic Stenciling Instructions, applying two coats of white acrylic paint. Allow 2 hours drying time between coats. After sanding lightly with #400 sandpaper and wiping clean, apply two coats of light blue acrylic paint to the top edge of the stool.

2. With technical fountain pen and india ink, trace the following design onto a sheet of tracing paper. Be sure to include the corner line. The design requires two stencils. The unshaded areas are #1 units, and the shaded areas are #2 units.

3. Following step E in Basic Stenciling Instruc-

tions, trace #1 units onto a piece of architects' tracing linen. (See Photograph 6-37.) Remove the linen and repeat procedure for #2 units. (See Photograph 6-38.)

Photograph 6-37

Photograph 6-38

4. Cut out both stencils according to directions in step F.
5. Position stencil #1 on top of the stool, with corner mark over the lower right-hand corner of the stool. Follow Color Suggestions chart or choose your own colors. Paint all #1 units (see Photograph 6-39), and clean brush immediately. After this area has dried, move the stencil over to the upper left-hand corner and stencil the kite. (See Photograph 6-40.) Remove the stencil, and clean with mineral spirits. Clean and dry the brush. Allow the stool to dry for about 30 minutes.
6. Follow same procedure to paint #2 units. (See Photograph 6-41.) Make sure that pants align with legs, sleeve with wrist, collar with

Photograph 6-39

Photograph 6-40

neck, and hair with face. Follow chart for colors. After you have stenciled the two clumps of grass, reposition the stencil to do the grass beneath the kite. Stencil a shrub of dark green grass between shrubs of light green, if you wish. Allow 30 minutes drying time before repositioning stencil. (See Photograph 6-42.)

Photograph 6-41

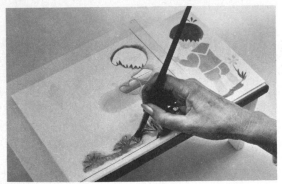

Photograph 6-42

Color Suggestions

Part	Color	Brush
face, neck, hands, and legs	fleshtone	#6 stencil brush
flower petals	pink	#2 stencil brush
flower centers	yellow	#2 stencil brush
cowlick and kite tail	terra cotta	#2 stencil brush
kite	light yellow	#6 stencil brush
suit	blue	#6 stencil brush
hair	terra cotta	#6 stencil brush
stems	green	#2 stencil brush
2 clumps of grass	light green	#2 stencil brush
1 clump of grass	dark green	#2 stencil brush

7. With a #1 or liner brush and terra cotta paint, outline the face, neck, hands, legs, and kite. Paint a line for the kite string, extending from kite to the hand. Paint in eyelashes.

8. Apply two coats of varnish to the entire stool, allowing 24 hours between coats.

220

Stenciled
Appliqué Shirt

The design for this shirt is stenciled on white broad-cloth, cut out, and appliquéd onto the shirt. The reason for this is that colors show up much better on white backgrounds than on darker backgrounds. If you wish, however, choose a light-colored shirt and stencil the design directly onto it.

Materials

man's work shirt, denim or chambray, in light blue
½ yard broadcloth, in white
flat or steam iron
several sheets tracing paper, 8½ by 11 inches
masking tape
technical fountain pen
waterproof india ink, in black
pencil
architects' tracing linen
1 sheet of glass, 8 by 10 inches
surgical, decoupage, or embroidery scissors

X-acto knife

1 large sheet of wrapping paper

paper towels

drawing board, 20 by 24 inches

thumbtacks

textile paints, in yellow, blue, red, green, black, and white

extender

stencil brushes, #2 and #6

brush-cleaning solution

mineral spirits

straight pins

½ yard Stitch Witchery

pressing cloth

embroidery needle, #7

embroidery floss, in colors to match or contrast with paint colors

thread, #50, in white

Instructions

1. Wash, dry, and press the ½ yard of white broadcloth. All the sizing must be removed from the material if the textile paints are to work well.

2. Following instructions in the Helpful Hints chapter, enlarge design pattern by 50 percent. If you are using the grid method of enlarging, each square should measure 1 inch. Trace enlarged design pattern parts onto tracing paper with technical fountain pen and india ink.

3. Most of the design parts require more than one stencil and different sizes of architects' tracing linen. Follow table below for stencil designations and sizes of linen to cut. Starting with the first stencil on the list, cut the linen to the size designated, position over appropriate tracing paper design pattern, and trace design with technical fountain pen and india ink. Remove architects' tracing linen and proceed to the next stencil on the list. For those stencils that are marked A, trace the entire shape. These are the outline stencils. (See Photographs 6-43 to 6-48.)

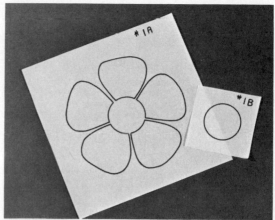

Photograph 6-43

Photograph 6-44

Photograph 6-45

221

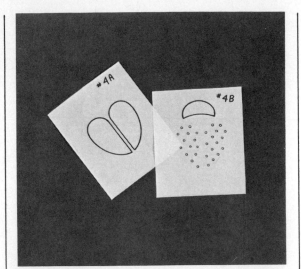

Photograph 6-46

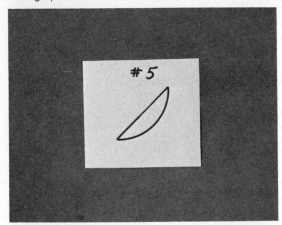

Photograph 6-47

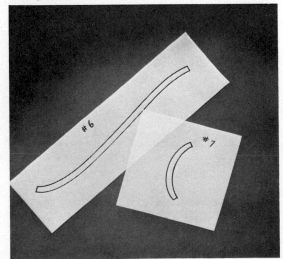

Photograph 6-48

Sizes of Architects' Tracing Linen

Stencil	Sizes of Linen to Cut
1A	9 by 9 inches
1B	3½ by 3½ inches
2A	5½ by 5½ inches
2B	5½ by 5½ inches
2C	2 by 2 inches
3A	4½ by 4½ inches
3B	2 by 2 inches
4A	5 by 6 inches
4B	5 by 6 inches
5	2 by 4 inches
6	3½ by 14 inches
7	4 by 4 inches

4. Following directions in step F of Basic Instructions, cut out all stencils.

5. Refer to step C in Basic Stenciling Instructions before stenciling the design shapes. Cut the broadcloth to fit the drawing board. Fasten one side of the broadcloth to the drawing board with thumbtacks, stretch taut, and fasten the other side. The cloth must be stretched tight in order to do stencil work properly. Follow chart below for stencils, stencil brushes, colors, and amounts of each shape to make. Shapes 7 and 8 are placed alongside each other to make a whole leaf. When working on shapes that are repeated, work on one stencil at a time. For example, for shape 3, stencil #2A for all three shapes before stenciling #2B. Mix red paint with white and add extender to get pink shades. Mix blue with white and extender to get light blue. Mix green with white and add extender to get light green. (See Photographs 6-49 through 6-55.) Clean the brush between

Photograph 6-49

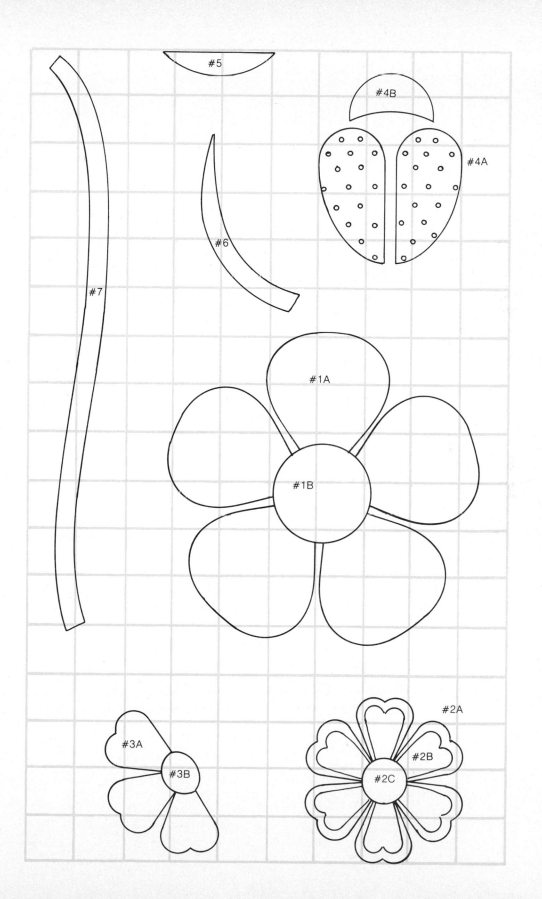

#5

#4B

#4A

#6

#7

#1A

#1B

#3A

#3B

#2A

#2B

#2C

223

Photograph 6-50

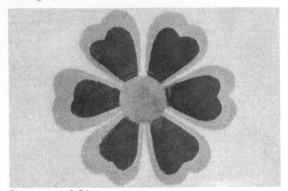

Photograph 6-51

Photograph 6-52

Photograph 6-53

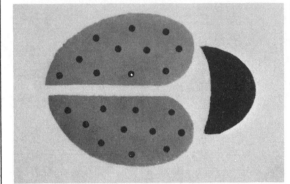

Photograph 6-54

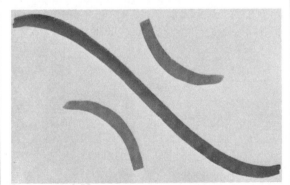

Photograph 6-55

224

color applications or use a different brush for each color. Clean each stencil with mineral spirits.

Stenciling Instructions

Shape Number	Amount	Stencil	Stencil Brush	Color
1	1	1A	#6	yellow
		1B	#6	blue
2	1	2A	#6	yellow
		2C	#6	blue
3	3	2A	#6	light pink
		2B	#6	dark pink
4	2	2A	#6	light blue
		2B	#6	dark blue
		2C	#6	dark pink
5	1	3A	#6	yellow
		3B	#6	blue
6	1	4A	#2	red
		4B	#2	black
7	29	5	#6	light green
8	29	5	#6	green
9	1	6	#6	green
10	1	7	#6	green

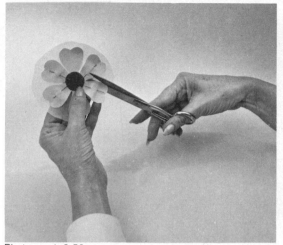
Photograph 6-56

6. Cut out all flowers, leaves, stems, and ladybug from the broadcloth. Follow the directions that come with the textile paints to set colors.

7. With straight pins, attach all cutout pieces to Stitch Witchery. Trim outlines so that the edges of the Stitch Witchery will not show. (See Photograph 6-56.)

8. Follow Diagram 6-3 to arrange the design on the back of the shirt, and attach with straight

Front view

Back view

Diagram 6-3

225

Photograph 6-57

Photograph 6-58

pins. Make sure that the Stitch Witchery is directly under each part and not protruding from the edges. Place a pressing cloth over the design. Following directions on the Stitch Witchery package, apply an iron to adhere the appliqué pieces to the shirt. Turn the shirt over. Arrange and attach the design to the front of the shirt in the same manner. (See Photograph 6-57.)

9. Using embroidery needle and floss, make buttonhole stitches around the outline of each appliqué, as shown in Diagram 6-4. Remove pins. (See Photograph 6-58.)

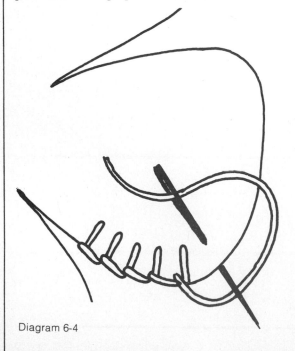

Diagram 6-4

Stenciled Appliqué Shirt

Wildflower
Snack Tray

This attractive snack tray may be used to serve hors d'oeuvres or simply to display in your china cabinet.

Materials

1 metal tray, ⅝ inch deep, 8 by 8 inches Rustoleum

sandpaper, #400 and #600

lint-free cloth or tack rag

4 jars acrylic or oil paints, 2-ounce size, in olive green, dark blue-green, brown, and white

1 paintbrush, ½ to 2 inches wide, sable or camel's hair

2 sheets tracing paper, 10 by 10 inches

masking tape

technical fountain pen

waterproof india ink, in black

pencil

architects' tracing linen

1 sheet of glass, 8 by 10 inches

surgical, decoupage, or embroidery scissors

X-acto knife

stencil brush, #2

brush-cleaning solution

mineral spirits

liner or #1 brush

1 can clear vinyl varnish

paste wax

soft cloth

Instructions

1. Follow directions in step A of Basic Stenciling Instructions to prepare the metal tray. Apply one coat of olive green paint to entire tray, and allow to dry thoroughly. Sand lightly with #400 sandpaper, wipe clean with a lint-free cloth or tack rag, and apply a second coat of olive green. Sand lightly and wipe clean.

2. Following directions in the Helpful Hints chapter, enlarge design by 15 percent. If you are using the grid method of enlarging, each square should measure 1 inch. Place a sheet of tracing paper over the enlarged design, and trace with technical fountain pen and india ink. Three stencils will be needed for this design. The unshaded areas are #1 units, the dotted areas are #2 units, and lined areas are #3 units.

3. Cut three 8- by 8-inch squares of architects' tracing linen. Following directions in step E of

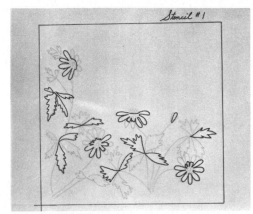

Photograph 6-59

Basic Instructions, trace #1 units onto one piece of tracing linen, #2 units on a second piece, and #3 units on a third. (See Photographs 6-59, 6-60, and 6-61.)

4. Following step F in Basic Instructions, cut out the three stencils. Make a 1-inch-long diagonal cut at each corner of the linen so that the

stencil will lie flat in the bottom of the tray.
5. Mix blue paint with a small amount of white to make a medium blue, and mix dark blue-green with brown and a touch of white to make a medium olive green. Position stencil #1 on the bottom of the tray. With the #2 stencil brush, apply the blue to flower petals and olive green to leaves. Clean and dry the brush after use of each

color. Remove the stencil, clean it, and allow paint to dry. (See Photograph 6-62.)

6. Mix dark blue-green paint with brown to

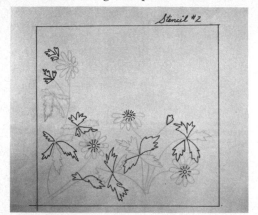

Photograph 6-60

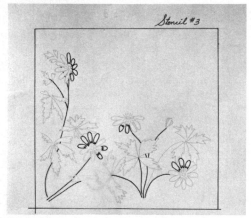

Photograph 6-61

Photograph 6-62

make a dark olive green. Position stencil #2 on the bottom of the tray, making sure that the flower centers are correctly located. Apply white to all flower centers and dark olive green to the leaves. Remove the stencil and allow the paint to dry. (See Photograph 6-63.)

7. Mix dark blue-green and a little white to make a shade of blue that is slightly darker than the blue made for stencil #1. Position stencil #3 in the bottom of the tray, and apply blue to flower petals. Apply dark olive green to stems. Remove the stencil and allow the paint to dry. (See Photograph 6-64.)

8. With the #1 or liner brush and the appropriate color, complete any stems that are not

Photograph 6-63

properly connected and touchup where necessary. Allow the paint to thoroughly dry.

9. Apply two coats of varnish to the tray, allowing 24 hours between coats. After the second coat has dried for 24 hours, sand with #400 sandpaper, wipe clean with a lint-free cloth or tack rag, and apply two more coats of varnish at 24-hour intervals. Allow the final coat of varnish to dry for 24 hours, sand lightly with #600 sandpaper, and wipe clean. Apply a coat of paste wax and wipe with a soft cloth.

Photograph 6-64

230

7

Theorem Painting on Velvet

Theorem painting is simply another term for stenciling. Stenciling is a technique that involves separating a design into groups of units; tracing each group of units onto a stiff piece of paper; cutting out the units; placing the cutout paper over a wood, paper, metal, or fabric surface; and applying color over the cutout sections in the paper. Theorem painting on velvet, therefore, is stenciling onto velvet surfaces.

When the early settlers left England and came to America, they brought with them the art of painting on velvet. From the 1790s to the early 1800s, painting on velvet was considered an integral part of the curriculum in finishing schools. Since velvet was a difficult material on which to work and since most of the young ladies were not adept at freehand painting, a stenciling approach to painting on velvet was introduced in 1830. It was called theorem painting because of the logical, formulated manner in which designs were separated into units. This was the start of a new art in the United States. However, the very first theorem painting on velvet designs were done in England in 1805.

The stencils used for the early works were made of thin paper that had been treated with linseed oil, dried thoroughly, and coated on both sides with varnish for strength. The designs were traced onto the stencils, the stencils were cut out, and the designs were transferred to velvet. There is some controversy over the type of velvet that was used, since the velvet backgrounds on early works are a creamy beige color. Some experts say that ordinary white cotton velvet was used and that the creamy beige quality is the result of a normal aging process. Others say that the velvet was dyed in tea water to create that color. In any case, the velvet was stretched on a work surface and brushed well to remove dust from the nap. The design was stenciled with watercolors and stiff short-handled brushes. After the paint had dried thoroughly, the velvet was brushed again. Details and finishing touches were done freehand, after stenciling.

From 1830 to 1860, theorem painting on velvet was particularly popular throughout New England. Many well-preserved works can be seen at the Abby Aldrich Rockefeller Folk Art Collection, in Williamsburg, Virginia; The New York State Historical Association, in Cooperstown, New York; the Shelbourne Museum, in Vermont; and Old Sturbridge Village, in Massachusetts.

Theorem Painting on Velvet Materials and Tools

With a few exceptions, the tools and materials needed to do theorem painting on velvet are basically the same as those needed to do stenciling.

The first major difference is, of course, the velvet. Purchase either cotton velvet or velveteen in the white or creamy beige color. Make sure that the material has not been treated with a fabric protector. After you have cut the velvet to the appropriate size, you will be stretching it out and attaching it to a sheet of heavy cardboard or posterboard. Sheets of many different sizes will be needed in the following projects.

The next step will be to trace the design pattern onto tracing paper. Purchase large rolls of tracing paper so that you will be able to cut sheets to the sizes you need. The designs are traced onto the tracing paper with a technical fountain pen, #00 point size, and waterproof black india ink. Also needed will be sheets of thin paper, such as notebook paper, to be used as masks for the velvet. The stencil is made with architects' tracing linen. The waterproof type is best. If, however, you must purchase the old-fashioned starch sizing type, be careful not to get it wet. Moisture will distort the linen. After the design has been traced onto the architects' tracing linen, it will be cut out. Tools used for cutting stencils are surgical, decoupage, or embroidery scissors; an X-acto knife; and a dental or paper punch. When working with the X-acto knife, you will need a sheet of glass to place over your work surface. Use the

#11 blade of the X-acto knife, and sharpen it often with a carborundum stone. Make sure that the edges of all scissors you use are clean and sharp. Dental punches or paper punches are useful for punching small holes in the design.

Most of the projects in this chapter require transparent oil paints. For the most part, alizarin crimson, Indian yellow, and Prussian blue are the only colors you will need. Make sure that the colors you have selected are transparent or semi-transparent. Opaque colors tend to cake on the velvet. To test them for transparency, apply some color to a sheet of glass and hold it up to the light. Colors are mixed with a palette knife on disposable palette pads or sheets of waxed paper.

To apply paint to velvet, you will need small pieces of wool flannel or 3- by 3-inch polyurethane sponges. An alternative to using either of these methods is to use #2 and #6 stencil brushes. You will also need a #1 liner brush or scroller brush. These are used for detail work.

Additional items needed are scissors, old paintbrushes for applying glue, a ruler, a pencil, masking tape, straight pins, a needle, turpentine, and various colors of thread.

Basic Theorem Painting on Velvet Instructions

The goal of theorem painting on velvet work is to make an exact reproduction of a colored design in the "soft look" style of velvet painting. Read the following instructions before beginning your projects.

A. Preparing the velvet: If you want your velvet backgrounds to have the creamy beige quality found in the older works and you have not been able to purchase that color, dye the white velvet. Place two tea bags in a gallon of hot water and let it stand for about 10 minutes. Agitate the water by dipping the tea bags up and down a few times. Squeeze the tea bags to remove their water and dispose of them. Dip the velvet into the warm tea water and gently agitate it so that the water will

soak through the material. Lift the velvet out of the water and, if possible, hang it outside to dry. The velvet should dry straight and free of wrinkles. If it should wrinkle, use a steamer or steam it over a teakettle or bathtub full of hot water.

Cut the velvet and a sheet of heavy cardboard or posterboard to appropriate size. Tightly stretch the velvet across the cardboard; secure it to the back side with masking tape. (See Photograph 7-1.)

Photograph 7-1

B. Selecting the design: Baskets or urns of flowers and fruits and other types of still-life designs are typical subjects for theorem painting on velvet. But landscapes, figure studies, or any design that you have the ability and patience to separate into stencils can also be theorem painted.

C. Tracing the design: Place a sheet of tracing paper over the design and secure it with masking tape. With the technical fountain pen and india ink, carefully trace the entire design onto tracing paper. Be sure to include all details. Untape and remove the tracing. Draw a border around the design, about 1 inch beyond the extremities. This will be used as a register mark. (See Photograph 7-2.)

D. Separating the design into units: Place the

233

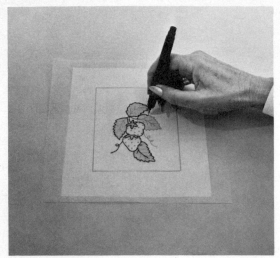

Photograph 7-2

tracing paper design on your work surface. Starting at the center of the design and working toward the outside, pencil a light #1 on all parts of the design that do not touch one another. These are the #1 units. Go over the design a second time, placing a light #2 on units that do not touch one another, but may touch #1 units. Continue in this manner until every part of the design has been included in a group of units. (If you wish, units may be separated according to color rather than relative position.) If there are three groups of units, there will be three stencils. In the projects that follow, I have already designated units by patterns of shading. When you are using designs from other sources, however, you

Diagram 7-1A

will have to separate them into units by yourself. (See Diagrams 7-1A and B.

E. Tracing the design onto tracing linen: For each stencil, cut a piece of architects' tracing linen that will be large enough to cover the design and the border around it. Position one of the pieces of linen on top of the traced design and secure it with masking tape. With the technical fountain pen and india ink, trace all #1 units and the border. (See Photograph 7-3.) Pencil in a #1 on top of the linen. Remove the linen and place a second piece on top of the traced design. Secure with masking tape. Trace all #2 units and the border in the same manner. (See Photograph 7-4.) Continue this procedure until all groups of

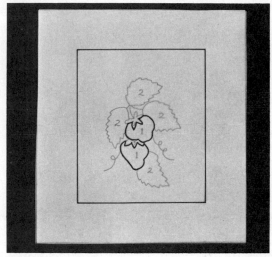

Photograph 7-3

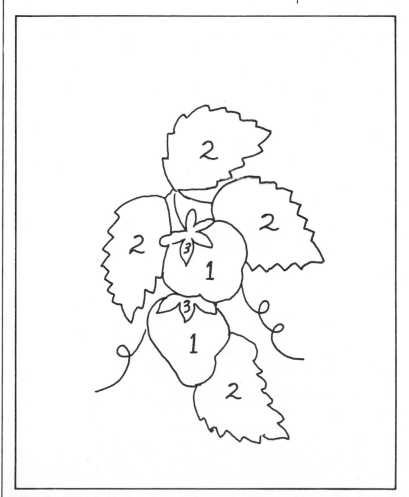

Diagram 7-1B

235

Photograph 7-4

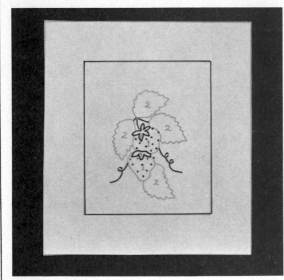

Photograph 7-5

units have been traced onto a piece of linen. (See Photograph 7-5.)

F. Cutting the stencil: The best way to start the cut is to punch a hole in the center of the unit with an X-acto knife. Switch to surgical, decoupage, or embroidery scissors for the actual cutting. Hold the scissors with the thumb and third finger in the handles and the blade resting against the index finger. Insert the blade through the linen from the underside. Keeping the blades in a perpendicular position to the linen, feed the linen into the throat of the scissors. Do not move the scissors. (See Photograph 7-6.)

For tiny holes, punch through with a dental punch, X-acto knife, or darning needle. If you are using the darning needle or X-acto knife, however, you must then snip around the hole with scissors. It may even be necessary to turn the linen over and sand down the trimmed edges. When working with an X-acto knife, it is a good idea to place linen over a sheet of glass.

G. Masking the velvet: Cut a piece of thin paper, such as vellum or notebook paper, to the same size as the velvet. Place this paper over the tracing paper design pattern and trace the border. Cut along the border on the notebook paper. The area within the border should be exactly the same size as the area within the border of each stencil. Position this mask over velvet and secure with masking tape. (See Photograph 7-7.) The mask serves two purposes. It protects the edges of the velvet from getting dirty and serves as a register for your stencils.

H. Mixing the paints: Place a small amount of your transparent oil paints on the palette. Three colors—alizarin crimson, Indian yellow, and Prussian blue—are the only colors you will need. From them you can mix a multitude of colors. Memorize the basic color formulas that follow.

Color	Formula
green	Indian yellow + Prussian blue
orange	Indian yellow + alizarin crimson
brown	Indian yellow + Prussian blue + alizarin crimson

236

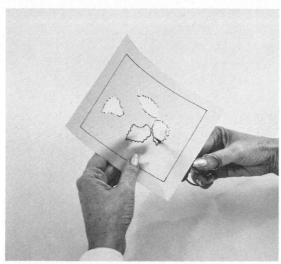

Photograph 7-6

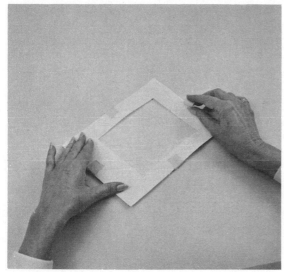

Photograph 7-7

In most painting work, varnish is added to transparent oil paints to control their intensity level. In other words, if you wanted a light orange, you would mix Indian yellow with alizarin crimson and add varnish. When working on velvet, however, varnish cannot be used. The intensity of the color must be controlled by the pressure exerted in applying the paint.

I. Stenciling: Position stencil #1 on the velvet, aligning its border with the outline of the mask. Secure with masking tape, as shown in Photograph 7-8. There are three ways in which paint can be applied to velvet. The first method is to wrap a piece of wool flannel around your index finger and dip it into the paint. Another method is to dip a stencil brush into the paint. The third method is to hold a 3- by 3-inch polyurethane sponge by its corners, thus forming a ball shape, and dip the ball section into paint. (See Photograph 7-9.) Although I prefer the third method, you may use either one. After you have dipped the flannel, sponge, or stencil brush into the paint, rub off the excess onto the palette. Working off the surface of the stencil into the cutout sections, apply the paint with a light, but brisk, oscillating motion. Try to work the color into the nap of the velvet.

An important aspect of theorem painting on velvet work is the shading effect. To achieve this, you must learn to control pressure levels when applying paint. Increase the pressure slightly where you want dark shading and decrease it where you want light shading. Changes in shading, however, should be gradual. Light areas should fade into the velvet background. It is also important that you use very little paint, since the application of too much paint will cause caking. The Color Suggestion charts within each project will specify color and shading patterns to be followed.

After you have stenciled all #1 units, remove stencil #1. (See Photograph 7-10.) Allow approximately 10 minutes drying time for the

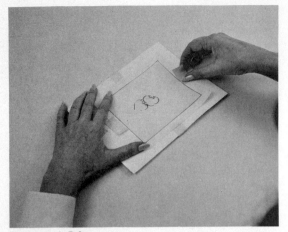

Photograph 7-8

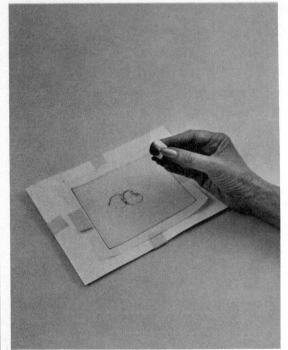

Photograph 7-9

paint. Place stencil #2 on the velvet, aligning the outline with mask, and secure with masking tape. Apply the color to the velvet in the same manner. (See Photograph 7-11.)

Once you have stenciled leaves, you are ready to model center and branch leaf veins. Cut a curved edge on a piece of architects' tracing linen and place over leaf opening, from top to bottom. Stencil off the curved edge of the linen. This will create a dark-shaded, modeled center vein. To do branch veins, move the curved linen to several positions on the leaf, intersecting the center vein.

After all #2 units have been stenciled, remove stencil #2, allow the paint to dry, and position the third stencil. Continue in this manner until all stencils have been completed. (See Photograph 7-12.)

J. Detailing the design: Selected areas of a design may be detailed with a liner brush and paint. This tends to make the design look more like a hand-painted work. (See Photograph 7-13.)

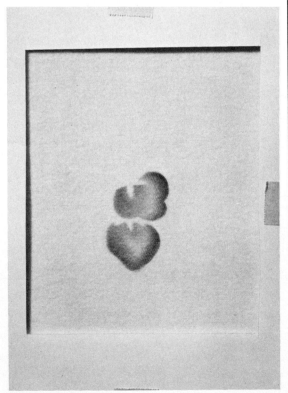

Photograph 7-10

Photograph 7-11

Photograph 7-13

Photograph 7-12

Violet Bouquet Picture

This attractive picture may be displayed on a wall or placed on a table or bureau in a standing frame.

Materials

1 sheet heavy cardboard or posterboard, 6 by 8 inches
1 piece cotton velveteen, 8 by 10 inches, in white
masking tape
1 sheet tracing paper, 6 by 8 inches
technical fountain pen
waterproof india ink, in black
scissors
¼ yard architects' tracing linen
1 sheet of glass, 8 by 10 inches
surgical, decoupage, or embroidery scissors
X-acto knife
1 sheet notebook paper, 8 by 10 inches
transparent oil paints, in alizarin crimson, Indian yellow, Prussian blue, and cerulean blue
disposable palette pad
stencil brushes, #2 and #6; polyurethane sponges, 3 by 3 inches; or wool flannel, small pieces
#1 liner brush or scroller brush
turpentine
1 frame, to fit around cardboard
1 sheet of glass, nonglare, to fit inside frame

Instructions

1. Follow directions in step A of Basic Instructions to prepare the velveteen.
2. Place a sheet of tracing paper over the design and secure in place with masking tape. Use the technical fountain pen and india ink to trace the entire design. Include all details and the border. Three stencils will be needed for this design. The unshaded areas are #1 units, the dotted areas are #2 units, and the lined areas are #3 units.
3. Cut three 6- by 8-inch pieces of architects' tracing linen. Place one piece over tracing paper design and secure in place with masking tape. Referring to step E in Basic Instructions, trace all #1 units and the border. Identify this stencil with a #1 and remove. (See Photograph 7-14.) Follow same procedure for second and third pieces of architects' linen. Be sure to trace the borders around each. (See Photographs 7-15 and 7-16.) Allow ink to dry.

Photograph 7-14

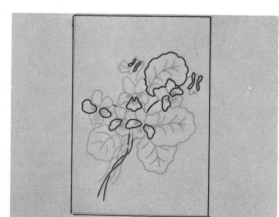

Photograph 7-15

Photograph 7-16

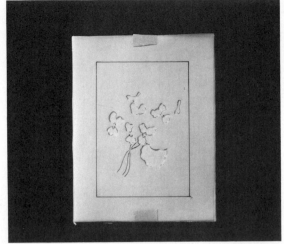

Photograph 7-17

Photograph 7-18

4. Following step F in Basic Instructions, cut out each of the three stencils.

5. Cut a sheet of notebook paper to the same size as the cardboard. Center the traced design on this sheet of paper and trace the border. Cut out the center of the paper, carefully following the traced border. Position the paper mask over the velveteen, align carefully, and secure to the back of the cardboard with masking tape. Do not tape to the face of the velveteen.

6. Position stencil #1 over the velveteen, aligning the border with the outline of the mask, and secure in place with masking tape. (See Photograph 7-17.) Place a dab each of alizarin crimson, Indian yellow, Prussian blue, and cerulean blue on your palette. Following steps H and I of Basic Instructions and Color Suggestions chart, mix colors and stencil #1 units. Paint three stems in a medium green. Use cerulean blue for the flower petals. Cut a piece of tracing linen with a slightly curved edge, and place on top of leaf opening. With medium green, model in the center vein of the leaf, stenciling off the edge of the tracing linen. Do the branch veins in the same manner. (See Photograph 7-18.) Remove stencil #1, and allow paint to dry before proceeding.

7. Position stencil #2 over the velvet, align with the mask, and secure with masking tape. Following the same procedure as before, stencil all #2 units. Paint two stems in a medium green. Model the veins into the leaf in the same manner as before. (See Photograph 7-19.) Remove stencil #2 and allow paint to dry.

8. Position stencil #3 over the velvet. Follow same procedure to stencil and model the veins. (See Photograph 7-20.) Remove stencil #3 and allow drying time for paint, as before.

Color Suggestions

Stencil #1

Part	Color	Shading
flower petals	medium blue	edges dark, centers light
leaf	medium green	upper edge dark, lower edge light

Stencil #2

Part	Color	Shading
flower petals	medium blue	edges dark, centers light
leaf	medium green	edge dark, center light

Stencil #3

Part	Color	Shading
leaves	medium green	upper edges dark, centers light, lower edges medium
flower petals	medium blue	edges dark, centers light

9. With a #1 liner brush, make a very fine outline around leaves, flower petals, and stems. Use a darker shade of the appropriate color. Paint a few fine lines of a darker shade of cerulean blue down the centers of the lower flower petals. (See Photograph 7-21.) Remove paper masks, and clean brushes with turpentine.

10. Assemble frame around cardboard, with glass in front of velveteen design.

Photograph 7-19

Photograph 7-20

Photograph 7-21

243

Basket of Fruit
on Velvet

This beautiful Victorian-style still life is done on a light beige velvet. The soft and delicate coloring is truly representative of this traditional folk art.

Materials

1 sheet heavy cardboard or posterboard, 12 by 15 inches
1 piece cotton velveteen, 14 by 18 inches, in beige
masking tape
1 sheet tracing paper, 9 by 12 inches
technical fountain pen
waterproof india ink, in black
scissors
⅓ yard architects' tracing linen
1 sheet of glass, 8 by 10 inches
surgical, decoupage, or embroidery scissors
X-acto knife
1 sheet notebook paper, 12 by 15 inches
transparent oil paints, in alizarin crimson, Indian yellow, Prussian blue, cerulean blue, and mauve
disposable palette pad
stencil brushes, #2 and #6; polyurethane sponges, 3 by 3 inches; or wool flannel, small pieces
#1 liner brush or scroller brush
turpentine
1 frame, to fit around cardboard
1 sheet of glass, nonglare, to fit inside frame

Instructions

1. Follow directions in step A of Basic Instructions to prepare the velveteen.

2. Enlarge design by 30 percent, according to directions in the Helpful Hints chapter. If you are using the grid method of enlarging, each square should measure 1 inch. Place a sheet of tracing paper over the enlarged design, and secure in place with masking tape. With the technical fountain pen and india ink, trace the entire design. Be sure to include the border and all details. The design will be done with four stencils. The unshaded areas are #1 units, the dotted areas are #2 units, the lined areas are #3 units, and squared areas are #4 units.

3. Cut four 9- by 12-inch pieces of architects' tracing linen. Place one piece of linen over design, and secure with masking tape. Referring to step E in Basic Instructions, trace all #1 units onto linen. Remove linen and repeat procedure

for #2, #3, and #4 units. Be sure to include borders and details on each.

4. Cut out each stencil following step F in Basic Instructions.

5. Cut a sheet of notebook paper to the same size as the cardboard. Center the traced design over the notebook paper, and trace around the border. Cut the center out of the paper, following the outline. Position this mask on the velveteen, with edges aligned, and secure with masking tape. (See Photograph 7-22.)

6. Position stencil #1 on the velveteen, aligning the border with the outline of the mask. Secure with masking tape as shown in Photograph 7-23. Place a dab each of alizarin crimson, Indian yellow, Prussian blue, cerulean blue, and mauve on your palette. Refer to steps H and I in Basic Instructions and Color Suggestions chart

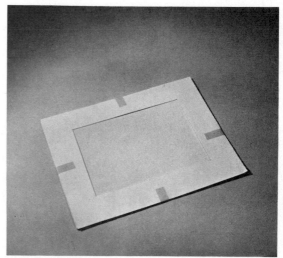

Photograph 7-22

245

Photograph 7-23

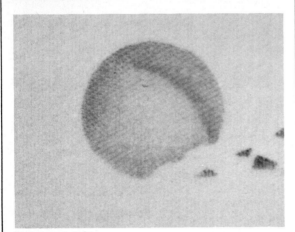

Photograph 7-24

Photograph 7-25

for mixing paints and stenciling instructions. Place the curved edge of a piece of architects' tracing linen over apricot openings and model a dark crease, as shown in Photograph 7-24. Place the curved edge of another piece of linen over each leaf opening and model in the center and branch veins. When you are done with all #1 units, remove the stencil and allow paint to dry. (See Photograph 7-25.)

7. Position and secure stencil #2. Follow same procedure and allow to dry. (See Photograph 7-26.) Remove stencil #2.

8. Position stencil #3 over design pattern and secure with masking tape. Follow same stenciling procedure. Do flower petals with cerulean blue. (See Photograph 7-27.) Remove stencil #3 and allow paint 10 minutes drying time.

9. Position stencil #4, secure with masking tape, and follow the same procedure for stenciling. (See Photograph 7-28.)

Color Suggestions

Stencil #1

Part	Color	Shading
basket weaves	milk chocolate brown	edges dark, centers light
orange	medium orange	edge dark, center light, left edge muted with green
apricots	reddish orange	edges dark, centers light
whole leaves	medium green	bases dark, tips light
pea pod	medium green	tips medium, center light
partial leaf (upper left-hand corner)	dark green	none
partial leaf (left center)	dark green	base dark, tip medium

Photograph 7-26

Photograph 7-27

Stencil #2

Part	Color	Shading
basket weaves	milk chocolate brown	edges dark, centers light
pear	orange yellow	edge dark, center light
lemon (left center), flower center, and flower center borders	medium yellow	muted with light green
cherries and partial apple	red	edges dark, centers light
leaves	medium green	bases dark, tips light
partial leaves and peas	light green	none

Stencil #3

Part	Color	Shading
basket rim and flower center borders	dark milk chocolate brown	edges dark, centers light
front apple and cherries	medium red	edges dark, centers light
flower petals and plum	blue	edges dark and accented with mauve, centers light
whole leaves	medium green	bases dark, centers light
partial leaves	light green	none

247

Stencil #4

Part	Color	Shading
basket rim	dark milk chocolate brown	edges dark, centers light
flower petals	blue	edges dark and muted with mauve, centers light
partial apple	red	above leaf light, muted with mauve to either side of leaf
cherries	red	none
whole leaves	medium green	bases dark, centers light

Photograph 7-28

10. With a liner brush, accentuate the details of the design with a darker shade of the appropriate color. (See Photograph 7-29.) For example, you may do flower petals, leaves, fruits, pea pod, peas, and basket weaves. Clean the brush each time you change the color. The paint may be thinned with a bit of turpentine so that it will work easily on the brush. Allow paint to dry and remove the paper mask.

11. Assemble frame around cardboard and place nonglare glass in front of velveteen.

Photograph 7-29

Basket of Fruit on Velvet

Daisy Velvet Pillow

This velvet pillow may be done with transparent oil paints or fabric paints. The advantage to using fabric paints is that they can be made colorfast.

Materials

1 sheet heavy cardboard or posterboard, 20 by 20 inches
1 piece cotton velveteen, 18 by 18 inches, in white
masking tape
1 sheet tracing paper, 16 by 16 inches
technical fountain pen
waterproof india ink, in black
scissors
1 yard architects' tracing linen
1 sheet of glass, 8 by 10 inches
surgical, decoupage, or embroidery scissors
X-acto knife
1 sheet notebook paper, 18 by 18 inches
pencil
ruler
fabric paints in yellow, blue, red, and Mexican violet; or transparent oil paints, in alizarin crimson, Indian yellow, and Prussian blue
disposable palette pad
stencil brushes, #2 and #6; polyurethane sponges, 3 by 3 inches; or wool flannel, small pieces
#1 liner brush or scroller brush
extender (for fabric paints)
turpentine
straight pins
½ yard cotton velveteen, in powder blue
thread, in powder blue
2 yards cable cord, ⅛ inch in diameter
sewing machine
kapok or other stuffing material of your choice
embroidery needle, #7

Instructions

1. Pin or tape velveteen to cardboard so that it will be stretched taut.
2. Following directions in the Helpful Hints chapter, enlarge design pattern by 50 percent. If you are using the grid method of enlarging, each square should measure 1 inch. Trace the enlarged design onto a sheet of tracing paper. Be sure to include the border. Design should measure 14 by 14 inches from border to border. Four stencils will be needed. The unshaded areas of the design are #1 units, the dotted areas are #2 units, the

lined areas are #3 units, and the squared oval-shaped flower centers are #4 units.

3. Cut three 15- by 15-inch pieces of architects' tracing linen and one 4- by 4-inch piece. Place one of the larger pieces over design pattern, and secure with masking tape. Follow directions in step E of Basic Instructions to trace #1 units onto linen. Be sure to include the border. (See Photograph 7-30.) In the same manner, trace #2 and #3 units onto pieces of architects' tracing linen.

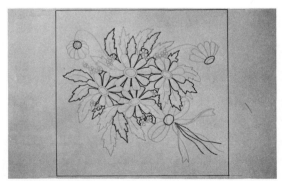

Photograph 7-30

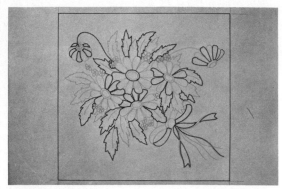

Photograph 7-31

Photograph 7-32

Photograph 7-33

(See Photographs 7-31 and 7-32.) Trace the flower centers onto the small piece of linen.

4. Follow directions in step F in Basic Instructions to cut out all four stencils.

5. Cut the sheet of notebook paper to the same size as cardboard. Center the enlarged tracing paper design on the notebook paper, and mark the four corners. With a pencil and ruler, connect the four marks. You now have a 14- by 14-inch square. Cut around the outline on the paper. Place this paper mask over your velveteen, and secure it in place with masking tape.

6. Place stencil #1 over the velveteen, aligning its border over the cutout in the mask. Secure in place with masking tape. Place a dab each of red, blue, and yellow paint on your palette. Following directions in steps H and I of Basic Instructions and Color Suggestions chart, mix paints and stencil all #1 units. If using fabric paints, extender should be used as a thinning agent. Cut a curved edge on a piece of tracing linen. Place over leaf openings, from top to bottom. Stenciling off the edge of the linen, make a dark center vein, as shown in Photograph 7-33. Do branch veins, intersecting the center vein, in the same manner. (See Photograph 7-34.) Remove stencil #1, and allow 10 minutes drying time. (See Photograph 7-35.)

7. Position stencil #2 over velveteen, aligning border with mask. Secure with masking tape. Stencil all #2 units in the same manner as before. The leaves have been lettered in the Color Suggestions chart. Leaves A and B are the two leaves that are above the bow center and between two flowers. Continuing in a clockwise direction, leaves are lettered up to letter J. Flowers are lettered A, B, C, D, and E, starting from the top right-hand flower and continuing in a clockwise direction. The veins of leaves are modeled in the same manner as stencil #1 leaves. Use medium green to model veins in leaves A, B, E, I, and J. Use a medium light green for leaves C, D, and G. Use a medium blue for the center vein in leaves F and H. Remove the stencil and allow 10 minutes

252

Photograph 7-34

drying time. (See Photograph 7-36.)

8. Position stencil #3 over the velveteen, aligning the border with the cutout of the mask, and secure with masking tape. Follow same procedure to stencil #3 units. Remove the stencil, and allow to dry. (See Photograph 7-37.)

9. Using stencil #4, stencil oval-shaped centers in the three large flowers in the middle of the design. (See Photograph 7-38.)

Photograph 7-35

Photograph 7-37

Photograph 7-36

Photograph 7-38

253

Color Suggestions

Stencil #1

Part	Color	Shading
leaves and 3 flower centers	medium green	edges dark, centers light
flower center (upper right-hand corner)	dark brown	edge dark, center light and muted with medium green
bow center	medium blue	edge dark, center light
stems	medium green	left sides dark, right sides light

Stencil #2

Part	Color	Shading
leaves A, B, and E	medium green	edges dark, centers light
leaves C and D	very light green	edges dark, centers light
leaf F	very light blue	edge dark, center light
leaf G	light green	tip dark, base light
leaf H	light blue	edge dark, center light
leaves I and J	light green	edges dark, centers light
leaf A and B tips	light blue	none
flower B petals	medium yellow	edges medium, centers orange yellow
flower C petals	medium yellow	centers medium yellow, edges medium brown
flower D petals	medium yellow	edges medium brown, centers medium green
flower A and E petals	medium yellow	none
flower center	medium brown	edges light, center light and muted with medium green

Part	Color	Shading
ribbon loops	light blue	edges dark, centers light
streamers	dark blue	twist area dark, center and ends light
stems	medium green	left sides dark, right sides light

Stencil #3

Part	Color	Shading
small flower (upper left-hand corner)	light blue	edge dark, center light
remaining small flowers and ribbon loops	medium blue	edges dark, centers light
ribbon edges	light blue	none
flower petals (upper left-hand corner)	light yellow	edges medium, centers orange yellow
stem (upper right-hand corner)	medium green	none

Stencil #4

Part	Color	Shading
flower centers	medium brown	edges dark, centers medium green

10. With the #1 liner brush or scroller brush, detail the design. All leaves, small flowers, and the bow are outlined with a slightly darker shade of the color in which they were stenciled. A spot of yellow is placed in the center of each small blue flower. The petals of all large flowers are outlined with light brown. Some dots of dark brown and dark green should be put in the centers of large flowers. (See Photograph 7-39.)

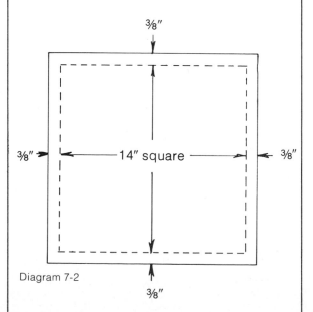

Photograph 7-39

11. Insert a pin through the velveteen at each corner of the mask. Disassemble mask, velveteen, and cardboard; place velveteen, facedown, on the work surface. On the back side, draw a light line connecting the four pin points. You should now have a 14- by 14-inch square outline. Measure ⅜ inch out from each of the lines, and lightly draw a second outline. This will be the seam allowance to be used when sewing the pillow together. (See Diagram 7-2.) Cut around the

Diagram 7-2

outer outline on the back side of the velveteen. Cut a piece of the blue velveteen to the same size.

12. Fold the remaining powder blue velvet on the bias, and cut along the fold. Make two strips by measuring 1¼ inch on the bias and cutting out. Position the two 1¼-inch-width strips together, as shown in Diagram 7-3, with velveteen

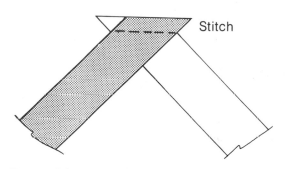

Diagram 7-3

sides facing. Stitch two pieces together. The resulting piece should be about 5 feet long. If it is shorter, add another piece in the same manner.

13. Fold the strip of bias material in half, lengthwise, with the velveteen side out. Place a piece of ⅛-inch-diameter cable cord inside the fold. With the edges of the material even and using the zipper foot on your sewing machine, sew down the length of the material. Make stitches close to the cord, as shown in Diagram 7-4. Further directions for welting can be found in your sewing machine manual.

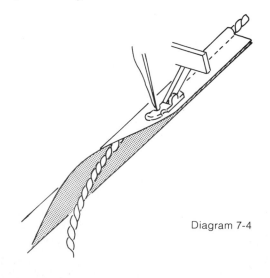

Diagram 7-4

255

14. Place the white velveteen on your sewing machine, design side up. Starting at the bottom center of the velveteen, leaving about ½ inch of the welting loose, align the edges of the welting with the velveteen. Use the zipper foot on the machine to stitch near to, but not crowding, the cord. When you come to a corner, cut the welting material almost to the cord so that it will

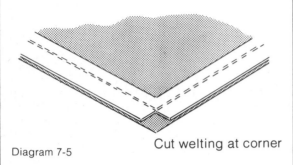

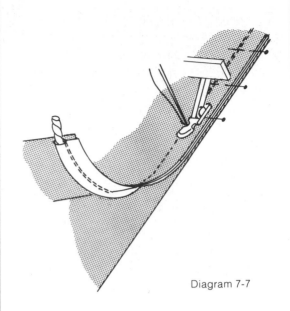

Diagram 7-7

Diagram 7-5

Cut welting at corner

bend around the corner. (See Diagram 7-5.) Finish at the bottom center with a crossed joint, as shown in Diagram 7-6.

15. Place the powder blue velveteen, faceup, on your work surface. Place the white velvet, design side down, on top of it, with the edges even. Pin or baste together. Leave a 4-inch section on one side unpinned. Using the stitching that holds the welting to the white velvet as a guide, stitch around the velvet with the zipper foot of your machine. Make stitches as close to the cord as possible. (See Diagram 7-7.) Start at one side of the opening and stitch around to the other side.

16. Invert the pillow slip so that it is right side up. Stuff with kapok and close up the opening by taking small stitches with a needle and thread.

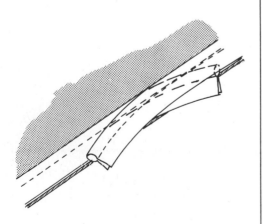

Diagram 7-6

Daisy Velvet Pillow

Strawberry Belt

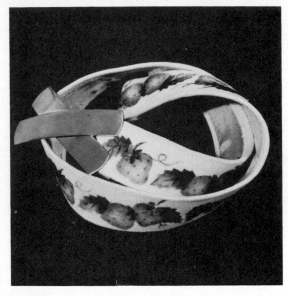

This belt can be stenciled with either fabric colors or transparent oil paints. Since fabric color allows the fabric to be washed, it is the preferred medium. Although quality of color in transparent oil paints is richer, fabric paints are quite adequate.

Materials

permanent form belting, 1½ inches wide, 6 inches longer than waist measurement

tape measure

scissors

⅛ yard velveteen, in white

ironing board

iron

Stitch Witchery

pressing cloth

grosgrain ribbon, 1¼ inches wide, the same length as belting

thread, in white

embroidery needle, #7

1 sheet tracing paper, 8½ by 11 inches

masking tape

technical fountain pen

waterproof india ink, in black

⅛ yard architects' tracing linen

pencil

1 sheet of glass, 8 by 10 inches

surgical, decoupage, or embroidery scissors

X-acto knife

fabric paints, in red, yellow, and blue; or transparent oil paints, in alizarin crimson, Indian yellow, and Prussian blue

disposable palette pad

stencil brushes, #2 and #6; polyurethane sponges, 3 by 3 inches; or wool flannel, small pieces

#1 liner brush or scroller brush

extender (for fabric paints)

turpentine

1 belt buckle, in style of your choice

Instructions

1. If you have chosen a belt buckle for a waist-size belt, cut off the extra 6 inches on the belting. Cut a point on the through end of the belting if buckle requires one.

2. Cut a piece of white velveteen to measure 1 inch longer and 1 inch wider than the belting. Set the iron to the temperature recommended on the belting package, and press belting flat. Cut a strip of Stitch Witchery to the same length and

width as the belting. Place the belting on your ironing board, right side up, with the Stitch Witchery on top of it. Center the velveteen, right side up, over the belting, as shown in Diagram 7-8. Place a damp pressing cloth on top of the

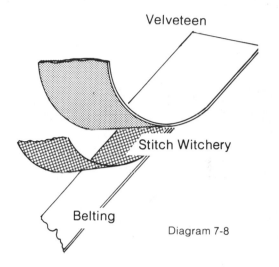

Diagram 7-8

velveteen, and press until the cloth is dry. Do not slide the iron; press one area and move to another, overlapping the first area slightly. Refer to the directions that come with Stitch Witchery for fusing two fabrics together.

3. Turn the piece over, and fold the velveteen around the edges to the back of the belting. (See Diagram 7-9.) Place grosgrain ribbon over velve-

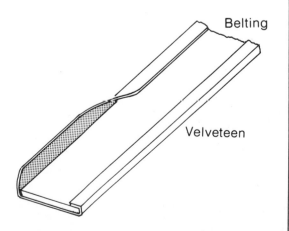

Diagram 7-9

259

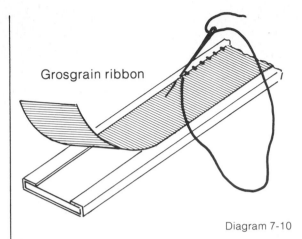

Grosgrain ribbon

Diagram 7-10

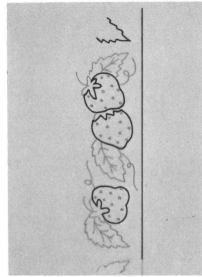

Photograph 7-40

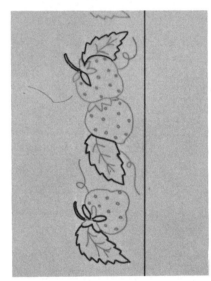

Photograph 7-41

teen, and whip together with a needle and thread, as shown in Diagram 7-10. If there is a point on the belting, cut the ribbon to the same shape. Cut the velveteen to the same shape, leaving a ¼-inch margin around the belting. Fold the velveteen around the point and whip to the ribbon.

4. Place a sheet of tracing paper over the design pattern. With the technical fountain pen and india ink, trace the entire design. Be sure to include all details and register line. The leaf above the first strawberry is used as a guide for spacing the design around the belt. It should be traced, therefore, but will not be stenciled. Three stencils will be needed for the design. The unshaded areas are #1 units, the dotted areas are #2 units, and the lined areas and strawberry seeds are #3 units.

5. Cut three pieces of architects' tracing linen. Place one of the pieces over design pattern, and secure it with masking tape. Following directions in step E of Basic Instructions, trace #1 units, index leaf, and register line onto linen. (See Photograph 7-40.) Follow the same procedure to trace #2 and #3 units onto second and third pieces of linen. (See Photographs 7-41 and 7-42.)

6. Following step F in Basic Instructions, cut out all stencils.

260

7. Place the belt on your work surface, velveteen side up. Starting 1 inch from the buckle end, position stencil #1 over belt. Align register line with bottom edge, as shown in Photograph 7-43. The stencil may be secured in place with masking tape or held in place with your hand. Place a dab each of red, yellow, and blue paint on your palette pad. Follow directions in steps H and I of Basic Instructions and Color Suggestions chart to mix paints and stencil #1 units. If you are using fabric paints, use extender as a thinning agent.

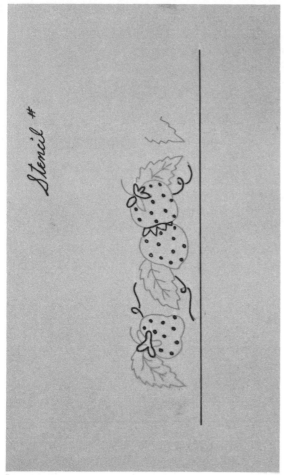

Photograph 7-42

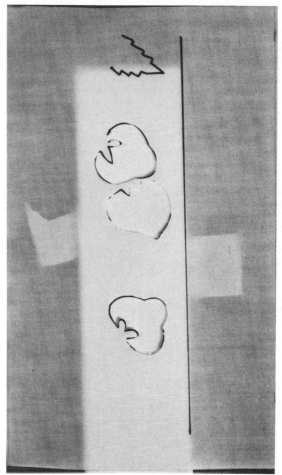

Photograph 7-43

Remove stencil #1 and allow to dry. (See Photograph 7-44.)

8. Place stencil #2 over the belt, aligning register line with lower edge and the curved edge in the right-hand leaf with the edge of the right-hand strawberry. Follow the same stenciling procedure. Place a curved piece of tracing linen over leaf openings, from top to bottom. Model in the center vein by stenciling off the curved edge. Place the linen so that it intersects the center vein, and model the branch veins. Remove stencil and allow to dry. (See Photograph 7-45.)

9. Place stencil #3 in position, and repeat stenciling procedure. Remove stencil #3, and allow to dry. (See Photograph 7-46.)

Color Suggestions

Stencil #1

Part	Color	Shading
strawberries	red	edges dark, centers light

Stencil #2

Part	Color	Shading
leaves and stems	medium green	bases dark, tips light

Stencil #3

Part	Color	Shading
seeds and tops	medium green	none

261

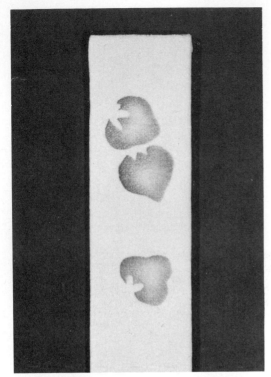

Photograph 7-44

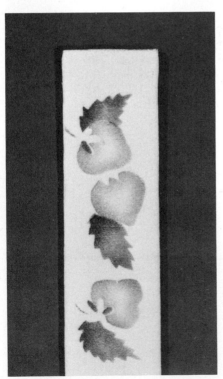

Photograph 7-45

Photograph 7-46

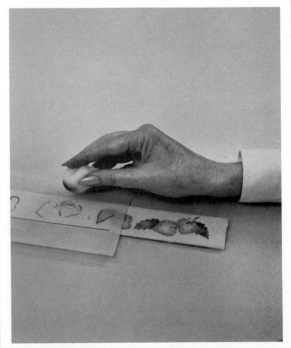

Photograph 7-47

Photograph 7-48

10. Replace stencil #1 on the belt. Align the index leaf with the left-hand leaf and the register line with the edge of the belt. (See Photograph 7-47.) Apply the color to stencils #1, #2, and #3 in the same manner as before. Continue stenciling around the belt, ending about 1 inch from the end.

11. With a #1 liner brush or scroller brush, outline each part of the design with a very narrow line. Use a darker shade of the appropriate color. (See Photograph 7-48.) Allow paint to dry.

12. Attach the buckle to the belt.

Portrait in Brown

This Mod study in brown looks charming when placed in a delicate gold frame. It is perfect for a teen-ager's room or family room.

Materials

1 sheet heavy cardboard or posterboard, 16 by 23 inches
1 piece cotton velveteen, 18 by 25 inches, in white
masking tape
1 sheet tracing paper, 12 by 18 inches
technical fountain pen
waterproof india ink, in black
scissors
½ yard architects' tracing linen
1 sheet of glass, 8 by 10 inches
surgical, decoupage, or embroidery scissors
X-acto knife
1 sheet notebook paper, 16 by 23 inches
pencil
ruler
transparent oil paints, in alizarin crimson, Indian yellow, and Prussian blue
disposable palette pad
#1 liner brush or scroller brush
stencil brushes, #2 and #6; polyurethane sponges, 3 by 3 inches; or wool flannel, small pieces
turpentine
1 frame, to fit around cardboard
1 sheet of glass, nonglare, to fit inside frame

Instructions

1. Prepare velveteen according to directions in step A of Basic Instructions.

2. Following directions in the Helpful Hints chapter, enlarge design by 50 percent. If you are using the grid method of enlarging, each square should measure 1 inch. Trace the enlarged design pattern onto tracing paper with technical fountain pen and india ink. Three stencils will be needed to do this design. The unshaded areas are #1 units, the dotted areas are #2 units, and the lined areas are #3 units.

3. Cut three 12- by 18-inch pieces of architects' tracing linen. Make sure all three pieces have perfectly square corners and straight sides and are exactly the same size. The outside dimensions of the piece are used to register the drawing. Place one piece of linen on top of the tracing paper

design, aligning the edges. Secure in place with masking tape. Following directions in step E of Basic Instructions, trace all #1 units onto tracing linen. Remove the first piece of linen. Following the same procedure, trace #2 units and #3 units onto pieces of linen.

4. Follow step F in Basic Instructions to cut out stencils.

5. Cut a sheet of notebook paper to the same size as cardboard. Center the enlarged design on the notebook paper and mark the four corners. Draw lines connecting the marks to form a 12- by 18-inch rectangle. Cut along the outline. Place this paper mask over the velveteen, aligning edges, and secure with masking tape. Tape around the edge of the cardboard to the back. Do not tape to the face of the velvet.

6. Position stencil #1 on the velvet, aligning its edges with the mask. Secure with masking tape. Place a dab of alizarin crimson, Indian yellow, and Prussian blue on the disposable palette. Follow steps H and I in Basic Instructions and Color Suggestions chart to mix paints and stencil #1 units. Remove stencil #1 and allow to dry. (See Photograph 7-49.)

Photograph 7-50

7. Position stencil #2 over the velvet, aligning edges. Follow same stenciling procedure as before. Remove stencil #2 and allow to dry. (See Photograph 7-50.)

8. Position stencil #3 on the velvet and stencil as before. After all units have been stenciled, remove stencil #3 and allow paint to dry. (See Photograph 7-51.)

Photograph 7-49

Photograph 7-51

266

Color Suggestions

Stencil #1

Part	Color	Shading
half of curls	reddish brown	edges dark, points along center light
half of curls	reddish brown	edges light, points along center dark
lips	reddish brown	none
pupil	dark brown	none
nostrils, eyebrows, and outline of eye	medium brown	none

Stencil #2

Part	Color	Shading
half of curls	reddish brown	edges dark, points along center light
half of curls	reddish brown	edges light, points along center dark
irises	reddish brown	none

Stencil #3

Part	Color	Shading
half of curls	reddish brown	edges dark, points along center dark
half of curls	reddish brown	edges light, points along center dark
cheek, chin, forehead, and eyebrow area	reddish brown	none

Photograph 7-52

9. With the liner brush, outline the curls with dark brown. A few dark brown lines are also drawn into the curls to give them shape. Put a very fine dark outline around the face, as shown in Photogaph 7-52.

10. Frame your picture, and place glass in front.

267

Helpful Hints

8

This chapter is devoted to the teaching of nine useful skills. It should be understood, however, that the methods described are those that I find easiest to do and are not, by any means, the only methods.

Enlarging Designs

The easiest way to get an enlargement of a design is to take it to one of the many blueprint companies that offer reproduction services. Tell them the size you want your design to be, and pick up the enlarged design the next day. The price is usually very reasonable. However, if you want to do the enlarging by yourself, the easiest method to follow is the grid method.

Instructions

1. Place a sheet of tracing paper over the design. Carefully trace design with a sharp, soft pencil or a technical fountain pen and india ink. Trace all details that you want to reproduce.

2. Draw either ¼-inch or ½-inch squares over the entire design. These are called grids. If the design is small, draw ¼-inch grids; if it is large, draw ½-inch grids. A good way to draw grids is to place a sheet of ¼-inch quadrille paper under the traced design. Trace every line for ¼-inch grids or every other line for ½-inch grids. (See Diagram 8-1.) Grids have already been drawn on those design patterns in this book that require enlarging. When enlarging designs from other sources, however, you will have to do this yourself.

3. On a second sheet of tracing paper, draw grids to the proportion to the original design that is needed. For example, if there are ½-inch grids on your traced design and you want your enlarged design to be twice as big, draw 1-inch grids. Those designs that have been reduced in this book can be enlarged to the proper size by drawing 1-inch grids.

4. Work on one section of the design at a time. For every point on the design that intersects the

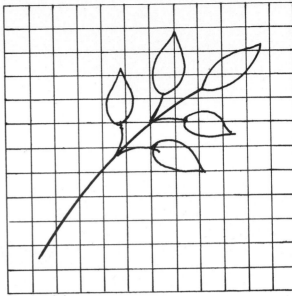

Diagram 8-1

small grid, make a dot on the enlarged grid in the corresponding position. Following the traced design, connect the dots. After you have reproduced the design in this section, move on to another, continuing until the entire design has been duplicated. Retrace the design, if necessary, to make lines cleaner and neater. (See Diagram 8-2.)

Constructing Shadow Box Frames

A shadow box frame is a shallow enclosure in which articles can be displayed. Most shadow box frames have a glass front, which enhances as well as protects the display. They are sold in decoupage shops, craft stores, and craft departments of discount and department stores. If you cannot find the right size or want a special frame, you can have them made at a frame shop. In many cases, however, you can convert an ordinary frame into a shadow box frame simply by adding depth. This is, of course, less expensive than having a special frame built for you. The following instructions will show you how to add an extension to a frame.

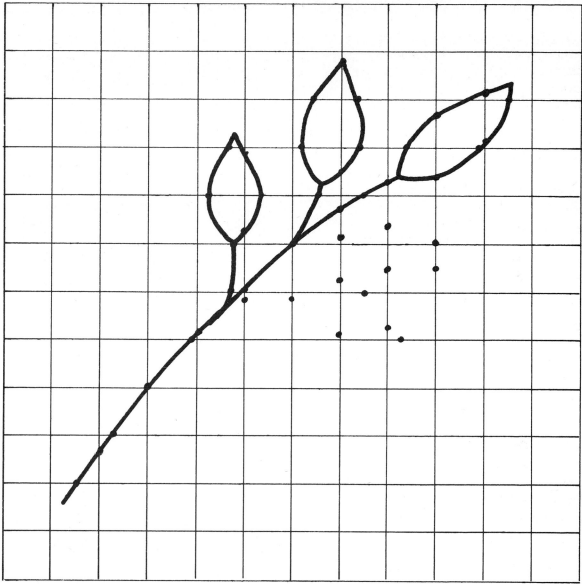

Diagram 8-2

Instructions

Square and Rectangular Shadow Box Frames

1. Place the frame, glass side down, on your work surface. Measure the frame from inside of the glass and decide upon the amount of depth you want to add. Measure the width of each side along the frame opening.

2. Cut four pieces of wood that are no wider than the width of the sides you have measured and that are thick enough to provide the depth you want. The length of two pieces should equal the width of the opening in the frame. The length of the other two pieces should equal the full length of the back of the frame.

3. With white glue, adhere the two smaller pieces between the two larger pieces to form a frame. This frame should fit perfectly around the opening on the back side. Sand the frame with

#350 garnet paper, seal with Treasure Sealer, and apply two coats of paint in the desired color. Both frames should be the same color. (See Diagram 8-3.)

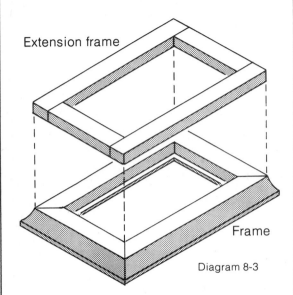

Extension frame

Frame

Diagram 8-3

4. Cut a piece of posterboard to the size of the outside dimensions of the extension frame. Apply white glue to the back side of the frame and adhere the posterboard to it. Be sure that the edges of the posterboard are even with the edges of the frame. Allow glue to dry. (See Diagram 8-4.)

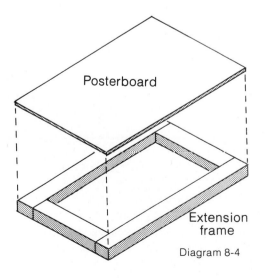

Posterboard

Extension frame

Diagram 8-4

5. Turn the frame over. Apply a thin coat of white glue to the inside surface of the posterboard. Adhere the posterboard backing of the design piece to the framed posterboard. It should fit snugly within the frame.

6. Cut four strips of 2-ply Strathmore paper to fit within the innermost edge. The widths of the strips should equal the depth of the entire frame. Paint one side of each strip with the color that was used for the posterboard background, or cover the strips with the same fabric that was used. To cover with fabric, place the fabric on the work surface, facedown. Put a thin coat of white glue on one side of each strip and adhere it to the fabric. Trim the fabric to leave a ¼-inch border around each of the strips. Apply glue to the back side of the strips, fold the material around the edges, and adhere.

7. With white glue, adhere the strips inside the frame extension, with one edge flush against the design background. (See Diagram 8-5.) If you

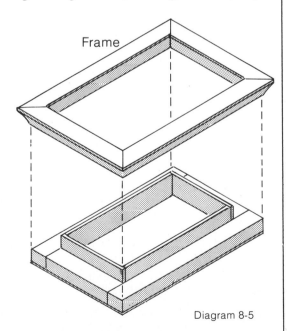

Frame

Diagram 8-5

wish, a piece of rattail in a matching color can be glued over each corner joint, and over the joint between the strips and the background.

8. Remove and clean the glass. Position back in

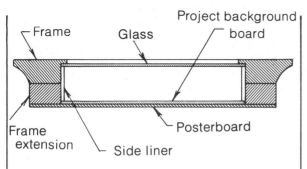

Diagram 8-6

the frame, and secure with glazier points. (See Diagram 8-6.) On small frames, place one glazier point at the top center, one at the bottom center, and one at each side. For larger frames, place two glazier points at the top, two at the bottom, and two at each side.

9. Put the front and back sections of the frame together and secure with screws. Drill clearance holes for the screws through the back frame and starting holes in the front frame. Place one on the top center, bottom, and each side. Do not use screws that will come through to the front of the frame.

10. Cut a piece of brown wrapping paper to the size of the back of the frame, and adhere in place with white glue. Rub the paper with a damp cloth and allow to dry.

Round and Oval-shaped Shadow Box Frames

1. Place the frame on a piece of wood that is thick enough to give the desired depth. Trace around the inside and outside of the frame with a pencil. Cut out both outlines.

2. Sand with #350 garnet paper, seal with Treasure Sealer, and apply two coats of desired paint.

3. Follow steps 4 and 5 in instructions for square or rectangular shadow boxes.

4. Cut a strip of Strathmore paper to the width of the entire depth of the frame and the length of inner circumference. Paint one side of the strip in the same color that was used for the background of the project. If the project has a fabric background, adhere the same fabric to this strip.

5. Clean the glass and position in the frame. Attach glass to frame with glazier points, and attach both frames with screws.

Making Mobiles

The type of mobile that we will discuss is the balanced beam or branch mobile. It is constructed with two or more beams, placed one above the other, and attached with nylon thread or light monofilament fish line. It is balanced in a seesaw fashion. The bottom beam has an ornament on each end, while higher beams have an ornament on one end. The opposite end is attached to the branch assembly below it.

Instructions

1. Cut a 6-inch piece of 16- or 18-gauge galvanized iron wire. Hang an ornament from one end of the wire with nylon thread or fish line. To attach the thread or fish line to the wire, make a small loop at the end of the wire with long-nose pliers, pass the thread through the loop, and tie. Another way is to wrap the thread around the end of the wire beam, tie a knot, and apply a drop of white glue. Repeat procedure for other end of wire. The ornaments may hang at either the same or different lengths below the beam. Tie a piece of thread or fish line around the beam, hold thread up from its end, and move it between the two ornaments until you find the point of balance. (See Diagram 8-7.) Secure the thread to the wire at this point with fast-drying white glue.

2. Cut a second piece of galvanized iron wire to an 8-inch length. Secure an ornament to one end in the same manner as before. Attach the thread of the bottom beam to the other end. Attach a piece of thread to the second beam, and move it to find the balance point.

3. Continue in this manner, making each successive beam 2 inches longer than the one beneath it. Make as many beams as you wish. Although the ornaments can hang at different lengths, the beams must be able to rotate with-

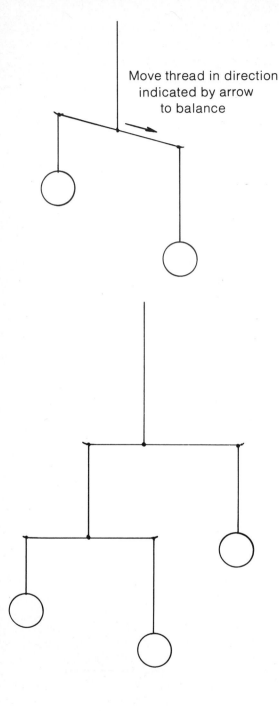

Move thread in direction
indicated by arrow
to balance

out tangling in the threads. Experiment with different lengths to make sure this will not happen.

Wiring Lamps

The sockets of all portable lamps, whether they are table, floor, or swag lamps, are wired in the same way. Here are the basic steps and precautions that should be taken when wiring them. Refer to Diagram 8-8 for clarification of parts.

Instructions

1. Use a ready-made lamp cord. This is usually a 6-foot cord with a molded male plug on one end. Swag lamp cords are longer but are made the same way. They are available as part of a swag lamp kit.

2. Disassemble the socket. If it is the kind that has two screws inside of it, remove them with a screwdriver to free the base. If there are no screws, press socket cover to remove. For table or floor lamps, put the harp retainer on the pipe and screw on the base of the socket.

3. When wiring a table or floor lamp, thread the cord through the hole in the base, up through the IPS pipe to the socket base. Be careful not to scrape the insulation and expose bare wire. The end of the wire should extend about 2 inches above the socket base. Take hold of the cord at the spot where it comes into the lamp base from the hole. While holding the cord at this point, pull it back out of the pipe. Tie a knot at the point, large enough to prevent the cord from being pulled. This serves as a strain relief. If the cord is pulled on, it will not put a strain on the wired connections. On a swag lamp, the chain acts as the strain relief.

4. Grab hold of the cord that extends beyond the socket base, and split the two wires in half for a distance of 2 inches. Most ready-made lamp cords are "zip" cords. These are very easily pulled apart. Strip the insulation off each wire for a distance of 1 inch, and twist the ends clockwise to gather any of the loose strands.

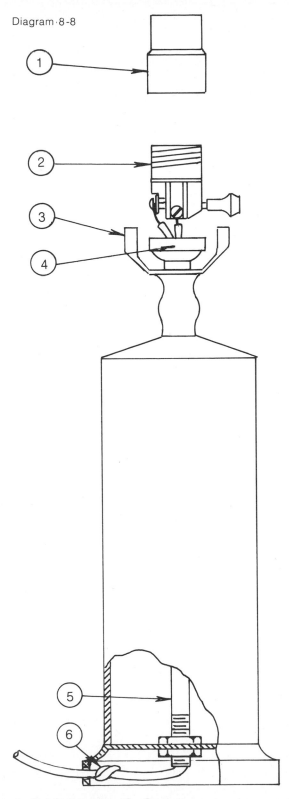

Diagram·8-8

1. Socket cover   2. Socket mechanism
3. Harp   4. Socket base
5. ⅛″ IPS pipe   6. Knotted cord

5. Loosen the two screws that are on either side of the socket. Place the end of one wire to the left side of one screw, wrap the end clockwise around it, and tighten the screw with a screwdriver. Be sure that there are no strands of wire left out. Turn the socket around and attach the other wire to the second screw in the same manner.

6. From the bottom of the base, pull the wire to remove the slack below the socket. Put the socket cover over the socket, and snap it into the base. Be sure to support the base of the socket when placing the cover on it.

Cutting Glass

Cutting glass can either be easy or difficult, depending upon how you go about it. We will concern ourselves with straight cuts in this section. Since curved cuts are somewhat difficult to do, it might be a good idea to have them done for you.

Instructions

1. Carefully measure the dimensions of the space to be paned.

2. Mark the glass to the same dimensions, favoring the low side of the dimension. This is to allow for a slight clearance.

3. Lay the glass on a flat surface. Hold the cutter in an upright position, with the handle between the first and second fingers, gripping the cutter with the thumb and first finger. (See Photograph 8-1.) Two types of glass cutters can be used to

Photograph 8-1

275

make straight cuts. A wheel-type cutter has a hard steel precision-honed wheel that is mounted in a handle on a pin axle. There are two or three notches, each ranging from $^3/_{16}$ to $^5/_{16}$ inch wide, next to the wheel. These are used to grip and break narrow strips of glass after they have been scored. When using a wheel cutter, dip the wheel into a light oil before cutting. The diamond scribe cutter is a sharp-pointed tool with an industrial diamond mounted at the point. It is excellent for making straight cuts.

4. Position a straight edge, such as a ruler, on your marks. Starting $^1/_{16}$ inch from the edge of glass, draw cutter across glass, against straight edge, with a firm, continuous stroke. Allow the wheel to drop off the edge of the glass. Make only one stroke; do not exert excess pressure. (See Photograph 8-2.)

Photograph 8-2

5. Grab hold of the glass at either side of the scored line. Holding the glass between your thumb and first finger, bend slightly to break. (See Photograph 8-3.) If the edge being broken off is narrow, use the notch at the side of the wheel cutter to bend it. Another method is to hold the large piece and tap off the narrow piece with the butt end of the cutter.

6. Practice the procedure for cutting glass on scrap pieces before you cut the project piece.

Photograph 8-3

Making Bows

The bows in the projects of this book vary as to size of loops, number of loops, and length of streamers, but can all be made in the same way. We will follow a six-looped bow from start to finish. To make a bow with any other number or size loops, mark off more or fewer segments of the required lengths. Make the bow in the same manner, adding or subtracting loops, as required.

Instructions

1. Mark a 33-inch length of satin ribbon into segments, as shown in diagram. Make a loop by bringing point A to the center. (See Diagram 8-9.) Use a small amount of white glue to adhere point A to the center. Make another loop by bringing point B to the center and adhering it with white glue. Turn the bow over.

2. Make two more loops by bringing point D and then point C to the center; adhere with white glue.

3. Turn the bow over, and make the last two loops by bringing point E and point F to the center and adhering with white glue.

4. Simulate a knot with a 1½-inch length of ribbon. Wrap it around the center of the bow, and fasten it to the back of bow with white glue.

Fitting Hinges

We will concern ourselves with fitting hinges on boxes, shadow box lids, and basket purses. By following a few basic steps and working slowly and deliberately, the task becomes relatively simple to do.

The spot at which to place hinges will usually depend on the type of box. On square or rectangular boxes, hinges are usually placed ½ to 2 inches from each corner. On hexagonal or octagonal boxes, hinges are usually positioned ¼ to ½ inch from each corner. Remember that hinges should be fit to the box before it has been painted.

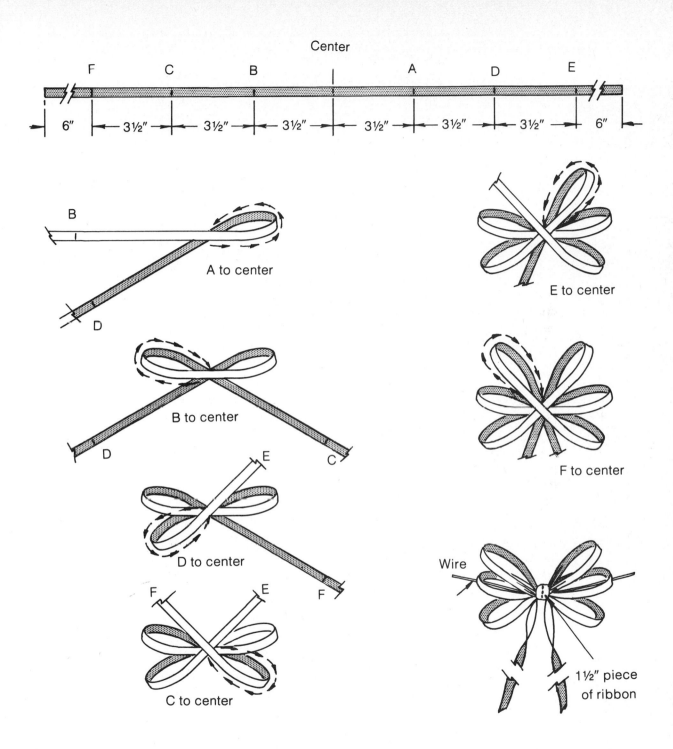

Center

F   C   B   A   D   E

6"   3½"   3½"   3½"   3½"   3½"   3½"   6"

B

A to center

D

B to center

D   C

E

D to center

F

F   E

C to center

E to center

F to center

Wire

1½" piece
of ribbon

Diagram 8-9

277

Instructions

Boxes

1. Remove the lid from the box.

2. Locate the points where the outside edges of the hinges are to fit. Measure from each corner of the side to the decided distance. With a pencil, mark the lip at this spot. (See Photograph 8-4.)

3. Place the edge of one hinge on one of these marks. Mark along this edge of the hinge, as shown in Photograph 8-5. Do the other hinge in

Photograph 8-4

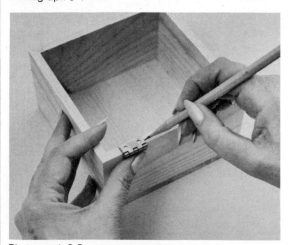

Photograph 8-5

the same manner. You should now have two pairs of marks on the lip that are perpendicular to the outside back edge. The marks should show slightly on this edge.

4. Put the lid on the box, and position so that all

edges will be even. Make a light mark on the edge of the lid, just above each of the marks on the lip. (See Photograph 8-6.) Remove the lid. Extend each of these marks across the lip of the lid.

Photograph 8-6

5. With an X-acto knife, cut each of the marks on the box lip. (See Photograph 8-7.) The depth of each cut should be equal to the thickness of the hinge. Notch out the area between each pair of cuts, making a flat-bottomed groove. The hinge flange or, in other words, one side of the hinge

Photograph 8-7

should fit perfectly within this area. (See Photograph 8-8.)

6. Place one of the hinges in the groove. Position so that its pinned joint will be just off the outside edge of the lip. Mark the hole pattern of the

Photograph 8-8

hinge onto the lip. Position the second hinge and
mark in the same manner.

7. With an awl, make a starting hole for the
hinge screws in the center of the hole marks.
Position the hinges. Drive in the screws with a
screwdriver, and fasten the hinges in place on the
box. (See Photograph 8-9.)

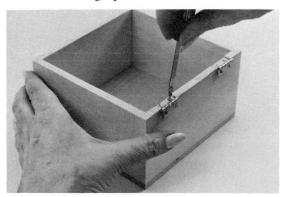

Photograph 8-9

8. Place a spacer, such as a book, under the lid of
the box. The idea is to hold the lid up so that it
will be the same height as the box. Position the
lid behind the box in what would be a fully open
position. Place the hinge flanges in the grooves in
the lip of the lid. Position the lid so that its
outside edge is just at the hinge joint. Mark the
holes.

9. With an awl, make starting holes for the
screws in the center of each mark on the lip of the
lid. Position the lid and attach screws. (See
Photograph 8-10.)

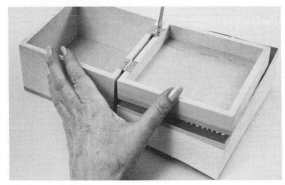

Photograph 8-10

Shadow Boxes

1. Shadow boxes are simply boxes with inverted
lids. In other words, the top of the lid becomes
the bottom of the lid. To make them, invert the
lid of the box you are using and follow directions
for attaching hinges to regular boxes. (See
Photographs 8-11 and 8-12.)

Photograph 8-11

Photograph 8-12

279

Basket Purses

1. The hinges of a basket purse are attached to the inside of the lid and the outside of the basket. Locate and mark the position on the inside of the lid that is to be hinged. Position hinges and mark holes.

2. With an awl, make starting holes for the hinge screws in the center of each marked hole. Secure the hinges to the inside of the lid with the screws. (See Photograph 8-13.)

Photograph 8-13

3. Place the lid on the basket purse with the unattached hinge flanges against the outside back rim of the basket. With a pencil, mark the hinge holes on the rim. Remove the lid.

4. With an awl, make starting holes for the screws at the center of each marked hole.

5. Put the lid on the basket, align the holes in the hinges with the starting holes, and secure with screws. (See Photograph 8-14.)

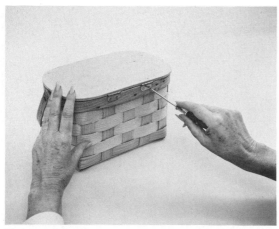

280

Photograph 8-14

Mitering Joints

A mitered joint is made by cutting two pieces at the angle where they join and fitting them together. The manner in which the joint is made will depend on the type of material you are working with.

Instructions

Gold Paper Braids

1. Cut the braid into lengths that will cover each side of the surface, allowing for an overlap at each joint. Place pieces over the surface. Lift overlapped pieces slightly above each joint, and cut through both pieces with scissors. Cut the line so that the angle formed by the overlap will be split in half. (See Photograph 8-15.)

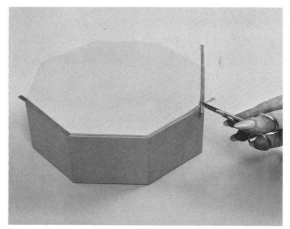

Photograph 8-15

Thin Strips of Wood

1. Follow the same procedure to miter corners of thin strips of wood. Cut corners with an X-acto knife. (See Photograph 8-16.)

Heavy Strips of Wood

1. Heavier strips of wood must be cut with a saw. If you are mitering corners for a square or rectangular piece, a miter box can be used. This is used to cut the ends of the wood at 45-degree angles. There are inexpensive miter boxes available at some craft shops and in hardware departments of discount and department stores. If a

Photograph 8-16

Photograph 8-17

miter box is not available, purchase a 45/90-degree carpenter's square. This is used to mark the ends of the strips at 45 degrees. Usually, heavy wood corners are cut with a small crosscut saw.

Multisided Surfaces

1. Since the sides may be of slightly different lengths, measure and identify each. To do this, cut a piece of tracing paper and place it over the surface, covering the lip. Secure in place with masking tape. With a pencil held at an angle so that you can mark with the side of the lead, trace along the inner edge of the lip. Be sure to locate each corner accurately. This will give you an outline of the inner dimension of the lid. Put a number on each side of the drawing and the same number on the corresponding side of the lid. (See Photograph 8-17.) Remove the drawing from the lid.

2. Place the tracing of the outline on your work surface. Place a ruler along the outline of each side, and with a lead pencil draw over it to straighten and give sharper definition.

3. Using a ruler and lead pencil, draw lines across the octagon or hexagon, connecting opposite points. These lines define the angle at which the sticks will be cut.

4. Place the sticks along the traced outline. Cut each stick at the angle where the drawn line intersects it. (See Photograph 8-18.) Keep each stick on its marked side until it is transferred to the corresponding numbered side of the lid. (See Photograph 8-19.)

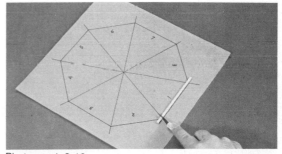

Photograph 8-18

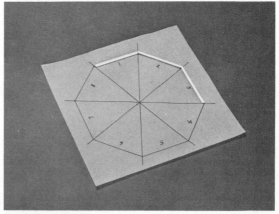

Photograph 8-19

281

Lining Boxes
and Purses

Metal leaf, painted, teapaper, and fabric are just some of the many types of linings that can be used for making purses and other types of boxes. Metal leaf and paint can be applied directly to the inside of the piece, following the instructions on the package or container. Read the following instructions for teapaper or fabric linings.

Instructions
Boxes

1. Measure the inside of the box along the bottom, and cut a piece of cardboard to fit.

2. Place the fabric you have selected facedown on your work surface. Apply a thin coat of white glue to the cardboard, and adhere it to the fabric. With scissors, cut the material even with the edges of the cardboard. Place the bottom liner inside the box.

3. Fold the material so that it is doubled, and measure its thickness with a scale or ruler. Measure the inside dimensions of the right and left inner sides of the box, and subtract the doubled fabric thickness from this measurement. If you wish to adhere gold cord around the inside top of the box, you must also subtract the thickness of the cord. Mark off an area on the shirt cardboard at this dimension and appropriate length to fit right and left inner sides. Draw strips on the cardboard and cut out. Using the two strips of cardboard to measure with, cut a piece of fabric for each, leaving a ¼-inch fabric border. Place the pieces of fabric facedown on your work surface. Apply a thin coat of white glue to one side of each piece of cardboard, and adhere to the center of the fabric pieces. Cut diagonally across each corner of the excess fabric. Apply a thin coat of white glue to the back side of the cardboard along its edge. Fold the material around the cardboard, and adhere in place. (See Diagram 8-10.)

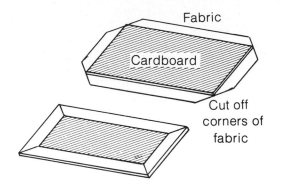

Diagram 8-10

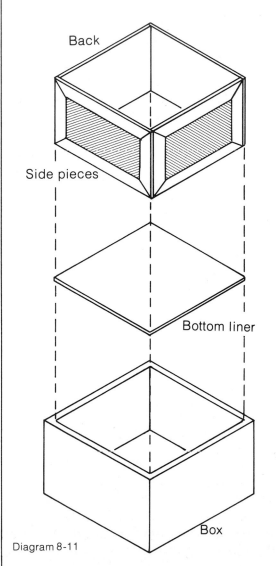

Diagram 8-11

4. Put the two right- and left-side lining pieces in the box. Measure the inside dimensions of the front and back sides. Cut shirt cardboard to the proper size and cover with fabric.

5. Measure and follow the same procedure for the lid of the box.

6. Remove all liners. Apply a small amount of white glue to the bottom, and adhere bottom lining in place. Glue the left and right sides and then the front and back sides. Adhere lining to lid in the same manner. (See Diagram 8-11.)

Basket Purses

1. Measure the inside circumference of the basket purse. The material used must be 1 inch wider than this measurement.

2. Measure down the inside front of the purse, across the bottom, and up the back. This measurement plus 1 inch is the required length of the material.

3. Fold the material in half, across the width. Measure from the folded end to a distance that is equal to half the width of the purse bottom. Draw a line at this point across the material. Turn the material over and draw a corresponding line. Starting at the open end of the folded fabric, sew a ½-inch-wide seam down each side to the folded end. (See Diagram 8-12.) With scissors,

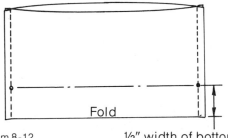

Diagram 8-12   ½" width of bottom

Fold

snip along the fold to the stitches. Press the seam open on each side with an iron. Fold one bottom corner in a triangular shape, as shown in Diagram 8-13, and stitch across the corner on the line. Turn the fabric over, and repeat procedure for other corner, as shown in diagram.

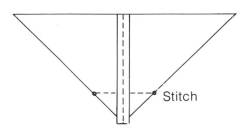

Stitch

Diagram 8-13

4. Place the liner bag in the purse, with the seams facing the sides of the basket and the bottom of the sack against the bottom of the purse. (See Diagram 8-14.) Fold a hem in the top edge of the fabric, making edges flush. The fold of the hem should be hidden between the lining and the purse. Apply white glue around the inner rim and adhere liner to inside of purse.

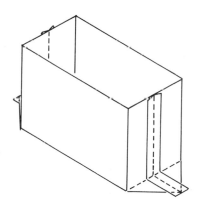

Diagram 8-14

283

Sources for Materials and Tools

On the following pages is an alphabetical list of supplies that are used in the projects throughout this book. Each supply is keyed by number or numbers to the immediately following list of sources for that supply.

1. art supply stores and departments of discount, department, hardware, and paint stores
2. bead stores
3. craft shops and departments of discount, department, and hardware stores and home building centers
4. decoupage shops
5. fabric stores and departments of discount, department, and dime stores
6. floral supply shops
7. hardware stores and departments of discount and department stores and home building centers
8. hobby shops
9. lamp supply stores
10. paint stores and departments of hardware, discount, and department stores and home building centers
11. stationers
12. supermarkets

absorbent cotton 12
acetate sheets 1, 8
acrylic paints 1, 3, 4, 8, 10
acrylic spray 1, 3, 4, 8, 10
aluminum foil 12
antiquing glazes 3, 4
awls 3, 4, 7
balsa wood 3, 8
bead wire 2, 3
beads 2, 3
beam or yardstick compass 1
Bond #527 All-Purpose Cement 3, 8
cable cord 5 (**notions department**)

carbon paper 11
cardboard 1
corsage pins 3, 6, 8
disposable palette pads 1
Dow Corning Silicone Adhesive 3, 4
Dow Corning Rubber Silicone Sealer 3, 4
drill bits 7
electric drills 7
enamel paints 10
fabrics of all types 5
felt 3
floral clay 3, 6
floral tape 3, 6
floral wire 3, 6
General Electric Silicone Seal 3, 4
glass 7
glass cutters 7, 10
glass domes 3
glazier points 7, 10
gold leaf kits 1, 3, 4
gold paper braid 3, 4
hammers 7
handsaws 7
hinges 3, 4, 7
india ink 1, 11
jewelry findings 2, 3
lace 5
lamp bases 9
lamp cylinders 3, 4, 9
lamp hardware 3, 4, 9
Liquid Leaf 3, 4
Liquid Pearl 3, 4
long-nose pliers 7
masking tape 1, 10, 11
metallic gold and silver braid 3, 4, 5
metallic gold and silver cord 3, 4, 5
miter boxes 7
needles 5 (**notions department**)
notebook paper 11
nylon thread 5 (**notions department**)
paintbrushes 1, 4, 8, 10
paint thinner 10

Mail Order Suppliers

Craft Suppliers:

Connoisseur Studio, Inc.
P.O. Box 7187
Louisville, Kentucky 40207

Hazel Pearson Handicrafts
4128 Temple City Boulevard
Rosemead, California 91770

Kraft Korner
5864 Mayfield Road
Mayfield Heights, Ohio 44124

Zim's Craft Supplies
P.O. Box 7620
Salt Lake City, Utah 84107

Early American Decorating Suppliers:

Carson and Ellis, Inc.
1153 Warwick Avenue
Warwick, Rhode Island 02888

Shell Suppliers:

Florida Supply House, Inc.
P.O. Box 847
Bradenton, Florida 33506

The Sea (no catalog and no mail order but good
   source for Californians)
525 North Harbor Boulevard
San Pedro, California 90731

BIBLIOGRAPHY

Abbott, R. Tucker. *Seashells of the World.* Golden Nature Guides. Edited by Herbert S. Zim. Racine, Wis.: Western Publishing Company, Inc., Golden Press, Ltd., 1962.

Ashton, Pearl F. *Everyone Can Paint Fabrics.* The Studio Publications, Inc., in association with Thomas Y. Crowell Company, New York and London.

Blanchard, Roberta Ray. *How to Restore and Decorate Chairs.* New York: Avenel Books.

Brazer, Esther Stevens. *Early American Decoration.* Springfield, Mass.: Pondeckberg Company.

Christensen, Erwin O. *Index of American Design.* New York: Macmillan Publishing Co., Inc., 1950.

Cramer, Edith. *Handbook of Early American Decoration.* Newton Centre, Mass.: Charles T. Branford Company.

Creekmore, Betsey B. *Traditional American Crafts.* New York: Hearthside Press, 1968.

DiValentin, Louis, and DiValentin, Maria. *Practical Encyclopedia of Crafts.* New York: Sterling Publishing Company, 1971.

Divine, J. A., and Blachford, G. *Stained Glass Craft.* New York: Dover Publications, Inc., 1972.

Dow, George F. *Arts and Crafts in New England 1704-1775.* New York: DaCapo Press, Inc., 1967.

Eaton, Allen H. *Handicrafts of New England.* New York: Bonanza Books.

Hall, Peg. *Early American Decorating Patterns.* Scituate, Mass.: Peg Hall Studios.

Hallett, Charles. *Furniture Decoration Made Easy.* Boston, Mass.: Charles T. Branford Company.

Hoke, Elizabeth S. *Painted Tray and Freehand Bronzing.* Plymouth Meeting, Mass.: Mrs. C. Naaman Keyser.

Jones, C. S., and Williams, H. T. *How to Make and Restore Victorian Objects d'Art.* Edited by Judy and John Freeman. Victorian Culture Series. Watkins Glen, N.Y.: Century House, Inc., 1968.

Krauss, Helen K. *Shell Art.* New York: Hearthside Press, 1965.

Lewis, Griselda. *Handbook of Crafts.* Boston, Mass.: Charles T. Branford Company.

Lichten, Frances. *Decorative Art of Victoria's Era.* New York: Charles Scribner's Sons.

Lipman, Jean. *American Folk Art in Wood, Metal, and Stone.* New York: Dover Publications, Inc.

Lipman, Jean. *American Folk Decoration.* New York: Dover Publications, Inc., 1972.

Little, Nina F. *American Decorative Wall Painting: 1700-1850.* New York: E. P. Dutton & Co., Inc., 1972.

Lord, Priscilla S., and Foley, Daniel J. *Folk Arts and Crafts of New England.* Radnor, Pa.: Chilton Book Company, 1970.

Sabine, Ellen S. *American Folk Art.* New York: Van Nostrand Reinhold Company, 1958.

Sabine, Ellen S. *Early American Decorative Patterns and How to Paint Them.* New York: Van Nostrand Reinhold Company.

Spears, Ruth Wyeth. *Painting Patterns for Home Decorators.* New York: Bonanza Books.

Stephenson, Jessie Bane. *From Old Stencils to Silk Screening.* New York: Charles Scribner's Sons.

Stix, Hugh, Stix, Marguerite, and Abbott, R. Tucker. *The Shell: Five Hundred Million Years of Inspired Design.* New York: Harry N. Abrams, Inc., 1968.

Stoddart, Brigitte. *Papercutting.* New York: Taplinger Publishing Co., Inc., 1973.

Toller, Jane. *Regency and Victorian Crafts: or, the Genteel Female, Her Arts and Pursuits.* New York: International Publications Service, 1969.

Travers, Louise Allderdice. *The Romance of Shells.* New York: M. Barrows & Co., Inc., 1962.

Wilson, Nadine C. *Guide to Decoration in the Early American Manner.* Rutland, Vt.: Charles E. Tuttle Co., Inc., 1965.

Yates, Raymond F. *Hobby Book of Stenciling and Brush Stroke Painting.* New York: McGraw-Hill Book Company.

INDEX